LABOR LAW

THIRD EDITION

SAMUEL ESTREICHER
Dwight D. Opperman Professor of Public Law & Director,
Center for Labor and Employment Law
New York University School of Law

MATTHEW T. BODIE
Robins Kaplan Professor
University of Minnesota Law School

CONCEPTS AND INSIGHTS SERIES®

FOUNDATION PRESS

860 Blue Gentian Road, Suite 350
Eagan, MN 55121
1-877-888-1330

Published in the United States of America

ISBN: 979-8-88786-787-8

For Abby—G-d has allowed me a second soulmate in one lifetime

S.E.

To Simon-Jon Koike, Jessica Rothberg, and Josh Zuckerberg, as we started on this road together

M.T.B.

SUMMARY OF CONTENTS

TABLE OF CONTENTS

LABOR LAW

THIRD EDITION

Chapter 1

INTRODUCTION TO U.S. LABOR LAW

Labor law addresses collective action by workers concerning wages, hours, and working conditions and employer conduct in such disputes. It is a legal regime that deals with the economic and legal relationships between sellers of labor, acting as a group, and actual or prospective purchasers of labor. Many times, employees will have chosen a labor organization—a union—to represent them collectively. But all employees have rights under labor law to engage in collective action for mutual gain, whether or not they are represented by—or even have any interest in joining—a union.

Labor law is one of three primary areas of workplace law, the others being employment discrimination law and employment law. Employment discrimination law concerns the legal prohibition of employment decisions based on an individual's race, sex, age, religion, national origin, disability and other status characteristics considered to bear no relationship to legitimate employer considerations.[1] Employment law covers the rights and obligations of individual employees as to minimum wage, overtime, health and safety, and a myriad other specific mandates, without regard to whether they are represented by labor unions. Labor law, by contrast, is principally about collective action.

Our federal system of labor law is based primarily on the National Labor Relations Act of 1935 (NLRA).[2] The NLRA was the first major government intervention in the employment relationship, building upon the 1926 Railway Labor Act (RLA) which regulated workplaces on the railroads (later amended to include air carriers).[3] The NLRA is a foundational law that has shaped both federal and state legislation and decisions dealing with the workplace. And it has had staying power, too. Employees seeking union representation follow the same basic procedures that employees did during the late 1930s. Laws governing labor relations in the federal sector and state and local government are often modeled in part after the NLRA.

---

1 To name just a few of the federal statutes that prohibit workplace discrimination by private and government employers: 42 U.S.C. § 1981; Title VIII of the Civil Rights Act of 1964, 42 U.S.C. § 2000e et seq.; the Age Discrimination in Employment Act, 29 U.S.C. §§ 621–633a; and the Americans with Disabilities Act of 1990, 42 U.S.C. § 12101 et seq.

2 29 U.S.C. § 151 et seq.

3 The Fair Labor Standards Act of 1938, dealing with minimum wage, overtime pay, child labor, and other matters was the second major New Deal intervention in the operation of private labor markets. See 29 U.S.C. §§ 201 et seq.

Other than occasional references to the RLA, our focus in this book is private-sector employment as regulated by the NLRA. The NLRA created the National Labor Relations Board (NLRB), the federal agency that administers the NLRA and regulates relationships between employees, employers, and unions. Federal labor law consists of the NLRA and the decisions interpreting that statute by the NLRB and federal courts. We will largely not address the labor relations of federal, state, and local government employees, which are subject to the government-sector labor laws of those jurisdictions.[4]

To understand the workings of American labor law, it helps first to understand the basic economic principles regarding both markets in general and labor markets in particular.

A. The Economics of Labor Markets

1. Labor Markets vs. Commodities Markets

Economists have long posited that in competitive markets where there are many buyers, many sellers, and few barriers to new entry, prices are set by the interplay of supply and demand forces. All other things being equal, for any particular good or service, those who can supply that item for sale will increase their efforts as the price goes up. In contrast, those who would buy that item will become less interested in the purchase as the price rises. At the intersection of these supply and demand forces, the market is said to be in "equilibrium" or to "clear": no purchaser has an incentive to pay more than the market-clearing price and no seller has an incentive to accept less than that price. If there are changes in supply—such as the location of new oil wells with respect to the price of crude oil—or changes in demand—for example, a recession in the economy or climate change amelioration dampening the need for oil—prices will change until a new equilibrium is reached.

The labor market, at its core, would seem to operate on the same basic principles. All other things kept constant, providers of labor (workers) will move into a particular labor market as wages (and other terms) for their services increase, while employers will decrease their demand for workers as wages rise. Here, too, an equilibrium wage is reached, where no additional job seeker will work for less and no employer is willing to pay more. Again, changes in supply—perhaps an influx of immigrant workers—or changes in demand—

[4] One principal exception on the federal level is the Postal Reorganization Act, 39 U.S.C. §§ 1201–1209, which established the U.S. Postal Service and provided for partial application of the provisions of the NLRA.

say, a boost in non-fossil fuel energy production—can change prices until a new equilibrium wage is reached.

Labor markets, however, operate somewhat differently than markets for commodities in a number of respects. First, labor is relatively immobile. Workers are often rooted in their communities and not able readily to uproot their families in pursuit of higher wages or better working conditions. Employers in some situations may set wages and benefits above the market-clearing level to attract better qualified, more responsible workers. These firms will also tend to key wage and benefit improvements to continued service in order to reduce turnover and encourage incumbent employees to train new hires.[5] Both of these factors make it difficult for employees to quit their current jobs and, in that sense, may enhance employer leverage over terms and conditions.

Second, because workers need their income to sustain themselves, they cannot reduce their services but instead will work additional hours in response to declining wages. Hence, the normal market correction for declining demand—reducing supply—may not work according to classic market principles. By contrast, sellers of commodities might hold on to their inventory or focus on other products, at least for a time, in response to declining prices.

A third important difference from commodity markets is that many of the terms and conditions of employment involve collective goods. Working conditions, such as workplace safety, are supplied to all workers and cannot be distributed to one group of workers in the plant rather than others. An improvement in working conditions often involves a collective benefit and, from the employer's standpoint, a collective cost not likely to be the subject of negotiation with individual workers. This is also true of improvement in wages for, as a practical matter to avoid coworker distress, the employer will likely have to extend the improvement to all workers who do the same or similar work.[6]

A fourth divergence is that it is harder to assess intangible elements of the position and the parties in markets for labor services than it is for markets for commodities. With the internet, it is easier now to disseminate views from employees and others about employers. Even so, without more detailed information it is hard to evaluate the reliability of these reports. An employer may, for instance, lay-off a significant number of workers for what appears no

---

[5] See George Akerlof & Janet Yellen, Efficiency Wage Models of the Labor Market (1986).

[6] See Samuel Estreicher, "Easy In, Easy Out": A Future for U.S. Workplace Representation, 98 Minn. L. Rev. 1615 (2014).

clear reason, but it is hard for applicants to the job to evaluate whether this action was based on economic necessity, poor management, or idiosyncratic behavior. Employers in many cases will not incur significant reputational costs for abusive conduct.[7]

Finally, workers are human beings. There are dignitary dimensions to fair treatment not likely to be captured in market-based determination of wages and working conditions. Today's young workers, for example, have shown an increasing interest in having a voice at their workplaces and care about the purposes to which their labor is put.

2. Modes of Regulation

Government interventions into the labor market seek to maintain decent, productive relations between employers and employees and protect workers from unfair work practices. There are essentially two approaches to the regulation of labor markets: (1) setting "minimum terms" which every employer must meet in hiring and retaining employees; or (2) establishing a process for collective bargaining by groups of employees over the terms and conditions of their employment. These are not mutually exclusive choices, as collective bargaining can occur above the "floor" set by minimum-terms laws.

a. "Minimum Terms" Laws

Many employment laws require certain minimum terms or prohibit other terms; the parties are not free to waive these provisions. The Fair Labor Standards Act of 1938 (FLSA),[8] enacted three years after the NLRA, is an example of a minimum-terms law that attempts to change the wages and hours of work available in most labor markets. The FLSA sets, for covered industries, a minimum wage that employers must pay even if workers are willing to offer their services for a lower wage. In the hope of encouraging the spreading of work opportunities among workers and limiting work hours, the law also requires that workers who work more than 40 hours in a week be paid an overtime premium of 150% of their basic wage. The FLSA does not, however, prevent employers from responding to a legally-imposed hike in minimum terms by cutting back employment levels, discharging some incumbent workers, adding hours of work for incumbents (even if paid at the overtime premium), or substituting capital (e.g., machinery) for labor. Proponents of the law point to studies suggesting that gradual

---

[7] See Samuel Estreicher, Employer Reputation at Work, 27 Hofstra Lab. & Emp. L. J. 1 (2009).

[8] 29 U.S.C. §201 et seq.

increases in minimum wages do not significantly reduce levels of employment and maintain that any lowering of hiring incentives is a tolerable cost for the social benefit of raising labor standards.[9] Opponents, however, argue that the minimum wage depresses employment, artificially restricts contractual liberty, and provides benefits irrespective of the economic means of the workers involved.[10]

Minimum-standards regulations extend beyond wages and hours to cover health and safety policies, antidiscrimination provisions, and pension benefits. Some laws impose social insurance payment obligations as a condition of employment. These include social security, workers' compensation, and unemployment compensation. Some of these laws are federal: the Patient Protection and Affordable Care Act (ACA) requires employers with 50 or more full-time or full-time equivalents to provide a certain level of health insurance coverage for their employees or pay a tax.[11] State or local employment laws add to federally-available benefits or create new sets of benefits, such as paid family and sick leave.

b. Collective Bargaining Legislation

The NLRA represents a different approach. It does not specify the minimum terms under which people may be employed. Rather, it establishes a process for collective bargaining. If employees choose collective representation, the employer must bargain with the employees as a group through their collective agent, i.e., their union. The economic relationship is thus dramatically altered. Instead of individually negotiating terms and conditions of employment with the employer or essentially permitting employers unilaterally to set terms subject to market forces, the employer must bargain in good faith over those terms with the union representing its employees.[12]

Most economists agree that union-represented employees are able to negotiate a somewhat higher wage and richer benefit package

---

[9] See, e.g., David Card & Alan B. Krueger, Myth and Measurement: The New Economics of the Minimum Wage (1995); David Card & Alan B. Krueger, Minimum Wages and Employment: A Case Study of the Fast-Food Industry in New Jersey and Pennsylvania: Reply, 90 Am. Econ. Rev. 1397 (Dec. 2000).

[10] See, e.g., Richard A. Epstein, The Regulatory Hour: The History, Law and Economics of Minimum Wage and Maximum Hours Legislation, 12 NYU J.L. & Liberty 477, 484 (2019).

[11] 124 Stat. 119; 26 U.S.C. § 4980H. Congress on December 22, 2017, enacted the Tax Cuts and Jobs Act of 2017 (Jobs Act), Pub. L. No. 115–97, 131 Stat. 2054, which, in pertinent part, kept the ACA in place but reduced the required-shared responsibility payment by individual taxpayers down to zero.

[12] Unions do not generally represent all of the workers of a company. Rather, they represent a particular "bargaining unit" of employees. A bargaining unit is a group of jobs held by employees who share a "community of interest" with their fellow employees. See Chapter 6.

than comparable unrepresented employees.[13] Instead of individuals relying on their own economic leverage, a union collectivizes the bargaining power of the employees it represents. The employer now has to negotiate with the employees as a group usually assisted by experienced union bargaining agents. Although there is no duty to make concessions or reach agreement, the NLRA imposes a duty of good-faith bargaining. The employer and the union have to deal with each other at least for the indefinite period of time required for good-faith bargaining. If the parties reach an agreement, they have to reduce the agreement to writing; that agreement becomes an instrument enforceable in the courts or arbitration.

If the parties do not reach agreement, the union may strike—a decision by workers to collectively withhold their labor. Under federal labor law, the employees on strike do not lose their status as protected employees, but the employer is permitted to attempt to maintain operations as a means of countering the union demands. The employer can hire replacement workers, either on a temporary or permanent basis. Strikers whose jobs have been replaced in this manner have conditional rights to be reinstated, which can occur when the parties reach a settlement of their dispute or when jobs open up. Through this process, the union attempts to negotiate a package of wages and other terms that is an improvement over the terms the employees would have obtained as individuals.[14]

Not all workers have the market power to gain such results through collective bargaining. If the employees can be replaced with other workers without much cost to the employer, the ability to inflict losses on the employer by striking is limited. Also, if the employer faces tough competition in the market for goods and services it produces, it cannot readily pass on higher labor costs to consumers without hurting its business position.

Sometimes unions are able to bolster their bargaining power by representing workers not just at one company, but rather at a significant number of companies competing with each other across an industry. Where the union is able to insist on uniform terms across competitors, each of the unionized companies is relatively insulated

---

[13] These comparisons are often difficult, but most studies agree that there is a consistent "union wage premium." See Barry T. Hirsch & John T. Addison, The Economic Analysis of Unions; New Approaches and Evidence (1986). Employers may reduce their workforce in response to union wage increases by investing in capital equipment, using third-party companies (called subcontractors) to do the work, or shifting production to regions of this country or other countries where labor standards are lower. Unions try to curb these effects by organizing all competitors in the same industry but are increasingly less able to do so. See Samuel Estreicher, Labor Law Reform in a World of Competitive Product Markets, 69 Chi.-Kent L. Rev. 3 (1993).

[14] See Samuel Estreicher, Collective Bargaining or 'Collective Begging': Reflections on Antistrikebreaker Legislation, 93 Mich. L. Rev. 377 (1993).

from competition on the basis of lower labor costs. Even non-union firms in that product market may decide to follow the wages and benefits paid in the unionized sector as a means of discouraging its own workers from seeking union representation. Economists might model this situation as one where the union, in effect, decides the wage level, and all employers must compensate their workers according to those terms. In these circumstances the union can be said to have taken labor costs "out of competition." The usual result is to set the wage above the equilibrium level that the market otherwise would set, creating a higher supply of workers, or seekers of work, in the union sector but fewer job opportunities because labor has become more expensive in that sector, thus driving down employer demand.[15]

Some labor law scholars have advocated laws requiring what is termed "sectoral bargaining"—bargaining on a sector-wide basis, where presumably all competitive firms in a product market are subject to the same labor terms.[16] This normally would require legislation. The term also has been used for regulatory frameworks where labor and management officials propose improvements in, say, minimum wages that are then ratified by government as legally binding.[17]

While economists agree on the general effects that unions have on labor markets, they disagree over whether those effects are beneficial to society as a whole. The traditional view of economists is that labor law, by "artificially" bolstering the bargaining power of unionized workers, reduces employment in the union sector and leads to an oversupply of workers in the non-union sector, reducing the overall efficiency of the market. These economists maintain that the higher costs of labor are borne by consumers in the form of higher prices and/or reduced quality of goods and services. This union-negotiated "cartel" is arguably not sustainable, however, as lower-cost producers draw business away from the union sector and unionized firms begin to break ranks.

There is, however, another side to the story that acknowledges union pressure on wages and working conditions but sees it in a more positive frame. First, some have argued that union wage increases are ultimately sustained by the productivity gains that firms enjoy

---

[15] Some unions, especially in the construction industry, may also directly control the labor supply through terms in the collective bargaining agreement restricting the employer's ability to hire additional workers without obtaining those workers from a union-maintained "hiring hall."

[16] See Kate Andrias, Union Rights for All: Towards Sectoral Bargaining in the United States, in Cambridge Handbook of U.S. Labor Law for the Twenty-First Century (Richard Bales & Charlotte Garden eds. 2019).

[17] See, e.g., California Assembly Bill (AB) 1228 (2023–2024).

from union labor. By raising labor costs, unions place greater pressure on employers to utilize resources more efficiently (including automation).[18] Second, even if the wage effect does not expand the economic pie, it benefits society by reducing inequality.[19] Some of the union gains are said to be drawn from the super-competitive profits of firms enjoying monopolistic or oligopolistic positions in the market; reducing such profits is a social good because these profits are not necessary to producing the firm's goods or services.[20] On this view, collective bargaining simply works a redistribution of compensation costs within the firm but need not alter the productive capacity of the firm. Union gains can also influence the expectations of workers in the non-union sector, and in that way raise worker expectations for their own terms and conditions.

Labor law also promotes participation values. The chance to participate in workplace decisions, on this view, helps develop better citizens and provide employees with a chance to have a voice in their everyday affairs. As the distinguished labor economist Albert Rees observed: "By giving workers protection against arbitrary treatment by employers, by acting as their representatives in politics, and by reinforcing their hope of continuous future gain, unions have helped to assure that the basic values of our society are widely diffused and that our disagreements on political and economic issues take place within a broad framework of agreement."[21]

The economics of labor markets and the effects of unions and collective bargaining on these markets remain the subject of vigorous public policy debate. Labor law enhances the bargaining power of workers by providing a legally protected means to organize and bargain collectively. Whether this power is beneficial, either to individual employees or society as a whole, remains contested terrain. Our labor laws are premised on the notion that the welfare of the United States is best served by facilitating collective bargaining and recognizing the rights of workers to engage in collective activity for their mutual gain or protection.[22] We now turn to the basic structure of U.S. labor law.

---

[18] See Kenneth Dau-Schmidt, A Bargaining Analysis of American Labor Law, 91 Mich. L. Rev. 419, 431–34 (1992).

[19] See Richard B. Freeman & James L. Medoff, What Do Unions Do? 78 (1984) ("[U]nion wage policies lower inequality of wages *within* establishments; union wage policies favor equal pay for equal work *across* establishments; and union wage gains for blue-collar labor reduce inequality between white-collar and blue-collar workers."). For a critique, see John T. Addison & Barry T. Hirsch, The Economic Analysis of Unions: New Approaches and Evidence (1986).

[20] Freeman & Medoff, supra, at 185–87.

[21] Albert Rees, The Economics of Trade Unions 187 (2d ed. 1977).

[22] See 29 U.S.C. § 151.

B. The Structure of U.S. Labor Law

1. Underlying Premises

The American labor relations system differs from its European and international counterparts in a number of ways. First, the system is based on an adversarial model. The law assumes that although both unions and employers are concerned with the welfare of the firm, they have conflicting interests on matters affecting compensation, work rules, and certain other conditions of employment. As examples, workers want higher wages and shorter hours, while employers generally resist any increase in labor costs; many workers prefer constraints on employer discretion in setting working conditions, while employers insist on retaining managerial flexibility. In recognition of this conflict of interest, the law is careful to keep unions and management in separate spheres. Companies governed by the NLRA are not permitted to have a role in initiating or supporting "labor organizations," a term that is broadly defined to include any mechanism by which employees "deal with" their employer on terms and conditions of employment.[23] And although employers can voluntarily recognize unions if shown evidence of majority support among the employees sought to be represented, an NLRB-conducted secret-ballot election is normally required absent the employer's voluntary recognition.[24] In such elections, management has a right to express its views in a non-coercive manner on the merits of unionization, even opposing the union's organizing bid.[25] In the rail and air transport industries governed by the RLA, the National Mediation Board conducts elections where voluntary recognition has not occurred.[26]

---

[23] For the definition of "labor organization," see NLRA § 2(5), 29 U.S.C. § 152(5); see, e.g., Crown Cork & Seal Co., 334 NLRB 699 (2001). Employer interference with or domination of such organizations is barred by § 8(a)(2), 29 U.S.C. § 158(a)(2). See generally Samuel Estreicher, Employee Involvement and the "Company Union" Prohibition: The Case for Partial Repeal of § 8(a)(2) of the NLRA, 69 N.Y.U.L. Rev. 101 (1994). The RLA does not have a similar prohibition. See Samuel Estreicher, Nonunion Employee Representation: A Legal/Policy Perspective, Ch. 9 (pp. 196–220), in Nonunion Employee Representation: History, Contemporary Practice, and Policy (Bruce Kaufman & Daphne Taras eds. 2000).

[24] As will be discussed further below, the NLRB may issue a bargaining order if the employer has undermined the possibility of a fair election through its improper practices.

[25] Under Section 8(c) of the NLRA, 29 U.S.C. § 158(c), expression of views, including expression of opposition to the inion, cannot constitute nor be evidence of an unfair labor practice, unless such expression contains a promise of benefit or threat of reprisal. Although the Railway Labor Act does not have a similar provision, courts have invoked the First Amendment to provide similar protection for such speech. See U.S. Airways, Inc. v. National Mediation Bd., 177 F.3d 985 (D.C. Cir. 1999).

[26] 45 U.S.C. §§ 151–188.

At nearly each point, the labor laws reflect a fundamental division of interest between labor and management. Unions can seek bargaining authority on behalf of nonmanagerial and nonsupervisory workers, but managers and supervisors are deemed representatives of the firm who have no right to form unions or insist on collective bargaining.[27] The scope of bargaining also reflects this division between spheres of influence: the parties must bargain over wages, hours, and working conditions, but decisions involving the disposition of assets and the strategic direction of the firm, including plant closings, are deemed to be part of management's realm of unilateral action. Management must bargain over the effects of such decisions but is not required to bargain over the decisions themselves.[28]

A second comparative differentiation is that the U.S. system is based on the principle of "voluntarism"—that substantive outcomes in collective bargaining should be the product of the preferences and bargaining power of the private parties involved, rather than government fiat.[29] The government has a role in establishing procedures for unions to obtain bargaining authority, requiring labor and management to bargain in good faith once such authority has been established, and setting a limited number of ground-rules for the conduct of bargaining and ensuing economic conflict. It does not, however, have the authority to require the parties to reach an agreement or make any concession.[30]

---

[27] The statutory exclusion of supervisors is contained in Section 2(11) of the NLRA, 29 U.S.C. § 152(11). In addition, the Supreme Court recognized an implied exclusion for "managerial" employees—employees who do not supervise others but have a role in formulating and implementing employer policy—in NLRB v. Bell Aerospace Co., 416 U.S. 267 (1974). For example, faculty of institutions of higher education are considered 'managerial' employees if they play a role in the formulation or administration of educational policy for their employers. See NLRB v. Yeshiva University, 444 U.S. 672 (1980).

[28] See First National Maintenance Corp. v. NLRB, 452 U.S. 666 (1981).

[29] The U.S. labor movement's historical attitude to "voluntarism" is undergoing a shift in favor of political action in support of extending "minimum terms" laws. See Samuel Estreicher, Trade Unionism Under Globalization: The Demise of Voluntarism?, 54 St. Louis U. L. J. 415 (2010).

[30] Congress made clear in § 8(d) of the NLRA, a product of the 1947 Taft-Hartley amendments to the statute, that the duty to bargain in good faith does not necessarily mean that the parties have to make any particular concession or reach agreement. In the government sector—where unions generally do not have the right to strike—some jurisdictions provide for compulsory arbitration as a final dispute mechanism. See Robert G. Howlett, Interest Arbitration in the Public Sector, 60 Chi.-Kent L. Rev. 815 (1994). For experience in federal public sector, see Samuel Estreicher, The Paradox of Federal Sector Labor Relations: Voluntary Unionism Without Collective Bargaining Over Pay and Employee Benefits, 19 Employee Rights & Employ. Pol'y J. 283 (2015).

Unlike several continental European countries,[31] there is no provision in U.S. law for the government to extend collectively-bargained standards to non-union companies.

In the U.S., employees can strike and picket (within certain limits) as means of placing economic pressure on employers. Employers may not discharge striking workers but may hire "permanent replacements" for those strikers; only if jobs open after the strike do these replaced strikers have preferential reinstatement rights. Disputes are resolved through these economic weapons rather than, as a general matter, through government intervention.[32] Government can, however, enact generally applicable laws that set minimum terms for all workers.[33]

Third, collective bargaining in this country is highly decentralized. American unions typically negotiate agreements with single companies that are often applicable only to a particular facility. Finding smaller units easier to organize, unions tend to seek bargaining authority on a plant-by-plant basis, often among a subgroup of workers in the plant.[34] Unlike German, French, and Swedish systems, regional bargaining between labor federations and multi-employer organizations in the United States is unusual; multi-employer bargaining units are formed only by consent and in many industries have unraveled. Coalition bargaining among unions representing different units of the same employer can occur only with the employer's consent. Unions attempt to maintain "pattern" settlements across firms that compete in the same product market but are finding this increasingly difficult in the face of a growing non-union sector and the competitive pressures of global markets.

Fourth, U.S. unions are predominantly multi-employer organizations representing employees of competing firms. Unlike Japan's enterprise unions,[35] employee associations representing only the employees of a particular firm are rare in the United States and tend over time to affiliate with national labor organizations that are

---

31 See Samuel Estreicher, Global Issues in Labor Law 180–82 (2007).

32 The federal government can intervene to deal with "national emergency disputes." Under §§ 206–210 of the Labor Management Relations Act of 1947 (LMRA), 29 U.S.C. §§ 176–180, the President can appoint a board of inquiry to report on the dispute and then may direct the Attorney General to bring an action seeking to enjoin a strike or lockout. Generally, the RLA seeks to forestall resort to self-help in labor disputes. See Douglas L. Leslie, The Railway Labor Act 220–24 (1995).

33 See Metropolitan Life Insurance Co. v. Massachusetts, 471 U.S. 724 (1985).

34 Under the RLA, owing to the interdependent nature of railway and air carrier operations, the National Mediation Board (NMB), which administers the election provisions of this law, will certify only carrier-wide units of a particular class or craft of workers. See Summit Airlines v. Teamsters Local No. 295, 628 F.2d 787 (2d Cir. 1980); Northern Illinois Regional Commuter R.R., 16 NMB 175, 179 (1989).

35 See Hirosuke Kawanishi, Enterprise Unionism in Japan (1992).

members of the central labor federation, the American Federation of Labor-Congress of Industrial Organizations (AFL-CIO). Enterprise-based works councils—functioning in most continental European countries as a second track for employee representation in addition to collective bargaining—are non-existent in the United States.[36]

Finally, American unions are institutionally insecure. The unions' vulnerability comes from the fact they face a growing non-union sector and are subject to various legal mechanisms that are designed to ensure union responsiveness to the rank-and-file employees. These include decertification elections; the employer's ability to test the union's continued majority support by filing an election petition or, in some cases, unilaterally withdrawing recognition; duty of fair representation suits brought by employees complaining of the union's representation in collective bargaining or grievance administration; the rights of non-union members to seek rebates of union dues used for political purposes; and union democracy requirements for the conduct of internal union elections and union discipline.[37] As a result of these pressures, union leaders must be politically attuned to the preferences of median voters within bargaining units—typically, long-service workers who are protected from lay-off by seniority rules.

2. Aspects of the Regulatory Framework

The following section provides a brief overview of private-sector labor law. It is designed to provide an introduction to the concepts (many quite complicated) that are further explored in subsequent chapters.

The principal U.S. labor law is, as noted, the National Labor Relations Act of 1935 (NLRA or Wagner Act). The NLRA applies to all employers in private industries "affecting commerce," with the

---

[36] Volkswagen for a time was interested in establishing a German-style works council at its Chattanooga, Tennessee plant. See Jack Ewing & Bill Vlasic, VW Plan Opens Door to Union and Dispute, N.Y. Times, Oct. 11, 2013, at B1. It negotiated a pre-election framework agreement with the United Automobile Workers (UAW) indicating the UAW's consent to such an arrangement if the UAW were to obtain bargaining authority at the plant. In March 2014, the employees at the Chattanooga plant voted against UAW representation. Later that year, the company promulgated a policy providing for consultation with employee organizations on a non-exclusive, members-only basis. See VW, Community Organization Engagement Policy (November 12, 2014), available at https://onlabor.files.wordpress.com/2014/11/vw-communityorganizationengagement.pdf. In June 2019, the UAW lost a second bid to obtain bargaining authority at the Chattanooga plant. See Gabrielle Coppola & Andrew Wallender, VW Tennessee Workers Reject Union, Dealing Blow to UAW, Bloomberg Business, June 14, 2019. In 2024, the UAW won a representation election at the Chattanooga plant. See Neal E. Boudette, VW Workers in Tennessee Vote for Union, a Labor Milestone, N.Y. Times, April 19, 2024.

[37] See Labor-Management Reporting and Disclosure Act of 1959 (LMRDA), 29 U.S.C. §§ 401–531.

exception of the railroad and airlines industries. Labor relations in the latter industries are regulated by the Railway Labor Act of 1926 (RLA).[38] Both the NLRA and RLA broadly preempt all state regulation of labor relations in the industries they cover.[39] The states have enacted "mini Wagner Acts" for private industries not regulated by federal law and public sector labor relations laws for the employees of state and local governments. The federal government has a separate labor relations statute for its employees.[40]

a. Administrative Agencies

Government agencies play an important role in the administration of the federal labor laws. In the case of the NLRA, the National Labor Relations Board (NLRB) has exclusive authority over the representation procedures and unfair labor practice provisions of the statute. The role of the courts is limited to suits by the NLRB for preliminary injunctive relief, actions by unions or management to enforce collective bargaining agreements,[41] and judicial review of final NLRB orders in unfair labor practice cases. In the case of the RLA, the National Mediation Board (NMB) conducts representation elections and plays an important role in mediating disputes. Unfair practices under the RLA are adjudicated in the federal courts.

Under the NLRA, charges of unfair labor practices (ULPs) are filed with regional offices of the NLRB. If, after investigation, the charges are believed to be meritorious, the General Counsel issues a complaint on the government's behalf. An adversarial, trial-type proceeding is conducted before an administrative law judge (ALJ), who hears the testimony, reviews the evidence, and makes initial findings of fact and conclusions of law. If no appeal is taken (which is rare), the ALJ's determination becomes the ruling of the agency. If a party appeals, the five-member Board sitting in Washington, D.C. considers the record and briefs and, on rare occasions, hears oral argument. The final decision of the Board is reviewable in the federal courts of appeals. The reviewing court must uphold the agency's decisions if its findings of fact are supported by "substantial evidence" on the record "considered as a whole" and its rulings of law are in conformity with the NLRA.

By contrast, under the RLA, the NMB's adjudicative authority is limited to representational disputes; the parties go directly to

---

[38] 45 U.S.C. §§ 151–188.

[39] In Canada, by contrast, the provinces exercise plenary authority over labor relations; the federal government regulates a limited set of industries considered to have a nationwide scope, such as transportation and communications.

[40] Federal Service Labor-Management Relations Statute, 5 U.S.C. § 7101 et seq.

[41] See Section 301 of the LMRA, 29 U.S.C. § 185(a).

federal district court to enforce other statutory obligations. The NMB also has a mediation role that the NLRB was not given.

Both the NLRA and RLA are based on the principle of exclusive representation (only the representatives chosen by a majority of the employees in a unit may bargain with the employer over terms and conditions of employment, to the exclusion of individual employees); and a legally mandated duty to bargain (both the exclusive representative and the employer are legally obligated to bargain in "good faith"). In the area of economic conflict, in part to avert work stoppages in the railroad and airline industries, the RLA places more substantial restraints on economic self-help than the NLRA; a strike or lockout cannot occur until the NMB essentially declares an impasse by proffering voluntary arbitration, and there are other mechanisms for maintaining the status quo.

b. Selection of Exclusive Bargaining Representative

Although "members only" unionism is permissible under both the NLRA and the RLA,[42] unions typically seek exclusive bargaining status either by securing voluntary recognition from the employer upon a showing of majority support, or petitioning the NLRB or NMB to hold a secret-ballot representation election. Such petitions require a preliminary showing of interest; the NLRB, as a matter of administrative practice, requires that 30 percent of the employees in an appropriate unit sign cards requesting a representation election. Traditionally, unions with a majority showing needed to file petitions if the employer chose not to voluntarily recognize them. But according to the Board's 2023 *Cemex* decision, the onus is on the employer to file a petition once a union has established its majority support (usually through authorization cards).[43] If the employer fails to file a petition within a reasonable time (generally two weeks), the Board will consider the union recognized as the representative of the bargaining unit.[44]

Once a petition for an election has been filed, the agency conducts a hearing to resolve contested issues, if any, concerning the scope of the bargaining unit, eligibility of voters, and other

---

[42] The generally-held view is that members-only unionism is lawful, and collective action by a members-only organization may be protected concerted activity under § 7 of the NLRA. The employer is under no duty to bargain, however, with the members-only union because the employer's duty to bargain is triggered only by an exclusive representative under § 9 of the Act. For a contrary view (not yet embraced by the NLRB or the courts), see Charles J. Morris, The Blue Eagle: Reclaiming Democratic Rights in the American Workplace (2005).

[43] Cemex Construction Materials Pacific, LLC, 372 NLRB No. 130 (2023). This approach has not (as of this writing) been reviewed by the courts.

[44] Id. at *25 n. 139. It should be noted that the *Cemex* decision is currently subject to several challenges in the federal courts of appeals.

procedural matters, and then schedules an election to determine if a majority of employees desire union representation. After the election is held, the agency considers challenges based on the conduct of the election campaign. If the petitioning union was selected by a majority of the employees, and the agency has rejected challenges to the conduct of the campaign, the agency certifies the union as the exclusive bargaining representative. With some minor exceptions, a NLRB-certified union has no different status than a voluntarily recognized majority union.

In the election campaign, the employer is permitted to voice its opposition to unionism in general and to the particular union. The employer may not, however, discharge or discipline employees because of their support of the union, engage in threats of reprisal, or change the terms and conditions of work for the purpose of affecting the election outcome. Such conduct would provide grounds for setting aside the election if the majority of employees voted "no union." The Board has long had authority to issue a bargaining order if employer violations mar the conditions for a fair rerun election under *Gissel Packing Co.*[45]

c. *The Process of Collective Bargaining*

Under the NLRA, once the union has been certified or lawfully recognized as the majority representative, the parties are under a duty to meet and confer at reasonable times and engage in "good faith" bargaining. There is no legal obligation, however, to make concessions or reach agreements. The duty to bargain is limited to "wages, hours and other terms and conditions of employment." These are considered "mandatory" subjects over which the parties must bargain (and provide information to substantiate bargaining positions) and over which they are free to press disagreements in good-faith bargaining to the point of "impasse," i.e., negotiation deadlock. Bargaining is not required over subjects like plant closings, advertising budgets, and capital investments that are considered to lie within the realm of exclusive "entrepreneurial control".[46] Bargaining is also not required over subjects that are within the union's exclusive control because they concern the union's relationship with the represented employees, such as employee votes on strike authorization and contract ratification. Parties have no

---

[45] See NLRB v. Gissel Packing Co., 395 U.S. 575 (1969). The new *Cemex* ruling provides that the NLRB may order the employer to bargain with a union that previously demonstrated support from a majority of the unit when the employer has committed labor law violations sufficient to justify overturning the election—a lower standard than *Gissel*. Cemex Construction Materials Pacific, LLC, 372 NLRB No. 130 (2023).

[46] See First National Maintenance Corp. v. NLRB, 456 U.S. 666 (1981).

duty to bargain over "permissive" subjects, and these subjects may not be a basis for bargaining deadlock.

The party in control of employment terms and conditions, typically the employer, retains the right to make unilateral changes over permissive subjects.[47] As will be discussed further in Chapter 7, some subjects are permissive as bargaining is not required but the non-controlling party, typically the union, may not insist on them to the point of impasse and the controlling party may not implement them without consent. This latter category includes attempts to alter the established framework of negotiations, such as proposals to bargain with coalitions of unions or to submit disagreements over the prospective content of labor contracts to arbitration (called "interest arbitration").

If the parties have reached an impasse over mandatory subjects, the NLRA permits resort to self-help after notice is given to the Federal Mediation and Conciliation Service (FMCS) and applicable state agencies and a 60-day "cooling off" period has expired. The employer may lock out its employees and/or unilaterally implement its final offer to the union. The union may exercise its right to strike, which is legally protected by both Sections 7 and 13 of the NLRA. Strikes can occur both before and after impasse.

Although the employer may not discharge striking workers, it can, in the interest of maintaining operations, hire permanent replacements even without a showing that it could not maintain operations by other means.[48] If permanent replacements have been hired, however, strikers remain employees and have preferential rights to job openings as they occur, once the strikers have offered unconditionally to return to work. If the strike is in protest over the employer's unfair labor practices (ULPs), however, the employer may not hire permanent replacements, and strikers who unconditionally offer to return to work can displace replacement workers. Also, if the employer resorts to a lockout (i.e., locking out the strikers from access to the facility), it may not permanently replace locked-out employees. The Supreme Court has recognized the right of employers to hire permanent replacements for economic strikers since 1938, but the decade of the 1980s witnessed a significant increase in the use of this bargaining tactic.

---

[47] See NLRB v. Wooster Division of Borg-Warner Corp., 356 U.S. 342 (1958). Where the pressure comes from internal union rules backed by union discipline, the union may be the controlling party in the event of impasse. See Scofield v. NLRB, 394 U.S. 423 (1969).

[48] See NLRB v. Mackay Radio & Telegraph Co., 304 U.S. 333 (1938); Samuel Estreicher, Collective Bargaining or 'Collective Begging': Reflections on Antistrikebreaker Legislation, 93 Mich. L. Rev. 377 (1993).

The framework for collective bargaining in the railroad and airline industries resembles that of the NLRA but differs in at least two important respects. First, bargaining occurs on a carrier-wide (in airlines) or system-wide (in rail) basis, because the NMB will generally certify only carrier- or system-wide units for particular crafts or classes of workers. Second, there are substantial statutory impediments to changing agreements. The parties to a collective bargaining agreement are under a statutory duty "to exert every reasonable effort to make and maintain agreements."[49] A party commences the process of seeking changes in agreements by serving the other side with what is called a "Section 6 notice" containing its proposals. The parties are then obligated to engage in direct negotiations. If no agreement is reached, either party may request mediation by the NMB, or the agency can intervene on its own. The NMB has authority to prolong bargaining (virtually free of judicial review), as long it believes further talks may be productive. As a practical matter, the NMB determines when the parties are at an impasse by making an offer of voluntary binding arbitration of the dispute; if the offer is refused, the agency declares that its mediation efforts have failed. The parties are then obligated to maintain the status quo for 30 days, in order to permit the President to establish an emergency board. If the President does not do so, the parties are free to engage in a strike or lockout to pressure the other side. Emergency boards are common in rail disputes but have seldom been appointed in airline disputes since the 1960s.

d. Restrictions on Boycotts and Picketing

One of a union's critical economic weapons is to protest against the employer in order to put economic pressure on their business. Such protests have traditionally taken place in the context of a union picket line., Despite picketing's role in conveying speech, the Supreme Court has held that regulation is permitted due to the combination of protected expression (the message on the pickets) and regulable conduct (signaling to allied labor groups to not cross the picket line).[50] The First Amendment does, however, play a role in informing how the NLRA is interpreted so as not to apply to labor activity like handbilling that does not ordinarily signal to allied groups that they should withhold their services or patronage.

The 1947 Taft-Hartley amendments to the NLRA in the Labor Management Relations Act (LMRA) added union ULPs. It is a union ULP to engage in secondary picketing targeting companies not directly involved in the primary dispute to discourage their

---

[49] 45 U.S.C. § 152.

[50] Teamsters, Local 695 v. Vogt, 354 U.S. 284 (1957).

employees from performing work for their employer as a means of placing pressure on the primary employer who may be relying on the secondary employer's product or services. It can also be a ULP to discourage customers of the secondary employer from patronizing the store entirely. The basic secondary-boycott provision, found in NLRA § 8(b)(4)(B), specifically allows for picketing of the primary employer even if that picketing has secondary effects—for example, by discouraging outside delivery drivers from crossing the picket line to make their deliveries. But picketing aimed at secondary employers violates the NLRA, which directs regional NLRB offices to give such cases priority and seek a injunction under § 10(*l*) "forthwith." [51] On the other hand, efforts to inform consumers about a labor dispute through leafletting or other methods outside of picketing do not signal to other workers to withhold their services and are protected under a proviso to the Act[52] as well as by the First Amendment.[53] Picketing may also be allowed if it is directed at informing consumers, does not ask other employees to stop working, and does not threaten the target with financial ruin.[54]

Section 8(b)(7) of the NLRA,[55] a product of the 1959 Landrum-Griffin amendments in the Labor-Management Reporting and Disclosure Act (LMRDA), makes it a union ULP to picket for more than 30 days for the purpose of compelling the employer to recognize or allow organizing by the picketing union.

e. Administering the Labor Agreement

Once the parties have entered into a collective bargaining agreement, some mechanism is needed to resolve disputes arising under the agreement; of necessity, a general document cannot contain rules for all disputes that might develop. Such disputes often involve discharges and other acts of discipline challenged by the union under the "just cause" provision of the labor agreement, or disagreements over the meaning of particular terms governing seniority, overtime assignments, or the use of subcontractors. The preferred mechanism under U.S. labor law for resolving these "rights" (as opposed to "interest") disputes is a contractual grievance machinery involving stages of negotiations between union and management representatives, and, should disagreements persist,

---

[51] 29 U.S.C. § 160(*l*).

[52] 29 U.S.C. § 158(b)(4).

[53] Edward J. DeBartolo Corp. v. Florida Gulf Coast Building & Construction Trades Council (DeBartolo II), 485 U.S. 568 (1988).

[54] NLRB v. Fruit & Vegetable Packers, Local 760 (Tree Fruits), 377 U.S. 58 (1964); NLRB v. Retail Store Employees Union, Local 1001 (Safeco Title Insurance Co.), 447 U.S. 607 (1980).

[55] 29 U.S.C. §158(b)(7).

arbitration before a neutral arbiter. Such systems are referred to as a "grievance-arbitration" process. Typically, unions agree not to strike over rights disputes arising under the contract during the life of the agreement, in exchange for which employers agree to final and binding arbitration over rights disputes under the agreement. The Supreme Court has recognized a limited implied duty not to strike over grievances subject to arbitration.[56]

Arbitrators are chosen by the parties. Some agreements provide for regular resort to the same arbitrator or panel of arbitrators. More commonly, arbitrators are selected on an ad hoc basis from rosters compiled by the FMCS, a state labor relations agency, or the American Arbitration Association (a private organization providing arbitration services). Under the RLA, the parties are required to establish boards of adjustment to hear grievances.[57] Hearings before arbitrators are considered more informal, quicker, and less costly than proceedings in court. Although some unions (like the International Association of Machinists) continue to use non-lawyer staff in arbitrations, the process is becoming increasingly judicialized, and reliance on lawyers is now common. The arbitrator's award is considered a "final and binding" resolution, with the legal grounds for challenging an award quite limited. Absent arbitrator bias, an indefinite award, or a strong showing that the arbitrator clearly exceeded their authority under the contract, the court must enforce the award.

Section 301 of the Labor Management Relations Act of 1947, a product of the Taft-Hartley amendments of that year, empowers the court not only to hear cases involving enforcement of arbitration promises or agreements but also has been held to authorize development of a federal common law of enforcement of labor agreements.[58] In three rulings issued the same day in 1960[59]—the so-called "*Steelworkers* Trilogy"—the Supreme Court established rules strongly supportive of labor arbitration. The Court announced a "presumption of arbitrability" under which any facially plausible claim of a contract violation within the scope of the arbitration clause of the agreement—even if of dubious merit—is presumed arbitrable, absent clear language in the agreement precluding arbitration. The Supreme Court also made clear that, since the parties bargained for

---

56 See Local 174, Teamsters v. Lucas Flour Co., 369 U.S. 95 (1962).

57 In rail, the statute establishes an industry-wide grievance apparatus, the National Railroad Adjustment Board.

58 29 U.S.C. § 185. See Textile Workers v. Lincoln Mills, 353 U.S. 448 (1957).

59 See United Steelworkers of America v. American Mfg. Co., 363 U.S. 564 (1960); United Steelworkers of America v. Warrior & Gulf Navigation Co., 363 U.S. 574 (1960); United Steelworkers of America v. Enterprise Wheel & Car Corp., 363 U.S. 593 (1960).

their own special dispute-resolver and contract-interpreter, the courts may not set aside an award absent clear proof that the arbitrator strayed beyond their contractual authority. Even where an award is claimed to be inconsistent with "public policy," the Court has insisted that, in order to overturn an award, the award must be in direct conflict with other "laws and legal precedents," rather than simply in tension with an assessment of "general considerations of supposed public interests."[60] The Court has left open whether the only basis for refusing to enforce an award on "public policy" grounds is when the arbitrator requires conduct that the employer on its own could not lawfully engage in.[61]

There can be situations where a challenge to an employer's decision, such as a discharge, can be framed both as a breach of the collective bargaining agreement and an unfair labor practice under the NLRA. The NLRB's policy in such cases is to require the union, which is the exclusive representative of employees for all claims under the labor contract, to exhaust the contractual grievance procedure before the agency will exercise its statutory jurisdiction. After completion of the grievance procedure, the agency will generally defer to the results of the labor arbitration if the statutory claim involves the same facts as the contractual claim and the arbitration award is not "clearly repugnant" to the policies of the labor law.[62]

f. Individual Rights Under the Collective Agreement

Once the employees have selected an exclusive bargaining representative, their ability to negotiate individual employment contracts is severely curtailed, unless the collective agreement allows individual bargaining (a practice common in the sports and entertainment industries).[63] Workers may be discharged if they engage in economic pressure like a walkout to compel employers to bargain with groups other than the exclusive representative.[64]

Concerning disputes arising under the labor agreement, individual workers file grievances with their union representatives. The union ultimately controls which grievances are taken up through the process to arbitration. If a grievance is taken to arbitration, the

---

60 W.R. Grace & Co. v. Rubber Workers, 461 U.S. 757, 766 (1983).

61 See Eastern Assoc. Coal Corp. v. United Mine Workers, Dist. 17, 531 U.S. 57 (2000); Paperworkers Int'l Union v. Misco, Inc., 484 U.S. 29 (1987).

62 Olin Corp., 268 NLRB 573 (1984); United Technologies Corp., 268 NLRB 557 (1984). The Board tightened up the standard for post-award deference in Babcock & Wilcox Constr. Co., 361 NLRB 1127 (2014).

63 See J.I. Case Co. v. NLRB, 321 U.S. 332 (1944).

64 See Emporium Capwell Co. v. Western Addition Community Organization, 420 U.S. 50 (1975).

arbitrator's award will generally be preclusive of any court action by the employee against the employer for breach of contract. Even if a grievance is not taken to arbitration, its resolution by the contractual process is "final and binding" and precludes a court action. There are two exceptions to the preclusive effect of the contractual dispute resolution process. The first is where the union breached its duty of fair representation. The exclusive representative, as a matter of law, is under a duty to fairly represent all employees in the bargaining unit. If a breach of this duty is shown, a court action for breach of contract against the employer may proceed.[65] The second exception is where the employee's claim is based on a statute creating individual rights that cannot be waived or modified by the collective bargaining representative, such as substantive protections under Title VII or other anti-discrimination laws.[66]

g. Relationship Between Represented Employee and Union Bargaining Agent

Federal labor law does not require workers to become members of labor unions even in firms where unions are the exclusive bargaining agency.[67] Indeed, the law prohibits "closed shops," i.e., agreements requiring workers to become union members as a condition of being hired or continuing employment. But union-security clauses (often called "union-shop" clauses) are lawful except in states which have enacted "right to work" laws barring such provisions.[68] Under a typical union-shop clause, the employer is permitted to hire whomever it wishes, but the individual hired must within 30 days pay that portion of dues that covers the costs of collective representation, even if they do not wish to be members of the union. Under a union-shop clause, all employees in the bargaining unit must pay their share of the costs of collective representation (sometimes known as agency fees), rather than to join the union as such, while those who do join the union must pay full dues.[69] Employees are free to resign from union membership at any

---

[65] See Hines v. Anchor Motor Freight, Inc., 424 U.S. 554 (1976); Vaca v. Sipes, 386 U.S. 171 (1967).

[66] Alexander v. Gardner-Denver Co., 415 U.S. 36 (1974). The Court has held that although the "presumption of arbitrability" does not apply to arbitration pursuant to CBAs of individual statutory rights, unions can in some circumstances require represented employees to pursue their individual statutory claims, at least initially, in arbitration. See 14 Penn Plaza LLC v. Pyett, 556 U.S. 247 (2009); Terry Meginniss & Paul Salvatore, The *Pyett* Protocol: Collectively-Bargained Grievance Arbitration as a Forum for Individual Statutory Employment Claims, in Beyond Elite Law: Access to Civil Justice in America (Samuel Estreicher & Joy Radice eds. 2016).

[67] See NLRB v. General Motors Corp., 373 U.S. 734 (1963).

[68] Such laws are permitted under § 14(b) of the NLRA, 29 U.S.C. § 164(b).

[69] See *General Motors*, 373 U.S. at 743–44; Marquez v. Screen Actors Guild, Inc., 525 U.S. 33 (1998).

time but are still subject to the union-shop provision requiring the payment of dues. Employees who object to a union's use of such funds for political purposes have certain rights under the NLRA and the RLA.[70]

For individuals who are union members (and most represented employees become members by virtue of the union-shop clause), the LMRDA imposes rules of internal union democracy. Under the LMRDA, union members have enforceable rights of free speech at union meetings and to run for union office (free of unreasonable restrictions) in fairly conducted elections. The law also limits the grounds for which unions can discipline their members and stipulates minimum standards of fairness in any union disciplinary proceedings. Union members can be subject to fines but cannot lose their jobs because of a violation of internal union rules.[71] They also have the right to resign their union membership at any time, even in the midst of a strike.[72]

h. *Labor Law and Business Change*

As a general matter, companies seeking to merge with other firms or to sell all or part of their assets are under no duty to bargain over the decision itself, although there is a duty to bargain over the "effects" of the decision on workers. Effects bargaining must be in time to permit meaningful bargaining but can take place after the decision is made. There may, however, be restrictions in the labor agreement requiring the employer to secure a purchaser who will assume the obligations of the unexpired agreements. Such restrictions are enforceable in arbitration, and unions may seek court injunctions to preserve the status quo pending arbitration.[73]

In mergers and sales of stock, the surviving entity or purchaser will generally be held to assume the obligation to bargain with the union and to comply with the terms of the unexpired labor agreement—absent a strong showing that employment conditions with the surviving entity or stock purchaser will so radically alter the preexisting employment relationship that the union cannot be considered any longer the exclusive representative of the workers in an appropriate unit.[74]

---

[70] See Communications Workers of America v. Beck, 487 U.S. 735 (1988).

[71] See NLRB v. Allis-Chalmers Mfg. Co., 388 U.S. 175 (1967); Scofield v. NLRB, 394 U.S. 423 (1969).

[72] See Pattern Markers' League of North America v. NLRB, 473 U.S. 95 (1985).

[73] See Howard Johnson Co. v. Detroit Local Joint Exec. Bd., Hotel & Rest. Emp. & Bartenders Int'l Union, AFL-CIO, 417 U.S. 249, 258 n.3 (1974); see, e.g., Local Lodge No. 1266, Intl. Assn. of Machinists v. Panoramic Corp., 668 F.2d 276 (7th Cir. 1981).

[74] See id.; John Wiley & Sons, Inc. v. Livingston, 376 U.S. 543 (1964).

In the case of asset purchases, however, the purchaser has fewer labor law obligations. There is no requirement to hire back former employees, absent proof that the purchaser refused to hire the seller's workers because of their union status.[75] The purchaser is under no obligation to assume the seller's unexpired contract, unless the purchaser hires substantially all of the seller's employees without predicating offers of employment on changes in terms and conditions of employment. The purchaser is also under no obligation to bargain with the union representing the seller's employees unless a majority of the purchaser's employees in the unit come from the ranks of the seller's workforce. This determination of majority status is made at the time the purchaser hires a "substantial and representative" complement, rather than the later point when its "full" complement has been hired.[76] However, a purchaser who buys a business with knowledge of the seller's unremedied unfair labor practices is subject to the NLRB's remedial authority.[77]

C. Chapter Preview

At this point in the book, you probably have more questions than answers: What is an unfair labor practice? How do we determine whether a bargaining unit is appropriate? What is the difference between mandatory and permissive bargaining subjects? These questions will be explored in more depth in the chapters to follow. Here is a brief overview of what is to come:

- Chapter 2 explores the history of U.S. labor relations, starting with the common law approach of the 19th and early 20th Centuries and extending up to recent history and its relative moment of union strength amidst an overall decline in union membership.
- Chapter 3 looks at the NLRB as an administrative agency and provides the history of a hypothetical case to explain the Board's processes.
- Chapter 4 sets forth the Board' jurisdictional boundaries and defines key concepts such as employee, supervisor, and joint employment.
- Chapter 5 tackles the critical concept of the unfair labor practice, including the role of motive, types of impact-related violations, the scope of "protected concerted activity," and remedies.

---

75 See NLRB v. Burns International Security Services, Inc., 406 U.S. 272 (1972).

76 See Fall River Dyeing & Finishing Corp. v. NLRB, 482 U.S. 27 (1987).

77 See Golden State Bottling Co., Inc. v. NLRB, 414 U.S. 168 (1973).

- Chapter 6 reviews the process through which a group of employees can choose a labor organization to represent them in collective bargaining, including the campaign period and the requirements for voluntary recognition.
- Chapter 7 discusses collective bargaining and the requirements on both sides to bargain in good faith.
- Chapter 8 describes the weapons of economic conflict available to be used by the parties: strikes, replacement workers, lockouts, boycotts, and picketing, including NLRA restrictions on secondary picketing.
- Chapter 9 explains the grievance-arbitration process and the role of courts in reviewing determinations made under that system.
- Chapter 10 discusses the ramifications of business change on labor law, including mergers, acquisitions, sale of substantially all assets, and bankruptcy.
- Chapter 11 concerns the relationship between labor law and antitrust, discussing statutory and non-statutory exemptions.
- Chapter 12 addresses the relationship between unions and their members, reviewing dues obligations, internal union discipline, the duty of fair representation, and federal regulation of internal union governance.
- Finally, Chapter 13 examines how courts have interpreted the NLRA to preempt state and local laws that concern labor matters, including activity regulated by the Act and activity intentionally left unregulated by the Act.

Labor law is a critical area of law that rewards deeper exploration. It establishes a system of workplace democracy that encourages collective bargaining and the peaceful resolution of industrial disputes. We hope this volume facilitates your understanding of this fascinating and important subject.

Chapter 2

HISTORICAL EVOLUTION OF U.S. LABOR RELATIONS SYSTEM

A. The Common Law of Labor Relations

Labor law as a distinctive area of law does not begin until the enactment of laws dealing with the establishment of the unions and regulation of union activities in organizing workers and applying points of pressure to employers. Courts dealt with these issues through application of the common law of torts and contracts. The Sherman Act of 1890, as amended by the Clayton Act of 1914, involved application of the antitrust laws against certain union activities.

This era has been termed "a common law of labor relations."[1] A major question for the common law model of labor relations is whether during the period up to the late 1930s in this country, when that model essentially prevailed, contract, tort, and general criminal laws adequately protected the legitimate interests of employers, workers, and the public—without at the same time suppressing legitimate, peaceful concerted activity by workers. Until the Thatcher administration of the 1980s,[2] the British addressed this tension by adding a set of tort immunities for unions to the common law model. Otherwise, the law did not regulate the formation of unions, impose rules for acquiring bargaining authority, or require employers to deal with these organizations.

In the particular historical context of the U.S. in the 19th and early 20th centuries, the common law model of labor relations produced, or failed to stem, widespread conflict and social discontent. With perhaps the exception of certain skilled trades groups, employers typically chose not to deal with unions. This often resulted in strikes by the workers (or organizations seeking to represent

---

1 The reference here is to the jurisprudence prevailing in the period before the enactment of affirmative federal legislation regarding labor relations. The term "common law of labor relations" is taken from Richard A. Epstein, A Common Law for Labor Relations: A Critique of New Deal Labor Legislation, 92 Yale L.J. 1357 (1983).

2 The British have substantially altered their labor relations law in the direction of the U.S. model with provision for representation elections, a legal duty to bargain with the elected or designated majority representative, and strike-ballot rights for union-represented employees. See Trade Union and Labour Relations (Consolidation) Act 1992, U.K. Public General Acts 1992, c.52, Part IV, Chapter 1; Samuel Estreicher, Global Issues in Labor Law 205–08 (2007); see, e.g., Declaration of Recognition Without a Ballot, The Parties: Unite the Union and Oscar Mayer Limited (U.K. Central Arbitration Comm. April 14, 2025).

them). When the strikes themselves were unable to halt operations, because the employer was able to maintain production through the use of technology, management personnel, or replacement workers, the strikers often maintained picket lines in front of the struck enterprise and attempted to dissuade employees of other employers from crossing those lines and, in some cases, urged consumers to boycott the goods produced by the struck enterprise (what is called a "secondary consumer boycott") or labor groups to refuse to handle the goods at other points of the processing and distribution process (what is called a "secondary producer boycott" or "secondary boycott").

Where these measures did not halt operations of the struck employer, the strike eventually died out and either the strikers lost their jobs or were permitted to return to work on the employer's terms. Where the employer anticipated a shutdown of operations, it might engage a strikebreaking force to physically assault the picketers or, more often, to force a safe path for replacement workers to go to work at the struck premises. Violence could also occur at the strikers' end as replacement workers would be threatened with violence and sometimes attacked to prevent them from crossing the picket line. Violent acts were not a monopoly of either side in these disputes.

Often the critical step occurred in court, as employers would seek an injunction halting the strike, the picketing, and the related boycotts. An injunction would typically kill the momentum of the strike. In some cases, once an injunction was obtained, the employer might attempt to sue the unions and their members for damages.

The courts then had to decide what role they should play in this conflict. Violence, of course, could be halted by injunctions backed up by tort and criminal penalties. But what about a peaceful strike or peaceful picketing? The law's initial response, as illustrated by the 1806 indictment in the *Philadelphia Cordwainers* case,[3] was to treat concerted demands by workers that they would work only at specified rates, as a criminal conspiracy. This approach was an overreaction to a new form of economic conflict. In 1842, the Supreme Judicial Court of Massachusetts, the leading industrial state at the time, announced in *Commonwealth v. Hunt*[4] the demise of the criminal-conspiracy doctrine in favor of a rule that presumed combinations of workers in unions to be a legitimate form of association in the absence of proof

---

[3] Commonwealth of Pennsylvania v. Pullis, 1806. The case is reprinted in 3 John R. Commons et al., A Documentary History of American Industrial Society 61–248 (1958).

[4] 4 Met. 111, 45 Mass. 111 (1842).

that the combination was for an unlawful purpose or employed unlawful means.

After *Commonwealth v. Hunt*, the emerging view of U.S. state courts was that unions themselves and the collective withholding of services by workers in support of economic demands (called the "primary strike" or "strike") were lawful.[5] The difficult question was what means the union could use to bolster its position when the employer tried to maintain operations in the face of the strike. Presumably, union members could ask their relatives and friends to withhold patronage from the struck employer. Could they also picket the premises? Plainly, any use of violence, including massing in front of the premises to prevent people from coming in or going out, was tortious and could be prohibited.

The emerging question was how should the law respond to peaceful picketing that was free of violence and mass assembly blocking access or egress? Here, too, the initial judicial response was to condemn such picketing as inherently coercive and tortious. In his famous 1896 dissent in *Vegelahn v. Guntner*,[6] Oliver Wendell Holmes, Jr., then a judge on the Massachusetts high court, took his colleagues to task for their refusal to recognize the legitimacy of this new form of economic conflict which inflicted harm on the employer no different in principle from the harm that companies visit on their competitors.[7]

Vegelahn illustrates not only the difficulty common law courts faced in applying traditional tort principles to the economic contest between labor and capital, but also the potency of the "labor injunction." As a general matter, employers did not pursue damages actions because individual employees were typically judgment-proof, unions as unincorporated association could not at that time be readily sued as entities, and relief would come too late to be of practical use. Injunctions were the employers' preferred remedy because if obtained promptly, the decree could kill the momentum of an organizing drive or a strike, often irreversibly, whether or not the injunction was subsequently overturned. Moreover, as equitable relief, injunctions could be obtained from judges without having to invite the judgment of the community in the form of a jury trial.

---

[5] In the 25 years after the decision in *Commonwealth v. Hunt*, no indictment against labor unions for criminal conspiracy appears to have been returned in Massachusetts. In other states, however, application of the criminal conspiracy doctrine continued for a time—e.g., State v. Donaldson, 32 N.J.L. 151 (Sup. Ct. 1867) (indictment charging defendants with criminal conspiracy to quit working for their employer unless he fired two named employees)—until the "labor injunction" emerged as an effective weapon against harms caused by or attributed to labor unions.

[6] 44 N.E. 1077 (Mass. 1896).

[7] Id. at 1081–82 (Holmes, J., dissenting).

Because a temporary injunction could be obtained *ex parte*, the procedure could result in unjustified and overbroad decrees and deputation of company officials to carry them out.

Writing in 1928, Harvard professors Felix Frankfurter and Nathan Greene's *The Labor Injunction* catalogued the abuses attending the use of injunctions in labor disputes—exposure which led to legislation curbing labor injunctions. In 1932, Congress passed the Norris-La Guardia Act[8] curbing the use of labor injunctions in federal courts; and some of the Northeast industrial states followed suit with laws limiting their use in state courts.

Another problem for the common law model, even after adoption of the approach of *Commonwealth v. Hunt*, was determining whether the union's objectives were lawful. Plainly striking for higher wages was proper, but what about striking for organizational objectives that might ultimately enhance the union's leverage at the bargaining table? In both *Cordwainers* and *Hunt,* the group had gone on strike to enforce what is called a "closed shop"—the requirement that the employer hire only members of the striking association. This objective involved more than the claim of freedom to associate; it included a demand to bar individuals who were not members of the group from working.[9] In its 1900 decision in *Plant v. Woods,*[10] the Massachusetts high court accepted the basic approach of the Holmes dissent in *Vegelahn* but sustained an injunction against a strike to enforce a closed shop: "The purpose of these defendants was to force the plaintiffs to join the defendant association, and to that end they injured the plaintiffs in their business, and molested and disturbed them in their efforts to work at their trade."[11] Holmes, dissenting, disagreed: "I differ from my brethren in thinking that the threats were as lawful for this preliminary purpose as for the final one to which strengthening the union was a means. I think that unity of organization is necessary to make the contest of labor effectual, and that societies of laborers lawfully may employ in their preparation the means which they might use in the final contest."[12]

B. The Antitrust Laws as a Weapon Against Labor

The physical output of American industry increased 14 times between 1870 and 1929, creating a demand for workers that attracted waves of immigration from Europe. In the prosperous years

---

8 47 Stat. 70 (1932), as amended, 29 U.S.C. §§ 101–115.

9 See Herbert Hovenkamp, Enterprise and American Law 1836–1937, at 227 (1991).

10 57 N.E. 1011 (Mass. 1900).

11 Id. at 1015.

12 Id. at 1016 (Holmes, C.J., dissenting).

following the depressed 1890s, the labor movement experienced a major period of growth, climbing from 447,000 members in 1897 to 2 million in 1904. Construction unions grew from 67,000 members in 1897 to 391,000 in 1904; transportation unions expanded from 116,000 to 446,000. The bituminous coal miners struck in 1897 and won the Central Competitive Field Agreement covering virtually the entire industry in Pennsylvania, Ohio, Indiana, and Illinois; the 1902 anthracite strike led to complete organization of the hard-coal fields.[13]

Many of the famous strikes of this period, such as the Carnegie Steel and Pullman disputes, were accompanied by considerable violence on both sides. Moreover, where unions took hold in an industry, it often was the result of an agreement with an association of employers that sought to control competition. Control was often imperfect, and union efforts to regulate wages and shop practices often spurred lower-cost, non-union competitors, leading to an unraveling of many of these agreements.

In the late 1890s and early twentieth century, union success provoked a counteroffensive by employers, and one by one the trade associations broke with the unions. Some of these associations, like the National Founders' Association, provided strikebreaking and industrial espionage services for its members. Others, like the National Metal Trades Association, helped maintain for its members an ample supply of skilled workers to help its members prevail during strikes.[14]

The passage of the Sherman Act[15] in 1890 provided employers with an important weapon for curbing labor unions. Although Congress was principally concerned with restraints of trade and other acts of monopolization by large business enterprises, the statute's language was sufficiently broad to potentially cover agreements between laborers to exert control over a labor market. In particular, § 1 of the Act states: "Every contract, combination in the form of trust or otherwise, or conspiracy, in restraint of trade or commerce among the several States, or with foreign nations, is declared to be illegal."

During the 1890s and early 1900s, vigorous national boycott campaigns, organized by the Hatters, Iron Molders, and other

---

[13] See David Brody, Workers in Industrial America: Essays on the Twentieth Century Struggle 24 (2d ed. 1993).

[14] See Howell Harris, Employers' Collective Action in the Open Shop Era: The Metal Manufacturers' Association of Philadelphia, c. 1903–1933, in The Power to Manage?: Employers and Industrial Relations in a Comparative-Historical Perspective (Steven Tolliday & Jonathan Zeitlin eds., 1991).

[15] 26 Stat. 209 (1890), as amended 15 U.S.C. § 1 et seq.

national craft unions, were successful in wresting concessions from previously resistant large manufacturers. These successes prompted the creation of the American Anti-Boycott Association (AABA), founded by two non-union hat manufacturers in Danbury, Connecticut—Dietrich Loewe and Charles Merritt. In 1902, Loewe refused to recognize the Hatters union, and all but ten of his men struck in support of the union. Loewe then hired a new workforce and resumed production, leading the American Federation of Labor (AFL), the dominant labor federation of the period, to place his firm on its "We Don't Patronize" list. Wherever Loewe's hats were sold, union agents or rank-and-file activists were on the scene, pressuring the local labor groups to put the retailer on their unfair list. In the first *Danbury Hatters* decision, *Loewe v. Lawlor*,[16] the Supreme Court held that the Sherman Act applied to combinations of workers, at least where the union boycotted goods that crossed state lines. Seven years later, a ruling enabled Loewe to collect treble damages from 248 Connecticut members of the union.[17]

Danbury Hatters involved a "primary" labor or producer dispute, between Loewe and his striking workers, and a "secondary consumer boycott," in which the union urged consumers to boycott not only Loewe but also third parties not directly involved in the dispute but who were wholesalers and retailers of Loewe's hats. The union had not called a secondary *producer* boycott where the union would be urging employees of Loewe's distributors or retailers to refuse to handle Loewe's hats.[18]

Danbury Hatters alarmed the labor movement not so much because of its impact on the consumer boycott tactic as for its implications for the central goal of AFL-affiliated unions—the industry-wide closed shop agreement. Through such agreements, the unions sought to control use of skilled labor and thereby attempt to prevent erosion of labor standards by new entrants into the industry.[19] The efficacy of these agreements depended on an ongoing

[16] 208 U.S. 274 (1908).

[17] Lawlor v. Loewe, 235 U.S. 522 (1915). Walter Merritt, son of the AABA cofounder who was counsel for the plaintiffs, searched state real estate and bank records to determine which of the union's Connecticut members had assets against which a judgment could be enforced. See David Bensman, The Practice of Solidarity: American Hat Finishers in the Nineteenth Century 202–03 (1985).

[18] Labor's supporters expressed outrage over the Supreme Court's application of the Sherman Act to labor disputes, and some commentators charged the Court with usurpation of the legislative role. See, e.g., Edward Berman, Labor and the Sherman Act 11–51 (1930). Others, however, have defended *Danbury Hatters* based on legislative history indicating that Congress had declined to pass amendments that would have exempted agreements between or combinations of laborers. See Hovenkamp, Enterprise and American Law, supra, at 229; 21 Cong. Rec. 2611–2612, 2728–2731 (1890); Alpheus T. Mason, Organized Labor and the Law, (1925).

[19] See Lloyd Ulman, The Rise of the National Labor Union 526–31 (2d ed. 1966).

union campaign utilizing secondary producer boycotts to ensure that all competitor firms in the industry agreed to abide by union pay and work rules. In 1913, the *Hitchman Coal & Coke Co. v. Mitchell* litigation resulted in a "perpetual injunction" against a claimed conspiracy between the United Mine Workers (UMW) and coal operators in western Pennsylvania, Ohio, Indiana, and Illinois, the so-called Competitive Coal Fields, to impose a closed shop on a nonunion West Virginia company. In 1917, the U.S. Supreme Court sustained the injunction.[20]

In 1914, President Woodrow Wilson issued a call for changes in the antitrust laws and for creation of a federal trade commission. Labor saw this as an opportunity to revive its campaign for a labor exemption from the antitrust laws. Wilson rejected the demand for a wholesale exclusion from antitrust scrutiny, and the Clayton bill that passed the House and became the Clayton Act[21] did not incorporate the AFL's broad exclusionary language. Nevertheless, labor's supporters noted that the Act expressly recognized that "the labor of a human being is not a commodity or article of commerce" and restricted labor injunctions, insisting that the measure in effect legalized the secondary boycott. In AFL president Samuel Gompers's terms, the Clayton Act was "Labor's Magna Carta."[22]

In *Duplex Printing Press Co. v. Deering*,[23] the Supreme Court dashed any hopes of a Labor Magna Carta. The case involved a Battle Creek, Michigan printing press manufacturer that was struck by the International Association of Machinists (IAM), an AFL affiliate. Duplex was an important IAM target because the other leading manufacturers of printing presses were under IAM contract and feared competition on the basis of Duplex's lower labor costs. The local strike was unable to stop production because most of the machinists at the Battle Creek facility refused to join the walkout. In order to put further pressure on Duplex, the IAM encouraged its members and supporters who worked for customers or deliverers of Duplex presses to strike their employers. The Court noted: "The acts complained of and sought to be restrained have nothing to do with the conduct or management of the factory in Michigan, but solely with the installation and operation of the presses by complainant's customers."[24] The Court upheld the injunction against the secondary producer boycott of Duplex's presses.

---

20 245 U.S. 229, 234–35 (1917).

21 38 Stat. 730 (1914), as amended, 15 U.S.C. § 12 et seq.

22 See Daniel R. Ernst, The Labor Exemption, 1908–1914, 74 Iowa L. Rev. 1151 (1989).

23 254 U.S. 443 (1921).

24 Id. at 462.

Labor had placed its hopes in two provisions of the Clayton Act: Sections 6 and 20.[25] The Court held that neither provision barred the injunction:

- Section 6 states that "[t]he labor of a human being is not a commodity or article of commerce" and that nothing in the antitrust laws would forbid or restrain labor organizations from "the[ir] legitimate objects." The *Duplex Printing* Court explained, however, that § 6 protected only "normal and legitimate objects," not a secondary boycott.
- Section 20 states that federal courts may not enjoin peaceful strikes or attempts to persuade employees to withhold their services in the course of a labor dispute. The Court explained that § 20 was of no avail because it did not apply to secondary boycotts where employees withholding or being asked to withhold their services were not employees of the struck employer. Justice Brandeis's dissent emphasized that there could be no antitrust or common law liability because the employees of customers and delivery companies who withheld, or were urged by the union to withhold, their services had a "common interest" with those on strike at Battle Creek in maintaining negotiated labor standards. Further, Congress had not in the Clayton Act restricted § 20 "to employers and working men in their *employ*."

In its 1925 decision in *Coronado Coal Co. v. United Mine Workers*,[26] the Court placed in question even the legality of the primary producer strike under the antitrust laws. In that case, an Arkansas mine that had been unionized reopened on a nonunion basis, provoking a violent strike. A jury returned a verdict of $200,000, which was trebled. On appeal, the Supreme Court initially remanded the case because it found evidence only of a "local" motive on the part of the UMW to reestablish a closed shop at the mine rather than an intent to restrain interstate commerce.[27] On remand, evidence was presented that the union's objective in organizing the Arkansas mine was to eliminate competition from nonunion mines that was undermining closed shop agreements in adjacent states. In

---

[25] 15 U.S.C. §§ 17, 52.

[26] 268 U.S. 295 (1925).

[27] United Mine Workers of America v. Coronado Coal Co., 259 U.S. 344 (1922).

its second *Coronado Coal* decision, the Supreme Court held this showing sufficient to demonstrate a violation of the Sherman Act.[28]

C. The Norris-LaGuardia Act of 1932 and Reexamination of the Antitrust Laws: Government Neutrality in Labor Disputes

Support for unionism and collective bargaining went into decline after the 1919 strike wave and the prosperity years of the 1920s. The "labor injunction" reached new heights (or lows) during the 1920s, with employers able to secure the judiciary's assistance in labor disputes by the simple expedient of requiring their employees to agree not to join a union or be involved in union activities during the term of their employment—the so-called "yellow dog contract." The presence of such a clause provided a predicate for enjoining union activity, as unions arguably sought to compel employees to breach those contracts. The Supreme Court facilitated this process by striking down legislation that outlawed such agreements.[29]

The labor injunction was used throughout the 1920s, with the courts in a sense assisting companies in their campaign to impose a nonunion shop throughout industry.[30] In one account, 1.25 million workers were required to sign yellow-dog contracts during the decade, and some court orders "covered large segments of an industry, like the notorious Red Jacket injunction granted by Judge John J. Parker in 1927, which effectively barred the UMW from organizing in virtually the entire West Virginia coal industry."[31]

Increasingly, the federal courts' exercise of their equity power clashed with an emerging sentiment in Congress in favor of labor organization and collective bargaining. The Railway Labor Act had been enacted in 1926 to carry forward the unionization of the railroads that had occurred during World War I. Largely at the behest of the labor movement, Congress passed the Davis-Bacon Act of 1931[32] to require payment of "prevailing wages"—typically, union-set wages and work rules—on public projects funded by the federal government. The Great Depression of 1929, the effects of which lasted until World War II, also increased public concern with the erosion of earnings and working conditions.

---

[28] 268 U.S. at 310.

[29] See Adair v. United States, 208 U.S. 161 (1908); Coppage v. Kansas, 236 U.S. 1 (1915).

[30] See, e.g., United Mine Workers v. Red Jacket Consol. Coal & Coke Co., 18 F.2d 839 (4th Cir. 1927).

[31] Irving Bernstein, The Lean Years: A History of the American Worker 1920–1933, at 200 (1960).

[32] 46 Stat. 1494 (1931), as amended, 40 U.S.C. § 3041 et seq.

This was the setting for the enactment of the Norris-LaGuardia Act on March 23, 1932. This statute, which remains in effect to this day, outlawed the yellow-dog contract and gave recognition for the first time to labor's claim that individual employees bargaining on their own could not exercise "actual liberty of contract."

The 1932 measure addressed many of the objections to labor injunctions raised by unions and their supporters. Section 4 barred federal courts from issuing any temporary or permanent injunctions or restraining orders against becoming or remaining a union member, engaging in strikes, nonviolent patrolling or other forms of publicizing labor disputes, peaceful assemblies for organizing in a labor dispute, or rendering advice or entering into an agreement to do any of the above.

Furthermore, § 7 imposed procedural conditions on the issuance of injunctions in labor disputes (defined broadly in § 13 so as to not to require that "the disputants stand in the proximate relation of employer and employee"[33]) in cases not covered by the protections of § 4. First, *ex parte* orders could be issued only when "a substantial and irreparable injury to complainant's property will be unavoidable," after the posting of adequate security, and only for a maximum of five days. Second, the issuance of any injunction required findings of facts supporting the normal requirements for the granting of equitable relief, including the lack of an adequate remedy at law, likelihood of success on the merits, likelihood of irreparable injury to the complainant's property, and the lesser impact on defendants from the grant of relief. Third, § 7 required a specific finding that public officers charged with protecting the complainant's property were unwilling or unable to do so without the issuance of the injunction. Fourth, the injunction could only be issued against the particular persons or organizations actually committing, threatening, or authorizing the unlawful acts being enjoined.

The Norris-LaGuardia Act afforded other procedural protections as well. Section 6 provided that no officer or member of a union or a union itself could be held liable for the unlawful acts of individual members or agents, except upon proof of actual participation in, authorization of, or ratification of the acts. Section 9 required injunctions to cover only the specific act or acts complained of and to be supported by findings of fact. Section 8 imposed a clean-hands doctrine barring injunctive relief when the complainant failed to comply with some legal obligation involved in the labor dispute or failed to make every reasonable effort to settle the dispute through private negotiation, government mediation, or voluntary arbitration.

---

[33] 29 U.S.C. § 113(c).

Section 10 required the certification of the appeal of temporary labor injunctions to the courts of appeals. Finally, § 11 required jury trials in all contempt proceedings under the Act other than those for contempt committed in the presence of the court.

The Norris-LaGuardia Act can be characterized as an attempt to perfect the common-law model for regulating labor disputes rather than as an effort to promote labor organizations directly. It was designed to afford unions an opportunity to organize free of the improper restraints of government.

Despite the fact that the express terms of the Norris-LaGuardia Act limit only the injunctive power of federal courts, the Act also had implications for the applicability of the antitrust laws in labor disputes. In *Apex Hosiery Co. v. Leader*,[34] the Court held that a primary strike which halted all production of hosiery by that company to be sold in interstate commerce did not violate the Sherman Act. Influenced by the passage of the Norris-LaGuardia Act and the NLRA, the Court (per Justice Stone) reasoned that attempts by labor unions to restrain competition in labor markets did not violate the antitrust laws. This case effectively revived the § 6 of the Clayton Act theory rejected in *Duplex Printing*. The decision is regarded as the Court's first recognition of labor's so-called "statutory exemption" from the antitrust laws when it "acts alone" and not in combination with business groups.

In *United States v. Hutcheson*,[35] the Court invalidated a federal indictment against the carpenters' union for instigating a work stoppage against the employer and its two construction companies because the employer had assigned work to the machinists' union rather than to the carpenters' union. Although it could easily have treated the case as a dispute involving the "proximate relation" of employer and employee and hence free of antitrust liability even under *Duplex Printing*, the Court (per Justice Frankfurter) broadly ruled that the Norris-LaGuardia Act's restriction on federal injunctions in labor disputes effectively limited the scope of federal antitrust liability:

> [W]hether trade union conduct constitutes a violation of the Sherman Law is to be determined only by reading the Sherman Law and § 20 of the Clayton Act and the Norris-LaGuardia Act as a harmonizing text of outlawry of labor conduct.
>
> Were then the acts charged against the defendants prohibited or permitted by these three interlacing statutes?

---

[34] 310 U.S. 469 (1940).

[35] 312 U.S. 219 (1941).

If the facts laid in the indictment come within the conduct enumerated in § 20 of the Clayton Act they do not constitute a crime within the general terms of the Sherman Law because of the explicit command of that section that such conduct shall not be "considered or held to be violations of any law of the United States." So long as a union acts in its self-interest and does not combine with non-labor groups, the licit and the illicit under § 20 are not to be distinguished by any judgment regarding the wisdom or unwisdom, the rightness or wrongness, the selfishness or unselfishness of the end of which the particular union activities are the means. There is nothing remotely within the terms of § 20 that differentiates between trade union conduct directed against an employer because of a controversy arising in the relation between employer and employee, as such, and conduct similarly directed but ultimately due to an internecine struggle between two unions seeking the favor of the same employer.[36]

D. Modern Labor Legislation: Affirmative Protection of Collective Representation

1. The Railway Labor Act of 1926 (RLA)

Rail unionism enjoyed tremendous growth during World War I. Following federal seizure of the rails in 1917, the Railroad Administration recognized the right of workers to organize and bargain collectively, and the unions obtained national agreements and bipartite national boards of adjustment for the first time.

The Transportation Act of 1920 returned the railroads to private operation and created a tripartite Railroad Labor Board to hear and decide disputes but with no means of enforcement. The rail carriers, however, began an "open shop" campaign, including the formation of company unions accompanied by yellow-dog contracts and discrimination against union activists.

A process of negotiation between the operating brotherhoods and the rail carriers led to enactment of the Railway Labor Act of 1926 (RLA).[37] The RLA made it the duty of the parties to exert every reasonable effort to "make and maintain agreements concerning rates of pay [and] working conditions" and to attempt to resolve differences by peaceful means.[38] A five-person Board of Mediation was created to attempt mediation if the parties could not come to

[36] Id. at 231–32.

[37] 44 Stat. 577 (1926), as amended, 45 U.S.C. §§ 151–188.

[38] 45 U.S.C. § 152.

agreement by themselves. The board was instructed to urge voluntary arbitration if mediation proved unsuccessful, and if arbitration were declined, to notify the President, who could empanel an ad hoc emergency board to investigate and publish findings. During the pendency of these various proceedings, and for 30 days after the report of the emergency board, the parties were under an obligation to maintain the status quo. The parties, however, were not obligated to accept the recommendations of the emergency board. The 1926 statute also provided for the creation of boards of adjustment to resolve grievances involving the interpretation or application of labor agreements, but these bipartite boards lacked a mechanism for breaking deadlocks.

Section 2, Third of the 1926 law provided that employees had a right to select their own representative "without interference, influence or coercion" from carriers,[39] although it lacked a procedure for determining representatives or requiring carriers to deal solely with the representatives of the majority of the employees. In *Texas & N.O. R. Co. v. Brotherhood of Railway and Steamship Clerks*,[40] the Supreme Court seemed to signal some greater receptivity toward federal regulation of private labor relations by upholding the constitutionality of this central provision.

A set of 1934 amendments established the National Railroad Adjustment Board (NRAB), an agency comprised of carrier and union representatives to adjust grievances and disputes arising out of the interpretation of labor agreements; these are denominated by the RLA as "minor" disputes, to be contrasted with "major" disputes involving negotiations for basic contract changes. In the event of a deadlock, the NRAB members are to select a neutral referee or have one assigned by the National Mediation Board (NMB), also created at this time. The 1934 measure also authorized the new NMB to resolve representation disputes and created a set of employer unfair labor practices to be enforced largely by the courts. (There is no corresponding set of union unfair labor practices, as there is under the NLRA by virtue of the 1947 Taft-Hartley amendments.)

In 1936, Congress brought the emerging airline industry under the RLA.[41] In lieu of the NRAB, the airline carriers and unions established system-wide boards of adjustment that handle grievances and other minor disputes. (Although the 1936 amendments authorize the NMB to establish a National Air Transport Board, neither airline carriers nor unions have expressed

---

[39] Id.

[40] 281 U.S. 548 (1930).

[41] Pub. L. No. 74–487, 49 Stat. 1189 (1936).

an interest in industry-wide settlement of "minor" disputes.) The other provisions of the RLA also apply to airline labor disputes.[42]

In 1966, Congress amended the RLA to provide for the establishment of special adjustment boards (now called Public Law Boards) at the request of either unions or carriers to hear minor disputes otherwise referable to the NRAB, and to limit sharply the scope of judicial review of awards.

2. The National Labor Relations Act of 1935 (NLRA)

The Democrats gained the White House in 1932 on the promise they would bring the economic hemorrhaging of the Great Depression to a halt. Franklin Delano Roosevelt's first New Deal administration embarked on an ambitious experimental program in the National Industrial Recovery Act of 1933 (NIRA). Industries were to organize themselves to eliminate cut-throat competition and stabilize prices. Private trade associations were to submit codes of fair competition to the National Recovery Administration. To boost purchasing power and reduce unemployment, the NIRA also called for the establishment of minimum-wage and maximum-hours standards in nearly every industry. Section 7(a) of the NIRA declared that "employees shall have the right to organize and bargain collectively through representatives of their own choosing, and shall be free from the interference, restraint or coercion of employers . . . in the designation of such representatives or in self-organization or in other concerted activities for the purpose of collective bargaining."

A burst of organizing and surge of strikes occurred soon after passage of the NIRA. Strikes in the last half of 1933 reached levels not seen since 1921. Workers formed unions, often without assistance from AFL organizers. Unions in mining and clothing revived. New federal labor unions, directly chartered by the AFL, began to appear in the rubber, electrical manufacturing, automobile, and petroleum refining industries. Dramatic and violent strikes occurred in 1934 among auto parts workers in Toledo, longshoremen in San Francisco, and truckers in Minneapolis. By the end of 1934, union membership rose to 3.5 million—a gain approximating the loss between 1923 and 1933.[43]

The NIRA provided no machinery for handling labor disputes. In August 1933, President Roosevelt created by executive order a National Labor Board (NLB) to conduct representation elections and hold hearings to determine whether firms had discriminated against employee organizers. The NLB, however, lacked any enforcement

---

[42] See 45 U.S.C. §§ 181–188.

[43] See Irving Bernstein, Turbulent Years: A History of the American Worker 1933–1941, chs. 2–3 (1969).

authority. In 1934, the NLB was replaced by the first National Labor Relations Board, and President Roosevelt appointed special boards in the automobile, steel, and petroleum industries.

The NIRA period would have a major influence on the shape and content of subsequent federal labor legislation. First, the NIRA experience pointed to the need for a strong administrative agency with enforcement authority rather than a body whose principal mission was to help adjust disputes. Second, despite President Roosevelt's acceptance of plural (i.e., minority union) representation in crafting a 1934 settlement in the automobile industry, the first Labor Board established the principle in *Houde Engineering Co.*[44] that the representative of the majority of workers in an appropriate unit would be the *exclusive* representative of the workers in that unit. Third, companies across the country formed in-house employee representation plans as a means of fending off organizing drives.[45] Some firms insisted they would deal only with their in-house employee committee, even where the independent union enjoyed the overwhelming support of the workers.[46]

On May 27, 1935, the Supreme Court invalidated the NIRA as both an unconstitutional delegation of legislative power and an invalid exercise of Congress's power under the Commerce Clause in *Schechter Poultry Corp. v. United States*.[47] The collapse of the NIRA edifice made more urgent the case for the proposed labor relations legislation that Democratic Senator Robert F. Wagner of New York, an ally of organized labor, had been shepherding through Congress. At the same time, the *Schechter* decision raised serious concerns about whether Wagner's measure could survive a constitutional challenge.

President Roosevelt signed the National Labor Relations Act (NLRA or Wagner Act) on July 5, 1935.[48] The centerpiece of the new law was § 7, which recognized the right of employees to engage in concerted activity to obtain union representation, collective bargaining, and "other mutual aid or protection." As a means of giving content to § 7 rights, the NLRA specified certain employer unfair labor practices in § 8.

---

44 1 NLRB (old) No. 12, at 39–44 (1934).

45 See U.S. Dept. of Labor, Bureau of Labor Statistics, Characteristics of Company Unions, 1935, Bull. No. 634 (1937).

46 See, e.g., the *Edward G. Budd Mfg.* and *Weirton Steel Co.* cases, described in James A. Gross, The Making of the National Labor Relations Board: A Study in Economics, Politics and the Law 1933–1937, at 37–39 (1974); Bernstein, Turbulent Years, supra, at 177–179.

47 295 U.S. 495 (1935).

48 49 Stat. 449 (codified at 29 U.S.C. §§ 151 et seq.).

Not all of labor was enthusiastic about the Wagner Act. Industrial unions that sought or organize workers on an industry-wide, wall-too-wall basis, forming first a Committee and then a Congress of Industrial Organizations (CIO), were strong backers. But craft unions of skilled workers, the mainstay of the American Federation of Labor (AFL), feared that the NLRA's reliance on an "agency model" of the role of unions vis-à-vis represented workers would stymie their traditional jurisdictional model, where unions would assert exclusive jurisdiction over a particular craft or skill groups irrespective of whether they obtained some form of authorization from the workers they sought to organize.[49]

The NLRA established a new independent federal agency, the National Labor Relations Board (NLRB or Board), to enforce the unfair labor practice (ULP) provisions of § 8 and to hold elections pursuant to § 9 to determine whether the majority of workers in an appropriate unit wished to be represented by a labor organization for purposes of collective bargaining. Voluntary recognition by employers of majority unions without elections was also permitted. A labor organization selected by employee vote (and certified by the NLRB) or recognized as the majority representative served as the exclusive bargaining agency with whom the employer was under a duty to bargain in good faith. Employers could play no role in the formation of labor organizations, and any support or domination would violate § 8(2).

During the first two years of its existence, the Board's operations were hampered by serious doubts that the NLRA's constitutionality would be upheld. In 1937, these doubts were laid to rest when the Supreme Court upheld the NLRA in *NLRB v. Jones & Laughlin Steel Corp.*[50] With the Court's imprimatur, the Act led to a substantial increase in labor activity between 1935 and 1947. The number of workers represented by unions rose from 3 million in 1935 to 15 million by 1947—including two-thirds of the NLRA-covered employees in manufacturing and over four-fifths of those in coal mining, construction, and trucking, as well as railroading (covered by the RLA).

Disputes over how best to organize workers in the growing mass production industries spurred the rift between the AFL and CIO. Affiliates of the latter group emphasized integrated production process over skills-based manufacture. CIO union leaders urged that craft organization could not effectively address the integrated

---

[49] This tension is ably presented in Christopher L. Tomlins, The State and the Unions: Labor Relations, Law, and the Organized Labor Movement in America 1880–1960 (1985).

[50] 301 U.S. 1 (1937).

operations of these industries. The challenge of the CIO stimulated new vigorous organizational campaigns by the AFL. The older federation soon made up for its loss of members to the CIO. Some AFL successes resulted from voluntary recognition by employers who wished to forestall bargaining with CIO unions, which were generally considered more militant than their AFL rivals. The rivalry between the two federations also blurred the distinction between craft and industrial unions, since the AFL, as a competitive measure, authorized federal local affiliates and allowed craft unions to charter industrial locals.

The AFL versus CIO rivalry also complicated the NLRB's administration of the Wagner Act. In determining appropriate units for elections and collective bargaining, the Board was continually faced with competing claims by AFL-affiliated and CIO-affiliated unions. The AFL charged that the Board's resolution of these claims indicated a pro-CIO bias, while employers alleged that the Board was biased in favor of organized labor *de tout*. These complaints ultimately contributed to the amendment of the Wagner Act by the Taft-Hartley Act of 1947. Taft-Hartley changed both aspects of the procedure for resolving representational issues and the internal structure of the NLRB.

World War II, like World War I, was a period of growth for the union movement. President Roosevelt promised to maintain the protections provided by the Wagner Act and the Fair Labor Standards Act of 1938, including minimum wages and premium pay for overtime. Unions, in turn, gave no-strike pledges designed to avoid interference with war production. Moreover, the prestige of the union movement was enhanced by the appointment of union leaders to important posts in mobilization agencies.

In 1942, the National War Labor Board (NWLB), a tripartite agency, was established "for adjusting and settling labor disputes which might interrupt work which contributes to the effective prosecution of the war." Later, its responsibility was extended to include wage stabilization as well as dispute settlement. The NWLB sought to "stabilize" wages without freezing them. Its basic guidelines were embodied in "the Little Steel formula," which in general sought to limit wage increases to those warranted by the 15 percent increase in the cost of living between January 1941 and May 1942. The NWLB's rulings also promoted adoption of union security (requiring payment of dues as a condition of employment) and grievance arbitration clauses and employee pension and health-care benefits in lieu of wage increases.

Following the war, the reconversion of the economy to a peace-time footing was accompanied by a wave of long and stubborn strikes;

these were the product of pent-up wage demands during the unions' wartime no-strike pledge. These strikes involved over 3 million workers in 1945 alone, and affected many important industries, including coal, electrical manufacturing, oil refining, longshore, railroads, and steel. In 1946, the government took vigorous action to end the most significant strikes—those in coal and railroads. The coal strike led to government seizure of the mines and to the imposition of fines on both United Mine Workers (UMW) President John L. Lewis and the UMW for violating an injunction against the strike. These strikes created widespread support for curbing the power of organized labor and contributed to the passage of the Taft-Hartley Act in 1947.

3. 1947 Taft-Hartley Amendments to the NLRA and the Labor Management Relations Act of 1947 (LMRA)

The Taft-Hartley amendments to the NLRA and the Labor Management Relations Act of 1947 (LMRA)[51] were in part a response to the strike wave of late 1945 and 1946 and the widespread public perception of abuse of union power.

The 1947 amendments significantly changed the NLRA in several ways. First, § 7, the Act's core provision, was amended to make clear that employees "shall also have the right to refrain" from the activities listed. Second, Taft-Hartley added § 8(b), establishing for the first time a number of union unfair labor practices under the NLRA. (Both the RLA and many state labor laws do not provide for union ULPs.) In addition to provisions paralleling certain of the employer ULPs set forth in § 8(a), Taft-Hartley also outlawed the secondary boycott and required the Board's regional offices to seek preliminary injunctions against such boycotts in federal court.[52] In contrast, § 10(j), also added in 1947, authorized but did not require the pursuit of injunctive relief in other unfair labor practice cases.[53]

Third, Taft-Hartley clarified in a new § 8(c) that the expression of views cannot constitute an unlawful labor practice (ULP) unless it contains a promise of benefit or threat of reprisal or force. Although the section in its terms protects union speech as well, it is often termed the "employer free speech" provision because it allows employers to express opposition to the union campaign or to unionization generally. Fourth, the new § 8(d) made clear that the Board lacked authority to infer that a party had not bargained in good faith from its failure to reach an agreement or to make particular concessions. Fifth, it made a set of election-related

---

51 61 Stat. 136 (1947), as amended, 29 U.S.C. §§ 141–197.

52 See NLRA § 10(1), 29 U.S.C. § 160(*l*).

53 29 U.S.C. § 160(j).

changes; it further amended the Act to exclude supervisors from the definition of covered employees; it admonished the Board not to equate its inquiry into an appropriate bargaining unit with the petitioning union's extent of organization; and it barred permanently replaced economic strikers from voting in NLRB elections (amended in 1959 to permit voting for up to one year from the commencement of an economic strike).

In another set of changes, Taft-Hartley outlawed the "closed shop" (where union membership is a prerequisite for employment), and permitted states to enact so-called "right to work" laws outlawing even the "union shop" (where union membership or its financial equivalent is required only after an initial period of employment).[54] Moreover, in states that did not enact such laws, the union-shop clause was lawful only if authorized by the affected employees in an NLRB election. (In 1951, this last provision was deleted, and employers and unions were permitted to require, without a prior election, the payment of union dues or its financial equivalent as a condition of employment after 30 days on the job, while employees were given the right to petition the Board for a "deauthorization" election to remove this union-security provision.[55])

Finally, in order to promote industrial peace, § 8(d) also required the party seeking termination or modification of the labor agreement to notify the Federal Mediation and Conciliation Service (FMCS) of any proposed contract modification or termination and mandated a 60-day "cooling-off" period. The LMRA authorized the President to invoke special procedures where strikes or lockouts were deemed to create a national emergency.[56] Also in LMRA § 301 Congress granted the federal courts jurisdiction to resolve disputes arising out of the application of collective bargaining agreements.[57]

To deal with the issue of union corruption, the LMRA included § 302 which bans employer payments to unions unless they fall within a list of exemptions.[58]

4. 1959 Amendments to the NLRA and the Labor-Management Reporting and Disclosure Act of 1959

In 1955 the AFL and CIO merged and became the AFL-CIO. The "no-raid" agreement in the constitution of the new organization provided that no AFL-CIO affiliate would attempt to organize

[54] See NLRA § 14(b), 29 U.S.C. § 164(b).

[55] See NLRA §§ 8(a)(3) and 9(e)(1) (as amended 1951), 29 U.S.C. §§ 158(a)(3), 159(e)(1).

[56] LMRA §§ 206–210 (codified at 29 U.S.C. §§ 176–180).

[57] 29 U.S.C. § 185.

[58] 29 U.S.C. § 186.

employees already represented or "claimed" by another affiliate, and further required the affiliates involved in any such dispute to submit to final and binding arbitration under AFL-CIO auspices.[59]

Public concern over labor corruption, fueled by an inquiry of a Senate select committee chaired by Senator McClellan, escalated in the 1950s. The hearings ultimately resulted in the enactment of the Labor-Management Reporting and Disclosure Act of 1959 (LMRDA or Landrum-Griffin Act),[60] a measure that broadly regulates the internal affairs of labor organizations. Title I established a "bill of rights of members of labor organizations." Title II imposed reporting requirements on labor organizations and their officers and employers. Title III provided for regulation of union trusteeships (the practice whereby a parent union can assume control over a subordinate labor organization). Title IV created safeguards for the conduct of internal union elections, and Title V recognized fiduciary obligations for union officers.

The Landrum-Griffin amendments also affected the NLRA. Certain perceived loopholes in the secondary-boycott prohibition (§ 8(b)(4)) enacted in 1947 were closed by outlawing "hot cargo" clauses.[61] Congress added another union unfair labor practice (§ 8(b)(7)) to outlaw extended picketing for a recognitional or organizational objective.[62] A new provision, § 8(f), was inserted to authorize building and construction industry employers to enter into "prehire" agreements with unions before the majority status of the union has been established.[63]

In addition, the 1959 amendments partially reinstated the voting rights of permanently replaced economic strikers, which had been entirely eliminated by Taft-Hartley. Congress amended § 9(c)(3) to authorize the NLRB to allow such strikers to vote in NLRB elections for a period of up to twelve months from the commencement of a strike.

---

59 See AFL-CIO Const. Articles XX, §§ 2, 3 and XXI, § 2, discussed in greater detail in Samuel Estreicher, Disunity Within the House of Labor: Change to Win or Stay the Course?, 27 J. Lab. Res. 505 (2006). Following the AFL-CIO merger and the no-raid pact, the percentage of "rival union" elections decreased dramatically. See Kye D. Pawlenko, Reevaluating Inter-Union Competition: A Proposal to Resurrect Rival Unionism, 8 U. Pa. J. Lab. & Emp. L. 65, 65 & nn.8–9 (2006) (only 6 percent of NLRB elections in 2004 had more than one union on the ballot, compared to 21 percent of elections in 1955); Jackson K. Maxwell, Solidarity Forever? Toward a Competitive Market for Organized Labor, 99 N.Y.U. L. Rev. 1436 (2024).

60 73 Stat. 519 (1959), as amended, 29 U.S.C. §§ 401–531.

61 See NLRA § 8(e), 29 U.S.C. § 158(e).

62 29 U.S.C. § 158(b)(7).

63 29 U.S.C. § 158(f).

5. The 1974 Health-Care Industry Amendments

In 1974, Congress amended the NLRA to extend its jurisdiction to nonprofit health care institutions, including hospitals, health maintenance organizations (HMOs), and nursing homes. (Jurisdiction over for-profit institutions was already clearly established.) The amendments provided special rules for resolution of disputes in the health-care industry, such as a requirement that a union give ten days' notice to the FMCS before going on strike.

6. Failed Labor Reform Proposals

In 1977, during the Carter administration, an attempt was made in the proposed Labor Reform Act of 1977 to strengthen NLRB remedies and speed up its election processes. After passing the heavily Democratic House by nearly 100 votes, it died in the Senate following a 19-day filibuster. Other significant efforts to amend the NLRA included bills in 1991 and 1993 that would have banned the hiring of permanent replacements for economic strikers, and the proposed Teamwork for Employees and Managers Act of 1995 (TEAM Act), which would have amended § 8(a)(2) to allow employers greater latitude in creating employee committees to discuss changes in working conditions. The TEAM Act actually passed both Houses of Congress but was vetoed by President Clinton in July 1996. Bills banning permanent replacements, like the Labor Reform Act, passed the House but died via filibuster in the Senate.

With the election of Democrat Barack Obama as President in 2008, the labor movement made a strong, concerted effort to enact the Employee Free Choice Act (EFCA).[64] EFCA had three titles: Title I provided for NLRB certification of unions without elections on the basis of a majority card-check (under present law, by contrast, the employer can insist on an election); Title II provided for mandatory interest arbitration in first-time bargaining situations; and Title III provided for enhanced remedies and penalties for employer unfair labor practices.[65] EFCA passed the House in 2007 but was unable to

---

64 S. 560, H.R. 1409, 111th Cong. (2009).

65 For a defense of EFCA, see Benjamin I. Sachs, Enabling Employee Choice: A Structural Approach to the Rules of Union Organizing, 123 Harv. L. Rev. 655 (2010); and Benjamin I. Sachs, Card Check 2.0, ch. 4, in Labor and Employment Law Initiatives and Proposals under the Obama Administration: Proc. of the N.Y.U. 62d Ann. Conf. on Labor (Zev J. Eigen & Samuel Estreicher eds. 2011). For a critique, see Andrew M. Kramer, Jacqueline M. Holmes & R. Scott Medsker, Two Sentences, 104 Words: Congress's Folly in First Contract Arbitration and the Future of Free Collective Bargaining, ch. 3, in Labor and Employment Law Initiatives and Proposals under the Obama Administration: Proc. of the N.Y.U. 62d Ann. Conf. on Labor (Zev J. Eigen & Samuel Estreicher eds. 2011). See also Samuel Estreicher, Labor Law Reform for the Long Haul, ABA J. Lab. & Empl. L. (forthcoming, 2025). For an evaluation of the potential for reform of NLRB processes and remedies without statutory change, see

marshal enough support in the Senate to ward off a threatened Senate filibuster.

Another effort at pro-union legislative reform came in 2021 with the election of President Biden. Called the Protecting the Right to Organize Act or PRO Act,[66] the bill's reforms included expanding the definition of covered employees, eliminating the use of permanent replacement workers for strikers, prohibiting "right to work" provisions under state law, and increasing penalties on employers for violating the Act, especially in the context of representation campaigns. The House of Representatives passed the PRO Act, but it could not overcome the threat of a filibuster in the Senate and did not become law.

E. The Sharp Decline in Private-Sector Unionism

The enactment of the NLRA in 1935 and the Supreme Court's upholding of the Act's constitutionality in the 1937 *Jones & Laughlin* decision were followed by sharp increases in union membership; the percentage of union members in the private-sector workforce jumped from 14 percent in 1935 to 23 percent in 1939, and to a peak of 36 percent in 1953.[67] The unionization rate then began a steady decline and by 1979 had reached 22 percent, identical to that in the year following *Jones & Laughlin*.

This decline accelerated even further in the 1980s; union density under the NLRA (i.e., the percentage of private-sector workers who are union members) fell from 20 percent in 1980 to 12 percent in 1990, and as of 2024 stood at 5.9 percent—a lower union density than existed prior to the NLRA's enactment.[68] Moreover, these percentages rise only a point or two if one includes employees who are covered by a collective bargaining agreement but are not themselves members of a union. The decline in union density cuts across all areas of private-sector employment, including traditional areas of union strength such as manufacturing and construction.[69]

Samuel Estreicher, Improving the Administration of the National Labor Relations Act without Statutory Change, 25 ABA J. Lab. & Empl. L. 1 (2009).

[66] H.R.842, 117th Cong. (2021).

[67] See Leo Troy & Neil Sheflin, Union Sourcebook: Membership, Structure, Finance, Directory A-1 (1st ed. 1985).

[68] See U.S. Dept. of Labor, BLS, Union Members—2024, USDL 25–0105 (Jan. 28, 2025); Barry T. Hirsch & David A. Macpherson, Union Membership and Earnings Data Book: Compilations from the Current Population Survey (2014) (Table 1c) (1973–2013).

[69] See Hirsch & Macpherson, supra, Tables 1c & 1d (manufacturing decline from 39 percent in 1973 to 28 percent in 1983 to 10.1 percent in 2013; construction decline from 31 percent in 1980 to 20 percent in 1993 to 14.1 percent in 2013).

Unions in recent years have had modest success organizing workers in service industries, the fastest growing sector of the economy. The percentage of private-sector service industry workers (including those in health-care as well as in the leisure and hospitality industries (i.e., hotels and restaurants)) belonging to unions was 5 percent in 2005 and 9.2 percent by 2024.[70] In 2024, unions represented 7.8 percent of workers in health-care and social-assistance industries.[71] In the last two decades, the total number of private-sector union members has dropped even as tens of millions of jobs have been added to the American economy. Although over 30 million jobs were added to the private-sector economy in the thirty years between 1983 and 2013, the number of union members in the private sector nonetheless declined by almost 3.5 million during that period.[72]

Competing theories attempting to explain this decline in union representation abound. The most prominent of these focus on: (1) structural changes in the American economy; (2) changes in workers' preferences ("demand-side" changes); (3) employer opposition; and (4) the effects of global product and labor market competition.

The "structural change" proponents argue that changes in the American economy such as the shift of jobs out of the traditionally union-heavy manufacturing sector and into the service sector and from the more heavily unionized Northeast and Midwest to the less union-friendly South and Southwest, as well as demographic changes in the workforce, best account for the decline in private-sector union density. Another important structural change is the growth of competition in product markets as a result of technological advancement, deregulation, and globalization.[73]

Other work attempts to explain the decline of private-sector union density by focusing on the changing preferences of American workers. Some studies have pointed to increased job satisfaction

---

[70] See U.S. Dept. of Labor, BLS, Union Members in 2005, USDL 6–99 (Jan. 20, 2006), Table 3; BLS, Union Members—2024, supra, Table 3.

[71] See BLS, Union Members—2024, supra, Table 3.

[72] See U.S. Dept. of Labor, BLS, Union Members in 2018, supra, Table 3; U.S. Dep't of Labor, Employment and Earnings (1983).

[73] See, e.g., Leo Troy, U.S. and Canadian Industrial Relations: Convergent or Divergent?, 39 Indus. Rel. 695 (2000); Leo Troy, Market Forces and Union Decline: A Response to Paul Weiler, 29 U. Chi. L. Rev. 681 (1992); see also Henry S. Farber & Bruce Western, Accounting for the Decline of Unions in the Private Sector, 1973–1998, 22 J. Lab. Res. 459 (2001). See generally Samuel Estreicher, Labor Law Reform in a World of Competitive Product Markets, 69 Chi.-Kent L. Rev. 3 (1993) (Kenneth M. Piper Lecture in Labor Law at IIT's Chicago-Kent School of Law).

among non-union workers.[74] One reason for this increased satisfaction may be the broad array of workplace regulations governing matters such as discrimination, safety, family and medical leave, plant closings, overtime, and pension benefits that also provide some job-related protection for all workers without need of unionization. Studies of employee preferences have focused on the American culture of individualism and its influence on U.S. workers.[75] Still other research suggests that American workers may want a different "product" than that currently offered by unions—that workers want a greater voice in workplace decisions but want that voice to be exercised as a part of a *cooperative* rather than a confrontational relationship with management.[76]

An opposing view identifies employer opposition to unions (both lawful and unlawful), in conjunction with the weak remedies available under the NLRA, as the principal cause of declining union density in private firms.[77] Proponents of this view point to an increase in employer ULPs, the growth of anti-union consultants, and the relative weakness of NLRB remedies to explain why employees are less supportive of union organization.[78]

A fourth explanation of the decline in private-sector union density emphasizes that many traditional union goals, including union wage premiums, shorter work weeks, staffing rules, and seniority systems, are increasingly difficult to achieve and maintain in an era of global product and labor market competition.[79]

The decline in private-sector union density is likely attributable to some combination of the above factors. For example, more

---

[74] See Henry S. Farber & Alan B. Krueger, Union Membership in the United States: The Decline Continues, in Employee Representation: Alternatives and Future Directions 105 (Bruce E. Kaufman & Morris M. Kleiner eds., 1993).

[75] Seymour Martin Lipset & Ivan Katchanovski, The Future of Private Sector Unions in the U.S., 22 J. Lab. Res. 229 (2001); Sharon Rabin-Margalioth, The Significance of Worker Attitudes: Individualism as a Cause for Labor's Decline, 16 Hofstra Lab. & Emp. L.J. 133 (1998).

[76] Richard B. Freeman & Joel Rogers, What Workers Want (1999); see also Richard B. Freeman & Joel Rogers, What Workers Want (updated ed. 2006).

[77] The classic statement of this position is found in Paul C. Weiler, Promises to Keep: Securing Workers' Rights to Self-Organization Under the NLRA, 96 Harv. L. Rev. 1769 (1983); see also Paul C. Weiler, Governing the Workplace: The Future of Labor and Employment Law (1990); Richard B. Freeman & James L. Medoff, What Do Unions Do?, ch. 15 (1984); Richard B. Freeman, What Do Unions Do?: The 2004 M-Brane Stringtwister Edition (Nat. Bur. Econ. Res., Working Paper No. 11410, June 2005), available at http://www.nber.org/papers/w11410.

[78] For the need for stronger labor-law remedies, see Weiler, Governing the Workplace, supra; James J. Brudney, Private Injuries, Public Policies: Adjusting the NLRB's Approach to Backpay Remedies, 5 FIU L. Rev. 645 (2010); Anne Marie Lofaso, The Persistence of Union Repression in an Era of Recognition, 62 Me. L. Rev. 199 (2010).

[79] See Estreicher, Labor Law Reform, supra.

competitive and increasingly global product markets may have stiffened employer resistance to unionization as well as affected workers' assessments of the potential costs and benefits of traditional union representation.[80]

The decline in private-sector union density is a worldwide phenomenon. In some European countries, the decline in union membership is masked by the effect of extension laws in extending contract coverage to a larger percentage of employees.[81] Even in Canada, with pro-unionization labor law in the federal sector and many of the provinces, union representation in private companies is declining, although the unionization rate is still considerably higher than in the United States.[82]

F. A Potential Renewal?

The COVID-19 pandemic has spawned a burst of union organizing in those retail and service industries where labor has traditionally had difficulty. Most notable is the organizing drive by Starbucks Workers United (SWU), which has won elections at over 500 Starbucks stores (as of December 2024). For most of the campaign, the company waged an aggressive effort to discourage their workers from voting for union representation that included numerous adjudicated ULPs.[83] In early 2024 Starbucks and SWU reached a framework agreement with the announced purpose of facilitating collective bargaining and, eventually, collective agreements.

Although not with the same breadth of success as SWU, unions have successfully organized stores at Apple, Chipotle, Trader Joes, and other retail stores. An unaffiliated union—the Amazon Labor Union—organized Amazon's JFK8 warehouse in New York and later affiliated with the Teamsters. Additionally, journalists and other workers at many smaller but prominent media companies have joined unions in the last few years. These new union members have not added appreciably to the percentage of the unionized workforce, which remains around six percent. But the high profile of these union victories auger a possible new future for organized labor in the U.S. private sector.

---

80 See id; see also Thomas A. Kochan et al., The Transformation of American Industrial Relations ch. 3 (2d ed. 1994).

81 See Samuel Estreicher, Global Issues in Labor Law 174–83 (2007).

82 See Samuel Estreicher, Trade Unionization Under Globalization: The Demise of Voluntarism?, 54 St. Louis U. L.J. 415, 425 n.26 (2010); Samuel Estreicher, "Think Global, Act Local": Employee Representation in a World of Global Labor and Product Market Competition, 4 Va. L. & Bus. Rev. 81 (2009).

83 Matthew T. Bodie, Labor Relations at the Woke Corporation, 79 N.Y.U. Ann. Surv. Am. L. 171 (2023).

Chapter 3

THE NATIONAL LABOR RELATIONS BOARD: STRUCTURE AND PROCESS

A. The NLRB's Structure

The National Labor Relations Board (NLRB) is the agency entrusted by Congress with the task of enforcing the National Labor Relations Act (NLRA or Act). Its two principal functions are conducting representation elections under § 9 and adjudicating and seeking redress from employer and union unfair labor practices (ULPs) under § 8. By contrast, the National Mediation Board (NMB) has a similar responsibility for conducting elections under Railway Labor Act and has a mediation role (unlike the NLRB), but RLA unfair practices are adjudicated in the federal courts, rather than at the NMB.

As a result of Taft-Hartley amendments, the NLRB is comprised of two largely separate units: the Board, representing the administrative and adjudicative wing, and the General Counsel's office, which represents the prosecutorial wing. The five members of the Board and the General Counsel are Presidential appointees confirmed with the advice and consent of the Senate. At the regional office level, the regional director (a career employee) acts an agent for the Board in representation cases—supervising hearing officers, making unit determination decisions, considering challenges to elections, and certifying election results. The regional director also acts as an agent for the General Counsel by supervising investigators and prosecutors in unfair labor practice (ULP) hearings and making recommendations to the General Counsel as to whether to issue a complaint.

1. The Board

The five-member Board[1] heads the agency. Like other so-called "independent" agencies, it is a multimember commission whose members sit for staggered five-year terms and cannot be discharged from their positions except for cause. By custom, three members of the Board are from the President's party and two from the opposing party. In representation cases the Board sometimes (but rarely) hears appeals from regional director decisions. Most of its work

[1] The term "Board" is commonly used to refer to both the NLRB as a whole and the five-member body at the head of the agency. For purposes of this section, we will refer to the five-member body as the Board, and the agency as the NLRB.

involves reviewing decisions of administrative law judges (ALJs) in ULP administrative adjudications. ALJs are agency employees responsible for presiding over the hearing and making an initial decision for the Board's review. The Board usually decides these cases on the briefs but occasionally schedules oral argument. The Board's decisions are final decisions of the agency. They are not self-enforcing orders but must be enforced by one of the U.S. Courts of Appeals.

The Board is the delegatee of Congressional authority and is the expositor of national labor policy under the NLRA. The Supreme Court recognized this special role in *Beth Israel Hospital v. NLRB*:[2]

> It is the Board on which Congress conferred the authority to develop and apply fundamental national labor policy. Because it is to the Board that Congress entrusted the task of applying the Act's general prohibitory language in the light of the infinite combinations of events which might be charged as violative of its terms, that body, if it is to accomplish the task which Congress set for it, necessarily must have authority to formulate rules to fill the interstices of the broad statutory provisions.[3]

In addition to reviewing ALJ decisions in ULP cases and hearing appeals from regional director decisions in representation cases, the Board can also issue regulations under § 6 which can deal with both agency procedures and substantive obligations. In addition, the Board must approve (absent delegation to the General Counsel) any application to seek § 10(j) preliminary injunctive relief from a district court.

2. The Division of Judges

The agency employees who preside at ULP adjudications are the ALJs of the Board's Division of Judges. ALJs are now appointed by the Board. Originally called "trial examiners," these civil-service officers preside over the ULP hearings and issue preliminary decisions containing proposed findings of fact and conclusions of law. If the ALJ decision is not appealed, it becomes the decision of the agency. ALJs are required to apply NLRB regulations and decisions but are not supervised by the agency's policymaking and prosecutorial personnel, nor may they participate in *ex parte* communications with such personnel.[4]

---

2 437 U.S. 483 (1978).

3 Id. at 500–01.

4 See Administrative Procedure Act (APA), 5 U.S.C. § 557(d).

3. General Counsel

The General Counsel's Office is the prosecutorial branch of the NLRB. The General Counsel (GC) is appointed by the President to a four-year term, but courts have upheld the president's power to terminate the GC before the end of the term without cause.[5] The GC oversees a set of internal departments and regional offices who prosecute complaints of § 8 violations on behalf of the GC. Under § 3(d) of the Act, the GC has virtually unreviewable discretion to decide whether to issue a ULP complaint.[6] If the GC does not issue a complaint, the charged violation can receive no further redress under the NLRA or state law (by virtue of federal labor law preemption, discussed in Chapter 13).

4. Regional Offices

The NLRB has 26 regional offices, as well as 22 subregional or resident offices, across the United States. The regional offices are under the purview of the General Counsel's office with respect to the prosecution of ULP claims. Acting on behalf of the GC, the regional offices conduct investigations into ULP charges, and regional directors authorize the complaints for ALJ adjudications (subject to discretionary appeal to the GC). The regional offices also act on behalf of the Board in representation cases (subject to limited appeal to the Board). When a regional director seeks to file for a § 10(j) preliminary injunction in federal court, she must have Board approval to do so, absent delegation from the Board to the GC. Under § 10(*l*), available against certain ULPs under § 8(b) as well as violations of § 8(e), the Regional Director is required to seek a preliminary injunction without having to obtain prior Board approval.

---

[5] On his first day in office, President Biden terminated GC Peter Robb before the end of Robb's term. Courts have upheld the president's right to terminate the GC, holding that "the President's removal power remains plenary in this case." NLRB v. Aakash, Inc., 58 F.4th 1099, 1106 (9th Cir. 2023); see also Exela Enter. Sols., Inc. v. NLRB, 32 F.4th 436, 441 (5th Cir. 2022) ("'[N]o provision of the NLRA protects the General Counsel of the NLRB from removal."). In January 2025, President Trump terminated both GC Jennifer Abruzzo as well as Board Member Gwynne Wilcox. Member Wilcox has sued, claiming that her termination is in violation of the statute. See 29 U.S.C. § 153(a). The question whether the president's executive authority under Article II of the Constitution includes the authority to remove appointees to multimember agencies (such as the NLRB, the SEC, and the FTC) at will despite Congressional removal protection is wending its way through the courts (as of this writing).

[6] But see Leedom v. Kyne, 358 U.S. 184 (1958) (recognizing a narrow exception for "nonstatutory review" if the NLRB is in clear violation of statutory commands).

5. Other Divisions

Both the Board and the General Counsel have internal divisions which handle specifics tasks within the agency. Divisions with prominent roles include:

- The Division of Advice (within the GC's office), which provides litigation advice and support for the regional offices, particularly on cases involving new or unsettled areas of the law;
- The Division of Enforcement Litigation (within the GC's office), which pursues actions to enforce the Board's orders;
- The Supreme Court and Appellate Court Branches (within the Board), which handle appeals of the Board's orders to the federal courts; and
- The Contempt, Compliance, and Special Litigation Branch, which represents the Board and the GC as to enforcement in all suits (except those based on §§ 10(e) and (f) of the NLRA) and conducts civil and criminal contempt litigation to obtain compliance with Board orders.

B. The NLRB's Processes

The NLRB's two principal functions are to prosecute and remedy ULPs and to conduct elections to determine whether a majority of employees in an appropriate unit wish to be represented by a union.

1. ULP Proceedings Hypothetical—Sarah Smith's Charge Against Big Bath & Beauty Stores, Inc.

An unfair labor practice (ULP) is a violation of one of the provisions of § 8 of the NLRA.[7] Section 8(a) covers those ULPs committed by employers, while § 8(b) covers ULPs committed by labor organizations. Consider the hypothetical case of Sarah Smith, an employee of Big Bath & Beauty Stores, Inc. (BBBS), who believes she was fired from her position as a sales clerk because of her support for Local 111, Sales Clerks Union (SCU), which is attempting to organize Smith and her coworkers at the store. Smith's allegations state a violation of § 8(a)(3) of the Act,[8] which makes it an unfair labor practice to discriminate against employees in their employment conditions because they have engaged in union activity. Whether in

---

[7] 29 U.S.C. § 158.

[8] Violations of § 8(a)(3) are also derivative violations of § 8(a)(1).

fact a violation occurred is usually a question of fact to be determined in an administrative adjudication.

Smith cannot file an action directly in federal court. The NLRB has exclusive authority to enforce the Act, outside of LMRA § 303 damages suits for certain union ULPs. If Smith wanted to proceed further, she would need to file a charge with the local NLRB regional office which would be investigated by a Board agent. The investigation usually begins with an interview of the charging party.

At the close of the investigation, the agent makes a recommendation to the Regional Director whether the charge should be dismissed or whether a complaint should issue against the charged party. A complaint is issued only if the Regional Director has reasonable cause to believe that a violation has occurred. If the Regional Director declines to issue a complaint, an appeal can be filed with the GC, but the GC's discretion not to issue a complaint is virtually unreviewable.[9] In non-routine cases, the Regional Director acts after consultation with the GC's office, especially the Division of Advice. In Smith's case, her affidavit provided enough evidence to support a prima facie case of an § 8(a)(3) violation: she told the Board agent about her union activity, her good workplace record, and her termination on (apparently) unsupported grounds in the midst of the union's campaign. The board agent requested information from BBBS; the store was willing to provide only a letter from its attorney saying that Smith was fired for "insubordination" without further specification. The agent recommended that a complaint issue, and the Director issued a complaint.

The next step is a hearing before an ALJ. At this hearing, the GC's Office (acting through field attorneys at the regional offices) represents the Government, and the respondent (employer) is generally represented by counsel. The charging party (in this case, likely to be represented by the union) is permitted to intervene. Witness statements made to Board agents are provided to the respondent shortly before the witness gives testimony, but there is nothing like the extensive pre-trial discovery or depositions characteristic of a civil case in federal court. The hearing is run like a trial. There is general adherence to the rules of evidence with both sides having an opportunity to present and cross-examine witnesses.

After the hearing, the ALJ issued a decision finding the testimony of Smith and her coworkers to be credible, and ruling in her favor as to the § 8(a)(3) claim. The ALJ ordered the traditional remedies: reinstatement of Smith to the same position at BBBS and back pay for the time she has been out of work, minus wages she

---

[9] NLRB v. United Food & Commercial Workers Union, 484 U.S. 112 (1987).

earned from other employment (or could have earned through reasonable diligence). The ALJ's decision can be appealed by filing "exceptions"—namely, specific points of law or fact where the ALJ is claimed to have erred. In this case, BBBS filed exceptions with the Board and the NLRB attorney filed a response in support of the decision. The Board then heard the appeal on the basis of the briefs and the record before the ALJ. Often the Board will delegate routine decisions to a three-member panel of the Board, and in many cases this panel may summarily affirm the ALJ's decision and incorporate the ALJ's written opinion in its opinion. More controversial cases are handled by the five-member Board. In our hypothetical, the Board affirmed the ALJ's ruling in Smith's case with a summary opinion.

Board decisions are not self-enforcing. The Board must petition a U.S. Court of Appeals for enforcement, if the charged party declines to comply. The respondent BBBS (and losing party in our hypothetical) could file a petition for review in any circuit in which that party "resides or is doing business," or in the D.C. Circuit, which is open to all appellants.[10] This venue choice allows respondents (often nationwide organizations) to circuit-shop for favorable law. The Board will generally opt for the circuit in which the ULP occurred, but often the respondent files first in the circuit of its choice.[11] In Smith's case, BBBS appealed to the D.C. Circuit, which issued an unpublished opinion affirming the Board's order. The only avenue left would be the U.S. Supreme Court, which is highly unlikely to grant review in any particular case, especially a routine fact-specific case as this one.

The overwhelming majority of NLRB charges are settled well before trial. Over 95 percent are resolved at the regional level, with 60 percent of the charges dismissed or withdrawn.[12] In fiscal years 2007 through 2009, less than five percent of cases reached an ALJ, less than three percent reached the Board, and less than two percent went to the courts of appeals.[13] In this same period, although the median time for a region to issue a complaint was within 100 days of the filing of the charge, it took significantly longer to reach an ALJ decision (296–338 days) and a Board decision (two years).[14] One way

---

[10] 29 U.S.C. § 160(f).

[11] See generally Samuel Estreicher & Richard L. Revesz, Nonacquiesence by Federal Administrative Agencies, 98 Yale L.J. 679, 706 & n.144 (1989).

[12] See 74 NLRB Ann. Rep. Table 8 (2009); 73 NLRB Ann. Rep. Table 8 (2008); 72 NLRB Ann. Rep. Table 8 (2007).

[13] See sources cited in note 12 supra.

[14] 74 NLRB Ann. Rep. Table 23 (2009).

to try to mitigate these lengthy delays[15] is through the Board's application for preliminary injunctive relief in U.S. district court under § 10(j) of the Act.[16]

2. Representation Proceedings: Local 111's RC Petition

Section 9 of the NLRA outlines the process through which employees can choose a union to represent them collectively. The Board's recent *Cemex* decision has changed the nuts and bolts of the process in important ways.[17] The decision is discussed briefly below and in Chapter 6. (As this volume went to print, this decision has not been reviewed by any federal court of appeals and may not survive the Trump II Administration.)

The NLRA is based on the principle of exclusive representation by the majority representative of the employees in an appropriate unit.[18] In a system based on members-only unionism, there would be no need for a representation process.[19] But under the NLRA as interpreted prior to *Cemex*, unless the employer voluntarily recognized a majority union in an appropriate unit, a union needed to file a petition in order to get the official NLRA-certification process started.[20] The petition would be necessary to present a question concerning representation (QCR).[21] Returning to our hypothetical with Smith and BBBS, remember that Local 111, Sales Clerks Union (SCU) was in the midst of an organizing drive for BBBS's sales clerks.

---

15 The problem of delay at the NLRB is assessed in Samuel Estreicher, Improving the Administration of the National Labor Relations Act without Statutory Change, 25 ABA J. Lab. & Emp. L. 1 (2009); Samuel Estreicher & Matthew T. Bodie, Administrative Delay at the NLRB: Some Modest Proposals, 23 J. Lab. Res. 87 (2002).

16 29 U.S.C. § 160(j).

17 Cemex Construction Materials Pacific, LLC, 372 NLRB No. 130 (2023).

18 See 29 U.S.C. § 159(a).

19 In European countries where members-only unionism tends to be the rule, the law provides some mechanism for registering unions but does not generally impose a duty on the employer to bargain with the members-only organization. In some countries, as in Germany, collective bargaining, as a matter of agreement rather than law, takes the form of multiemployer bargaining with a single union on a members-only basis. The legal compulsion, if any, comes from the prospect of administrative extension of collective agreements to unorganized sectors. See Samuel Estreicher, Global Issues in Labor Law 196–205 (2007).

20 Under § 9(c)(1)(A) a petition can be filed "by an employee or group of employees or any individual or labor organization acting in their behalf . . . ." Under § 9(c)(3), employers also can file petitions in certain circumstances.

21 Petitions include a request by the union for certification (RC petition), a request by an employer to sort out union claims to representation (RM petition), a request by employees to decertify the union (RD petition), or requests to clarify the unit at hand (UC petition) or to abandon any claim to representation (UD petition).

Local 111 could file an RC petition to start the representation process in motion.[22]

There are two substantive requirements that accompany the RC petition. First, the petitioning union must provide a description of the jobs held by a group of employees that the union wishes to represent, called the bargaining unit. A union could seek to represent all of a company's employees, outside of supervisors and managers,[23] or it could seek to represent a set of particular jobs if they are found to comprise a "community of interest." The second substantive requirement is that the union must have signatures from at least thirty percent of the employees in the petitioned unit on cards indicating that the employee wishes to be represented by that union (or, at least, have an election to determine the question).[24] The thirty-percent rule is an administrative threshold; § 9(c) requires only that the petitioner "allege that a substantial number of employees" wish to be represented by the union. The names of the signing employees are not released to the employer; however, the employer can provide handwriting samples to the Board if it suspects forgery.

The *Cemex* decision offers an alternative route for unions that have the support of a majority of the bargaining unit. Local 111 could request recognition from BBBS based on its card majority. If BBBS did not want to recognize the union and instead wanted a secret ballot election to be held, it would need to file its own representation petition within two weeks of the union's request.[25] If BBBS failed to recognize and failed to file the petition, BBBS would under *Cemex*

---

[22] Voluntary recognition is permissible under the NLRA provided the union is the majority representative of employees in an appropriate unit. Prior to the *Cemex* decision, the employer was under no duty to recognize the union without requiring proof whether it had a basis for doubting the union's majority support. See NLRB v. Gissel Packing Co., 395 U.S. 575 (1960); Linden Lumber Div, Summer Co. v. NLRB, 419 U.S. 301 (1974). The employer's duty ripened only when the union became a certified bargaining representative after winning an NLRB representation election. Under the Supreme Court's *Gissel* decision, the NLRB could order the employer to bargain with the union if the employer had committed serious ULPs precluding a fair rerun election and if the union had demonstrated majority support prior to the ULPs. See *Gissel,* 395 U.S. at 610–15. While *Gissel* remains good law, the Board's *Cemex* decision somewhat supersedes it. The *Cemex* Board decided that there is no need to show that the ULPs prevented a fair rerun election but did not clearly decide how serious the ULPs had to be to warrant a bargaining order. Cemex Construction Materials Pacific, LLC, 372 NLRB No. 130 (2023).

[23] The statutory exclusions for employees such as supervisors and managers are discussed in Chapter 4.

[24] Technically, the cards are only required to say that the employees wish to have an election to determine if the union should represent the employees of the unit. For other purposes, however (including the possibility of a bargaining order without an election where serious employer ULPs mar fair elections conditions or under *Cemex*), the card must state that the employee is authorizing the union to serve as the bargaining agent.

[25] Cemex Construction Materials Pacific, LLC, 372 NLRB No. 130 (2023).

forfeit its right to an election, and the Board would recognize the union as representative of the bargaining unit. (Prior to that decision, a union with support from a majority of the unit could request recognition from the employer, but the employer was under no obligation to recognize or even respond to the union.)

Once a petition has been filed by either party, the employer may contest the bargaining unit as described by the union. As discussed further in Chapter 6, the unit must be an "appropriate" unit for carrying on collective bargaining.[26] Suppose that Local 111 has filed an RC petition seeking to represent "[a]ll full-time sales clerks at the Big Bath & Beauty Store, Inc., Ridgemont location." The store at that location has ten employees: six full-time sales clerks, two sales assistants, an assistant manager, and a manager. BBBS objects to the proposed unit, contending that the assistant manager and the sales assistants should be included in the unit. The NLRB regional office will seek to reach some sort of settlement between the parties on the issue, which would result in a "stipulated election agreement" setting forth the agreed-upon bargaining unit and the timeline for the election. If the parties cannot agree, the Region will conduct a hearing on the appropriateness of the unit. The hearing is conducted by a staff member of the regional office, and the decision is made by the Regional Director. The decision can be appealed to the Board, but it is subject only to discretionary review at this stage, and such review is infrequently granted. To reach the Board and an appellate court, the parties must wait until after the election.[27]

In this case, Local 111 and BBBS reach a stipulated election agreement (which occurs 85 percent of the time).[28] The parties agree that sales assistants will be included in the unit, but the assistant manager will not. In accordance with the agreement, an election is held three weeks from the stipulated agreement. Elections are conducted by secret ballot and are usually held at the employer's premises. A Board agent secures the location, provides the ballots, and monitors the process. Generally, representatives from each

[26] 29 U.S.C. § 159(b)("The Board shall decide in each case whether, in order to assure to employees the fullest freedom in exercising the rights guaranteed by this subchapter, the unit appropriate for the purposes of collective bargaining shall be the employer unit, craft unit, plant unit, or subdivision thereof. . . .").

[27] In general, decisions in representation case proceedings are not final agency orders reviewable in the courts. See American Federation of Labor v. NLRB, 308 U.S. 401 (1940). Rather, the party objecting to those decisions (typically, the employer) must await the results of the representation election and convert the representation case determination into a ULP order (typically, an order to bargain with the union winning the election) which can be reviewed. In Leedom v. Kyne, 358 U.S. 184 (1958), the Supreme Court recognized a narrow exception for "nonstatutory review" (akin to mandamus) of agency determinations in violation of clear NLRA requirements.

[28] See, e.g., 70 NLRB Ann. Report Table 9 (2005).

party—one from the union,[29] one from the employer—sit alongside the agent and monitor the process. As individual employees come forward to vote, either representative can contest a voter's eligibility to participate in the election. An objection usually results in that employee's vote being placed in an envelope, set aside, and marked for later determination. After the other ballots are counted, these sequestered ballots are discarded if they ultimately would not affect the election's result. If the union receives fifty percent plus one of the votes cast,[30] it will be certified as the employees' exclusive representative.[31]

If necessary, the NLRB regional office will hold post-election hearings to review challenges to particular ballots or to the victorious party's conduct during the campaign period prior to the election. Post-election challenges can target behavior such as alleged threats to employees, promises of benefits, racially inflammatory speech, and other conduct that would tend to impede workers' expression of their true opinions about representation. After a hearing, the Regional Director decides the merits of the election challenges. This decision can also be appealed to the Board, but employers and unions cannot obtain direct review of the Board's ruling from a court. Instead, employers must wait until after the union has been certified and then refuse to bargain with the union. This refusal constitutes a ULP under § 8(a)(5). It is considered a "technical" refusal to bargain because the court of appeals will consider the validity of the representation case decision—a procedure authorized by § 9(d). Unions generally have no comparable means of converting a representation case decision into a union ULP. They can only seek extraordinary relief, akin to a writ of mandamus, in cases where the Board has clearly exceeded its authority.[32] Unions almost never seek such relief, as the judicial remedy (even if granted) would be limited to a new election, which the union can seek after a year in any event.[33]

---

[29] Or each union, if more than one is participating in the election. These representatives must be employees of the company.

[30] The union need only receive a majority of ballots cast.as opposed to a majority of the employees in the unit. In a 2010 rulemaking, the National Mediation Board (NMB), the agency responsible for holding representation elections under the RLA, revoked its longstanding requirement that a union must garner votes by a majority of eligible voters to win an election in favor of a requirement that the union need only obtain the majority of the votes cast. See 75 Fed. Reg. 26062 (May 11, 2010).

[31] Under § 9(c)(3) if there is more than one labor organization on the ballot and none of the choices receives a majority, a run-off election is held between the top two choices. This is now also the procedure under the RLA after the FAA Modernization Reform Act of 2012, § 1002, Pub. L. 112–95, 126 Stat. 12 (Feb. 12, 2012).

[32] See note 27 supra.

[33] See NLRA § 9(e)(2), 29 U.S.C. § 159(e)(2).

In our hypothetical case, Local 111 won the election, 5–2 (with one non-voter), but BBBS claimed that the union improperly promised employees free T-shirts[34] if the union won the election. After a hearing on the matter, the Regional Director found that the promise was not significant enough to constitute a violation of fair election conditions. The Board upheld that decision and certified Local 111 as the exclusive bargaining representative in the agreed-upon unit. Wishing to appeal that ruling, BBBS refused to bargain with Local 111, which then filed a ULP charge against BBBS. The Board then conducted a summary proceeding finding that BBBS had refused to bargain with Local 111 in violation of § 8(a)(5). BBBS petitioned for review in the circuit in which the alleged ULP occurred. The court of appeals reviewed the Board's underlying decision about the T-shirts and, agreeing with the ruling, enforced the Board's order.

If either party files a ULP charge during the election campaign, it can have the effect of delaying the election. Under the NLRB's "blocking charge" policy, the regional office will generally suspend the election proceedings while the ULP claims are investigated and, perhaps, litigated.[35] The Board's policy is designed to prevent the election from taking place in a cloud of uncertainty, as fair election conditions could by tainted by employer or (rarely) union ULPs. The effect of the "blocking charge" policy is to delay the holding of elections.[36] It is arguably better policy simply to hold the election and see if the election results moot the charging party's objections. If the charging party were to lose the election, the Board can consider whether a ULP actually occurred, whether it affected the election outcome, and, if so, whether to order a rerun election.[37]

---

[34] Cf. Owens-Illinois, Inc., 271 NLRB 1235 (1984) (election-day gift of union jackets held to be impermissible behavior).

[35] NLRB Casehandling Manual, Pt. 2, Representation Proceedings §§ 11730–11734 (1999).

[36] See Estreicher, Improving the Administration, supra, at 9 & n.28.

[37] For judicial criticism of the blocking-charge policy, see Templeton v. Dixie Color Printing Co., 444 F.2d 1064, 1068 (5th Cir. 1971); but see Surratt v. NLRB, 463 F.2d 378, 381 (5th Cir. 1972); Remington Lodging & Hospitality, LLC v. Ahearn, 749 F. Supp. 2d 951, 962 (D. Alaska 2010) (finding the blocking charge policy to have been applied appropriately). See generally Burton B. Subrin, The NLRB's Blocking Charge Policy: Wisdom or Folly?, 39 Lab. L.J. 651 (1988).

The Trump Board had proposed rulemaking which included a "vote-and-impound" procedure for processing representation petitions when a party has requested blocking the election based on a pending ULP charge. Instead of holding off on the election, the election would be held, but the Board would impound the ballots until the charges had been resolved. NLRB, Notice of Proposed Rulemaking, Representation—Case Procedures: Election Bars; Proof of Majority Support in Construction Industry Collective-Bargaining Relationships, 84 Fed. Reg. 39930, Aug. 12, 2019, https://www.govinfo.gov/content/pkg/FR-2019-08-12/pdf/2019-17105.pdf. The rule was not enacted but may be taken up again in the second Trump term.

3. Injunctions

The handling of ULP charges and representation petitions represents the bulk of the NLRB's work. However, in special cases, the agency seeks preliminary injunctive relief in the courts under §§ 10(j) and 10(*l*) of the Act.[38]

Section 10(j) authorizes the Board to petition the district court for "appropriate temporary relief" after issuance of a complaint alleging ULPs and will obtain such relief if the district court agrees it is "just and proper."[39] A petition for § 10(j) relief requires the approval of both the General Counsel's office and the five-member Board. In some years, the Board has delegated its authority to the General Counsel.

The Board has used the § 10(j) process where time is of the essence, such as in the case of unlawful discharges in the midst of organizing campaigns.[40] Through § 10(j), the Board can obtain interim reinstatement of the employee considered to be discriminatorily discharged within a much briefer period than a typical ALJ administrative proceeding.[41] The Board has also used § 10(j) to enjoin bargaining violations during initial contract negotiations and to expedite relief after an ALJ decision has been handed down.[42]

Section 10(j) is used sparingly. Although the Board has authorized up to 104 cases under § 10(j) in a given year, the norm is roughly half of that.[43] During the past twenty years, there have been between six and forty-five § 10(j) petitions submitted each year.[44] There can be significant variation between years; for fiscal year 2018, the Trump Board pursued only six § 10(j) actions, down from thirty

---

[38] 29 U.S.C. § 160(j), (*l*).

[39] In 2024 the Supreme Court ruled that the traditional four-part test for injunctive relief governed applications for § 10(j) preliminary injunctions. See Starbucks Corp. v. McKinney, 602 U.S. 339, 345 (2024).

[40] See Lafe E. Solomon, Memorandum, Effective Section 10(j) Remedies for Unlawful Discharges in Organizing Campaigns, GC 10–07, Sept. 30, 2010, at: https://apps.nlrb.gov/link/document.aspx/09031d4580989438.

[41] See Samuel Estreicher, Strikers and Replacements, 3 Lab. Lawyer 897, 917–18 (1987).

[42] See Ronald Meisburg, Memorandum, End-of-Term Report on Utilization of Section 10(j) Injunctive Proceedings, GC 10–05, Attachment 1, June 15, 2010, at: https://apps.nlrb.gov/link/document.aspx/09031d458037524a.

[43] As one example, from 1984 to 1993, the Board authorized between 37 and 62 § 10(j) actions per year. In 1994, the number jumped to 83, and it rose again to 104 in 1995. However, it dropped back to 53 in 1996 and 45 in 1998. See Fred Feinstein, The Challenge of Being General Counsel, 16 Lab. Lawyer 19, 28 & fig. 2 (2000).

[44] See NLRB, Injunction Activity under Section 10(j), https://www.nlrb.gov/news-outreach/graphs-data/litigations/litigation-injunction (last visited August 2, 2019).

the year before.[45] The Biden Board also has been sparing in § 10(j) actions, only seeking between seven and nineteen per year. Many commentators, including the authors, have advocated that the internal Board process for seeking § 10(j) relief be streamlined in order to promote its use, which is especially important where union supporters are discharged in the midst of the organizing campaign.[46]

Section 10(*l*), by contrast, concerns charges filed under §§ 8(b)(4), 8(b)(7) & 8(e), which prohibit secondary picketing and boycotts, certain instances of recognitional picketing, and so-called "hot cargo" clauses. With the exception of the latter, these exclusively involve union ULPs. If the Regional Director or Regional Attorney finds reasonable cause supports the charge, the official must bring an action in federal district court to enjoin such activity, without having to obtain Board authorization.[47]

4. Rulemaking

Unlike most other major administrative agencies, the NLRB prefers to make policy through case-by-case adjudication rather than notice-and-comment rulemaking. In 1989, the Board for the first time promulgated a rule, designating eight bargaining units that would be presumed appropriate in acute-care hospitals.[48] The rule was challenged by industry groups upon enactment but affirmed by a unanimous Supreme Court.[49] Despite the auspicious first result, the agency has been less successful in other rulemaking efforts. For example, its attempted presumptive single-location rule during the Clinton Administration foundered in the face of Congressional opposition.[50] In 2011, the D.C. Circuit struck down the Board's rule requiring employers to post conspicuous notices describing employee rights under the NLRA because the rule was deemed to compel employer speech in violation of § 8(c).[51]

Commentators have suggested that the Board engage in rulemaking more frequently, as the process provides more notice to

---

[45] Id.

[46] Estreicher & Bodie, supra, at 97–98.

[47] 29 U.S.C. § 160(*l*).

[48] 54 Fed. Reg. 16336 (1989) (designating units consisting of physicians, registered nurses, other professional employees, medical technicians, skilled maintenance workers, clerical workers, guards, and other nonprofessional employees).

[49] American Hospital Ass'n v. NLRB, 499 U.S. 606 (1991).

[50] For an insider's perspective on this effort and the ensuing Congressional resistance, see William B. Gould, Labored Relations: Law, Politics, and the NLRB 168–75 (2000).

[51] National Assn. of Manuf. v. NLRB, 717 F.3d 947 (D.C. Cir. 2013) (striking down 76 Fed. Reg. 54,006 (Aug. 30, 2011)).

the public and a chance to reduce policy oscillation.[52] Promulgation of a rule, however, also enhances the saliency of what the agency is doing, leading to continual legislative and judicial challenges, which have reduced the agency's appetite for rulemaking. For a time the Trump Administration Board pursued an aggressive rulemaking agenda, regarding topics such as the joint-employer standard, representation-case procedures, and graduate student employment status.[53] But these efforts did not lead to lasting policy changes. The joint-employer rule was undone by a finalized rule under the Biden Administration Board that significantly expanded the scope of joint employment.[54] The new Biden rule itself proved sufficiently controversial that Congress passed a resolution under the Congressional Review Act (CRA)[55] overturning the regulation,[56] and a federal district court enjoined the rule.[57] Other Trump-era rules have not fared better. The Trump Board rule rescinding the Obama Board's overhaul off election procedures was itself rescinded by the Biden Board, which largely returned to the Obama Board policies.[58] And the 2019 proposed rule eliminating the rights of graduate students to organize was withdrawn by the Biden Board within months of the change in administration.[59]

---

52 See, e.g., Samuel Estreicher, Policy Oscillation at the Board: A Plea for Rulemaking, 37 Admin. L. Rev. 163, 181 (1985); Estreicher & Bodie, supra, at 97–98. Judge Henry Friendly was also a noted critic of the agency's reliance on adjudication when changing Board law and urged the use of rulemaking in such circumstances. See NLRB v. Majestic Weaving Co., 355 F.2d 854, 860 (2d Cir. 1966); Bell Aerospace Co. Div. of Textron Inc. v. NLRB, 475 F.2d 485, 495–97 (2d Cir. 1973), rev'd, 416 U.S. 267 (1974). The Supreme Court in *Bell Aerospace* rejected Judge Friendly's approach, holding that the decision whether to engage in rulemaking rather than case-by-case adjudication is a matter within the Board's discretion subject to review only for abuse of discretion.

53 NLRB Office of Public Affairs, NLRB Rulemaking Agenda Announced, May 22, 2019, https://www.nlrb.gov/news-outreach/news-story/nlrb-rulemaking-agenda-announced.

54 Standard for Determining Joint Employer Status, 88 Fed. Reg. 73,946 (Oct. 27, 2023).

55 5 U.S.C. §§ 801–808.

56 H.J. Res. 98, Jan. 12, 2024. President Biden vetoed the CRA resolution. White House, Message to the House of Representatives—President's Veto of H.J. Res. 98, May 3, 2024.

57 Chamber of Commerce of United States v. NLRB, 723 F.Supp.3d 498 (E.D. Tex. 2024). The NLRB chose not to appeal the decision. Unopposed Motion for Voluntary Dismissal, NLRB v. Chamber of Commerce of United States, Case No. 24–40331 (5th Cir. July 19, 2024).

58 See Representation-Case Procedures, 88 Fed. Reg. 58,076 (Aug. 25, 2023). The Trump rule had also been largely invalidated by the D.C. Circuit on review. See AFL-CIO v. NLRB, 57 F.4th 1023 (D.C. Cir. 2023).

59 86 Fed. Reg. 14,297 (March 15, 2021).

C. The Relationship Between the Board and the Courts

The NLRA provides that federal courts of appeals review Board decisions, with the Supreme Court as the final authority. When reviewing factual determinations, courts will affirm the Board's findings "if supported by substantial evidence on the record considered as a whole."[60] Courts have interpreted this to require deference to the Board's factual findings if "it would have been possible for a reasonable trier of fact to reach the Board's conclusion."[61] This is not deference to the ALJ's decision; the ALJ is not a delegatee of Congressional authority. Rather, where deference is owed, it is owed to the five-member Board, which is the Congressional delegatee.[62]

Even though the courts have the last word on what the NLRA means, there are areas whether the agency's views are entitled to strong respect, where the NLRB has built up decades of experience administering the ins and outs of the law or where the best reading of the law is that Congress is inviting agency policymaking discretion, again within statutory limits. For example, it is a ULP under §8(a)(1) for an employer to "interfere" with the employee's exercise of protected group activity. But what does "interfere" mean? Congress plainly meant beyond employer torts under the common law as employees are business invitees and the statute expressly protects employee group activity. Do employees have the right to talk to each other about workplace issues and unions during non-work time at the employer's premises, absent a showing that such communications interfered with production or discipline? The Court (per Justice Reed) in *Republic Aviation Corp. v. NLRB*,[63] upheld the Board's rule of presumptive access as a reasonable policy within the Board's discretion. A decade later in *NLRB v. Babcock & Wilcox Co.*,[64] however, the Court (per Justice Reed again) disagreed with the Board's extension of this rule to non-employee union organizer access as going beyond statutory limits in treating non-employees who were not NLRA rights-bearers nor business invitees the same as employees.

Over time, two administrative law doctrines developed to help guide judicial review of agency statutory interpretation. The doctrine

---

60 29 U.S.C. § 160(f).

61 See Allentown Mack Sales & Service, Inc. v. NLRB, 522 U.S. 359, 370 (1998).

62 See Universal Camera Corp. v. NLRB, 340 U.S. 474 (1951).

63 324 U.S. 793 (1945).

64 351 U.S. 105 (1956).

of "*Skidmore* deference" or "*Skidmore* respect"[65] preserves judicial control of statutory interpretation but allows courts to be persuaded by longstanding agency views which reflect agency experience and expertise. Until recently, a second doctrine termed "*Chevron* deference"[66] was read to require courts to defer to reasonable agency views of the NLRA where the statute was ambiguous. In *Loper Bright Enterprises v. Raimondo*,[67] the Court rejected the *Chevron* doctrine as an abdication of judicial control over what the statute means but left the *Skidmore* framework, and recognition of the Board' reasonable policy-making discretion, undisturbed.

The future relationship between the courts and the NLRB remains uncertain in the wake of *Loper Bright*. Given the many cases before *Chevron* in which the Court expressed deference to the Board's determinations about federal labor law,[68] federal courts may continue to give the Board the opportunity to set labor policy within statutory limits, as in *Republic Aviation*. But empirical studies have shown that labor law remains highly contested terrain.[69] Some commentators blame courts for the conservative turn certain labor law doctrines have taken.[70] Others argue that the Board is at least partially to blame, as it has masked its policy decisions in findings of fact and malleable multi-factor tests.[71] Disputes over important matters of policy seem likely to continue into the future, given the Board's continued oscillation on important labor law doctrines, which

---

65 See Skidmore v. Swift & Co., 323 U.S. 134 (1944).

66 See Chevron U.S.A., Inc. v. NRDC, 467 U.S. 837 (1984).

67 603 U.S. 369 (2024).

68 See, e.g., Republic Aviation Corp. v. NLRB, 324 U.S. 793, 802 (1945) (sustaining the agency's framework where the Board had "fairly . . . explicated" its legal theory as to protected employee speech); NLRB v. Erie Resistor Corp., 373 U.S. 221, 236 (1963); NLRB v. United Insurance Co., 390 U.S. 254, 260 (1968) (upholding the Board's determination when "it made a choice between two fairly conflicting views"). NLRB v. Weingarten, Inc., 420 U.S. 251, 266–67 (1975) (same); NLRB v. Transportation Management Corp., 462 U.S. 393 (1983) (same); NLRB v. Curtin Matheson Scientific, Inc., 494 U.S. 775, 786–87 (1990) ("We will uphold a Board rule as long as it is rational and consistent with the Act, even if we would have formulated a different rule had we sat on the Board.").

69 See James J. Brudney, A Famous Victory: Collective Bargaining Protections and the Statutory Aging Process, 74 N.C. L. Rev. 939, 945–46 (1996), Peter H. Schuck & E. Donald Elliott, To the *Chevron* Station: An Empirical Study of Federal Administrative Law, 1990 Duke L.J. 984, 1013–22.

70 See, e.g., James B. Atleson, Values and Assumptions in American Labor Law (1983), Ellen Dannin, Taking Back the Worker's Law: How to Fight the Assault on Labor Rights (2006); Karl E. Klare, Judicial Deradicalization of the Wagner Act and the Origins of Modern Legal Consciousness, 1937–1941, 62 Minn. L. Rev. 265, 293–336 (1978); George Schatzki, It's Simple: Judges Don't Like Labor Unions, 30 Conn. L. Rev. 1365, 1366–70 (1998).

71 See Joan Flynn, The Costs and Benefits of "Hiding the Ball": NLRB Policymaking and the Failure of Judicial Review, 75 B.U. L. Rev. 387, 427–28 (1995).

can at times appear as political maneuverings rather than reasoned elaboration of the NLRA reflecting agency expertise.[72]

[72] See Samuel Estreicher, 'Depoliticizing' the National Labor Relations Board: Some Administrative Steps, 64 Emory L.J. 1611 (2015).

Chapter 4

NLRB JURISDICTION AND COVERAGE

In typical cases involving manufacturing workers at a large industrial plant or the service and maintenance crew for a large office building, the NLRB's jurisdiction over the matter is clear. However, as the boundaries of national commerce as well as our conception of "employment" have changed, there are cases in which the Board's authority will be contested. This Chapter provides an overview of the Act's coverage, which requires we look at the agency's jurisdiction and the definition of covered "employer" and "employee."

A. NLRA Jurisdictional Limits and the Definition of "Employer"

The NLRB can operate only within the limits of Congress's constitutional authority and the scope of authorization from Congress. In 1938 the Supreme Court upheld the Act as a Commerce Clause measure in *NLRB v. Jones & Laughlin Steel Corp.*[1] The Court observed that Congress defined the Board's jurisdiction in § 2(7) of the Act in broad, inclusive terms;[2] and that the Board's jurisdiction under the statute is coextensive with Congress's authority under the Commerce Clause. The NLRA, the Court held, was a proper exercise of the Congressional power to regulate interstate commerce, for even a local labor dispute could give rise to the requisite burdening of interstate commerce: "It is the effect upon commerce, not the source of the injury, which is the criterion."[3]

---

[1] 301 U.S. 1 (1937).

[2] NLRA § 2(7), 29 U.S.C. § 152(7): "The term 'affecting commerce' means in commerce, or burdening or obstructing commerce or the free flow of commerce, or having led or tending to lead to a labor dispute burdening or obstructing commerce or the free flow of commerce."

[3] *Jones & Laughlin*, 301 U.S. at 32. The broad reading of the commerce power in *Jones & Laughlin* remains intact, It should be noted, however, that a majority of the Justices in National Federation of Independent Business v. Sibelius, 567 U.S. 519 (2012) were unwilling to sustain the statutory requirement that individuals purchase health-care insurance under the Affordable Care Act as a Commerce Clause enactment.

As of this writing, there are several cases challenging on other constitutional grounds the structure and adjudicative process of the NLRB. One major issue is whether the President's executive authority under Article II of the Constitution includes the authority to remove without cause people appointed with the Senate's advice and consent to head multimember agencies like the NLRB even though Congress has provided protections against at-will dismissal. In Humphrey's Executor

In 1958 regulations, the Board set limits on its own jurisdiction related to the size of the employer's business:

> For employers engaged in a retail business: The employer must engage in at least $500,000 in business (as per annual gross volume).
>
> For employers engaged in a nonretail business: The employer must have at least $50,000 in annual "outflow" or "inflow" of business across state lines. Outflow refers to goods or services furnished or sold by the employer; inflow refers to goods or services furnished to or bought by the employer.

These limits have never been updated, but efforts to raise them to adjust for inflation have been unavailing. Section 14(c) permits states to exercise jurisdiction over employers who fall beneath these thresholds,[4] and many states include such small businesses under their state labor laws.

The Board's jurisdiction includes foreign corporations doing business in the United States[5] but does not include U.S. citizens permanently employed, even by American companies, outside of the United States.[6]

The Board's jurisdiction is also limited by emanations from the First Amendment. In *NLRB v. Catholic Bishop of Chicago*,[7] the Supreme Court held that the Board could not exercise jurisdiction over religious organizations as employers. The case involved teachers of lay subjects at parochial schools, and the Court interpreted the

---

v. United States, 295 U.S. 602 (1935), a case involving the Federal Trade Commission (FTC), the Supreme Court unanimously ruled that because the FTC and other so-called "independent" multimember agencies are not "purely executive," but instead exercise some "quasi-judicial" and "quasi-legislative" authority, Congress could provide protection against at-will dismissal. More recently, the Court has suggested that the President's removal authority may extend to multimember agencies exercising "substantial executive power," advancing a "unitary executive" conception of the President's powers under Article II. See Seila Law LLC v. Consumer Fin. Prot. Bureau, 591 U.S. 197 (2020). A related issue is whether ALJs are subject to at-will dismissal despite statutory protections. They are "inferior executive officers" under Lucia v. Securities and Exchange Comm'n, 585 U.S. 237(2018), but they are exclusively engaged in adjudicative tasks, where removal protection may be sustainable under Wiener v. United States, 357 U.S. 349 (1958) (discussing removal of members of the War Claims Commission).

[4] 29 U.S.C. § 164(c).

[5] Il Progresso Italo Americano Publishing Co., 299 NLRB 270 (1990).

[6] Computer Sciences Raytheon, 318 NLRB 966, 968 (1995) (citing McCulloch v. Sociedad Nacional, 372 U.S. 10 (1963)). There will be cases at the margin where the employment relationship is centered in the U.S. but the employees are on temporary assignment in another country. See, e.g., Asplundh Tree Expert Co. v. NLRB, 365 F.3d 168 (3d Cir. 2004).

[7] 440 U.S. 490 (1979).

NLRA not to reach church-operated schools in order to avoid any difficulties under the Free Exercise Clause that might arise from Board interference with their operations.[8]

B. Statutory Exclusions and the Definition of "Employee"

Employees expressly excluded from the Act's coverage by the provisions of § 2(3) (29 U.S.C. § 152(3)) include:

- Agricultural workers[9]
- Employees in "the domestic service of any family or person at his home, or any individual employed by his parent or spouse"[10]
- Public-sector employees[11]
- Railroad, airline, and other transportation workers covered by the Railway Labor Act (RLA)
- Independent contractors (§ 2(3))
- Supervisors (§ 2(11))[12]

While some of these categories are fairly easy to demarcate, others have proven more challenging to apply. Below we explore how the Board and courts have approached these exclusions.

---

[8] In Pacific Lutheran University, 361 NLRB 1404, 1408 (2014), the Board asserted jurisdiction over a case involving contingent (non-tenure track) higher-education faculty, stating it would decline jurisdiction on *Catholic Bishop* grounds only if the school "holds itself out" (1) as "providing a religious educational environment", and (2) "the petitioned-for faculty members perform[ ] a specific role in creating or maintaining the school's religious educational environment."

[9] California and Arizona, among other states, have enacted agricultural labor relations laws. See California Agricultural Labor Relations Act, Cal. Lab. Code §§ 1140–1166.3; Arizona Farm Labor Law, A.R.S. §§ 3–3101–3–3125; A.R.S. §§ 23–1381–23–1395.

[10] Illinois established a collective bargaining structure between representatives of home health-care workers and the state. See Harris v. Quinn, 573 U.S. 616 (2014) (holding that the state could not require these health-care workers to pay an agency fee under the First Amendment; earlier ruling that permitted such payments in the context of a government employee collective-bargaining agreement did not apply to persons who are not "full-fledged public employees, but [rather] others who are deemed to be public employees solely for the purpose of unionization and the collection of an agency fee"). In Janus v. AFSCME Council 31, 585 U.S. 878 (2018), the Court, overruling prior precedent, held that the First Amendment prohibited agreements that required any government employee represented in collective bargaining to pay their share of the costs of union representation if they opposed such representation.

[11] These include employees of federal, state, and local governments.

[12] Under NLRB v. Bell Aerospace Co., 416 U.S. 267 (1974), managerial employees are impliedly excluded from the Act. Under NLRB v. Hendricks County Rural Elec., 454 U.S. 170 (1981), confidential employees are only excluded if they perform "labor nexus" functions under the *Bell Aerospace* rationale.

1. Independent Contractors

The NLRA initially did not expressly exclude independent contractors, and the Board interpreted "employee" broadly to cover some workers who would traditionally have been in that category. In a 1944 decision, the Supreme Court affirmed an NLRB determination that news vendors who operated their own newsstand and sometimes hired their own help were nevertheless statutory employees because of the "economic realities" of their dependent relationship on the newspaper publishers. But Congress in the 1947 Taft-Hartley amendments rejected this interpretation. Section 2(3) now expressly excludes "any individual having the status of an independent contractor." The NLRA itself contains no definition of "independent contractor." Committee reports accompanying the amendment state that the applicable test is the common law "right to control" test, developed as a principle of agency law in the context of determining whether a user of another person's services is responsible for torts committed by that person pursuant to an agency relationship.

As formulated in § 220 of the American Law Institute (ALI)'s Restatement Second of Agency, which the Supreme Court has favorably referenced in a number of decisions, the putative employer's ability to control the physical conduct in the performance of the services—the "right to control" factor or test—is the dominant criterion for employee status.[13] However, § 220 includes nine other relevant factors as part of its test, including whether the worker is engaged in a distinct occupation or business, the skill required for the particular occupation, and whether or not the work is a part of the regular business of the employer.[14] The relationship between these factors has been the source of controversy and contention for the Board and courts of appeals.[15]

A recurring area of difficulty has been the employee status of delivery truck drivers. Drivers are given assignments and a time frame to complete delivery but are not closely supervised as to how they go about performing their tasks. They may own their

---

[13] On whether a contractual reservation of a right to control is sufficient for employer status under the common law, see Samuel Estreicher & Sara Spaur, Is Actual Control Required for an Employer-Employee Relationship? The Case Law Suggests Otherwise, Justia Verdict, Sept. 30, 2019.

[14] Whether the putative independent contractors perform tasks central to the user employer's core business is emphasized in the California Supreme Court's influential decision in Dynamex Operations West, Inc. v. Superior Court of Los Angeles, 4 Cal.5th 903 (2018), as codified in California Labor Code § 2775 et seq.

[15] For the view that independent contractors who supply principally their personal services without significant capital investment are covered by the "statutory" labor exemption to the antitrust laws, see Samuel Estreicher & Jack Samuel, Labor's Antitrust Exemption for Independent-Contractor Workers, 59 Wake Forest L. Rev. 1060 (2024).

equipment, even their own trucks. In *Roadway Package Systems, Inc.*,[16] the Board found delivery truck drivers working for a nationwide package delivery company to be employees, based on the drivers' lack of prior experience, their de facto exclusive arrangements with the company, and the uniformity of their operating procedures. The Board, however, considered the drivers in *Dial-A-Mattress Operating Corp.*[17] to be independent contractors because they had more flexibility in choosing and outfitting their trucks, which the drivers could also use for other jobs.

In *FedEx Home Delivery v. NLRB*,[18] the D.C. Circuit ruled that the right-of-control test has evolved into an inquiry over whether the workers have "significant entrepreneurial opportunity for gain or loss."[19] The court reversed the Board's determination that the delivery truck drivers were employees reasoning that the drivers retained important contractual rights, including the rights to sell their routes. In a 2014 case involving FedEx drivers, the Board responded by reiterating the importance of all of the factors that make up the "right to control" test.[20] Looking at the actual—rather than theoretical—entrepreneurial opportunities available to drivers, the Board held that they were employees.[21]

The first Trump Administration Board adopted a more expansive view of the entrepreneurial-control test in *SuperShuttle DFW*.[22] It overruled the Board's 2014 *FedEx II* decision because it had "impermissibly altered the common-law test" by denigrating the entrepreneurial-opportunities factor.[23] The Board explained that "employer control and [the contractor's] entrepreneurial opportunity

---

16 326 NLRB 842 (1998).

17 326 NLRB 884 (1998).

18 563 F.3d 492 (D.C. Cir. 2009).

19 Id. at 497. But see Matthew T. Bodie, Participation as a Theory of Employment, 89 Notre Dame L. Rev. 661, 718–20 (2013) (the FedEx drivers were employees because they were almost exclusively engaged in FedEx's core business).

20 FedEx Home Delivery, 361 NLRB 610 (2014) (*Fed Ex II*).

21 In *FedEx II*, the Board referenced the American Law Institute (ALI)'s Restatement of Employment Law, which provided a new formulation for the employment test. 361 NLRB at 621. Individuals providing services are independent contractors if "the employer controls the manner and means by which individual renders services, or the employer otherwise effectively prevents the individual from rendering those services as an independent businessperson." Restatement of Employment Law § 1.01 (2015). The Restatement specifies that an independent businessperson "in his or her own interest exercises entrepreneurial control over important business decisions, including whether to hire and where to assign assistants, whether to purchase and where to deploy equipment, and whether and where to provide service to other customers." Id. § 1.01(b). (The authors of this book were reporters for the Employment Law Restatement.)

22 SuperShuttle DFW, Inc., 367 NLRB No. 75 (Jan. 25, 2019).

23 Id. at *1.

are opposite sides of the same coin: in general, the more control, the less scope for entrepreneurial initiative, and vice versa."[24]

The Biden Board in *The Atlanta Opera*[25] returned to the agency's earlier multi-factor test that does not place special emphasis on entrepreneurial opportunities. It noted the continuing relevance of the common-law agency test as set forth in § 220 of the Restatement Second of Agency, stating that the right to control is only one factor among many and that there is "no shorthand formula or magic phrase that can be applied to find the answer."[26]

2. Supervisors

The premise, and promise, of the NLRA is that employees should have the right to bargain collectively with their employer over their terms and conditions of employment. Thus, the "employer" must have an existence distinct from its employees in order to bargain with them. The NLRA differentiates between managerial or supervisory employees who act as representatives of the company and those employees who do not. Some employees have a controlling interest in the company and are excluded from coverage as either executives or owners.[27] Other employees do not come within the core control group but supervise employees on behalf of the employer.

Congress in the 1947 Taft-Hartley amendments excluded supervisors from coverage under the NLRA. Under § 2(11), an excluded "supervisor" is "any individual having authority, in the interest of the employer, to hire, transfer, suspend, lay off, recall, promote, discharge, assign, reward, or discipline other employees, or responsibly to direct them, or to adjust their grievances, or effectively to recommend such action, if in connection with the foregoing the exercise of such authority is not of a merely routine or clerical nature, but requires the use of independent judgment."[28]

The § 2(11) definition for supervisor can be broken down into three elements:

(1) the exercise of one of the twelve supervisory functions (hire, transfer, suspend, lay off, recall, promote, discharge, assign, reward, or discipline other employees, or responsibly to direct them, or to adjust their grievances);

---

[24] Id. at *15.

[25] 372 NLRB No. 95 (June 13, 2023).

[26] Id. at 3–4 (quoting NLRB v. United Insurance Co. of America, 390 U.S. 254, 258 (1968)).

[27] Cf. Restatement of Employment Law § 1.02 (2015) (discussing the role of owners as employees under the common law).

[28] 29 U.S.C. § 152(11).

(2) the use of independent judgment in exercising the function or functions; and

(3) exercising that authority "in the interest of the employer."

Some of the twelve functions serve as hallmarks of supervisory status, such as the authority to hire and discharge. Others have been harder to pin down, such as the authority to assign tasks to other employees or the ability "responsibly to direct them."[29] A worker need only perform one of these twelve functions to meet this part of the test. Moreover, the statute specifies that it is enough "effectively to recommend such action."[30] The other two factors—independent judgment and interest of the employer—have also been difficult to apply in particular cases.

The basic policy judgment underlying § 2(11) is that an employer is entitled to the undivided loyalty of its representatives. This policy is also reflected in § 8(b)(1)(A), a Taft-Hartley provision that make it a ULP for a union "to restrain or coerce . . . an employer in the selection of his representatives for the purposes of collective bargaining or the adjustment of grievances."

In a series of cases stretching out over a decade, the Board and the Supreme Court wrestled with the question of whether registered and licensed practical nurses were supervisors for purposes of the Act. These cases involve an overlap between the supervisory exclusion and Congress's decision in § 2(12), another Taft-Hartley provision, to include professional employees as statutory employees.[31] In these cases, the nurses generally exercise some of the twelve supervisory functions, in that they are often responsible for assigning and directing the work of the nurses' aides. The Board has resisted finding supervisory status. Its initial approach was to rule that the nurses did not exercise authority "in the interest of their employer" but rather only as part of their professional responsibility to care for patients. In *NLRB v. Health Care & Retirement Corp. of America*,[32] the Supreme Court rejected the Board's reasoning: "Patient care is the business of a nursing home, and it follows that attending to the needs of the nursing home patients, who are the employer's customers, is in the interest of the employer."

In a second round of cases culminating in *NLRB v. Kentucky River Community Care, Inc.*,[33] the Board invoked the "independent

[29] Id.

[30] Id.

[31] 29 U.S.C. § 152(12).

[32] 511 U.S. 571, 577 (1994).

[33] 532 U.S. 706 (2001).

judgment" element of the statutory provision and treated as nonsupervisory "ordinary professional or technical judgment in directing less-skilled employees to deliver services." In this case, the registered nurses would at times direct the work of other employees (such as nurses' aides), although they had no authority to enforce their instructions through discipline. In effect, the Board tried to limit the scope of the "responsibly to direct" prong by requiring that the worker use something other than ordinary professional judgment in directing the employees. Without this limitation, the agency reasoned, almost all professional employees—who frequently direct clerical workers to work with them in their tasks—would be considered supervisors.

The Supreme Court in *Kentucky River* rejected this approach as well. It agreed with the Board that the "responsibly to direct" prong was ambiguous and that the employer might eliminate an employee's independent judgment through a set of detailed instructions.[34] But the Board's introduction of the "ordinary professional judgment" gloss, the majority stated, "insert[ed] a startling categorical exclusion into statutory text that does not suggest its existence."[35]

The Board signaled a different approach in the 2006 case of *Oakwood Healthcare, Inc.*[36] The agency defined the term "assign" in the statutory exclusion as "the act of designating an employee to a place (such as a location, department, or wing), appointing an employee to a time (such as a shift or overtime period), or giving significant overall duties, i.e., tasks, to an employee."[37] Thus, for example, "if a charge nurse designates [a licensed practical nurse (LPN)] to be the person who will regularly administer medications to a patient or a group of patients, the giving of that overall duty to the LPN is an assignment."[38] But short-term directives not part of a regular assignment, such as the charge nurse's ordering an LPN to immediately give a sedative to a particular patient, would not be sufficient evidence of supervision. In addition, the Board held that the putative supervisor also had to be held accountable for the performance of the employees she directs in order to fulfill the "responsibly to direct" factor.

---

34 Id. at 713–14.

35 Id. at 714. Interestingly, the Court suggested a line of inquiry that might lead to employee status in some cases: "Perhaps the Board could offer a limiting interpretation of the supervisory function of responsible direction by distinguishing employees who direct the manner of others' performance of discrete *tasks* from employees who direct other *employees,* as [§ 2(11)] requires." Id. at 720 (emphasis in original).

36 348 NLRB 686 (2006).

37 Id. at 689.

38 Id.

In these nursing cases, the unions wanted the nurses not to be considered supervisors, as the unions were seeking to represent them. In other cases, however, unions have sought to exclude individual employees as supervisors. The union may not want those employees to be voting in the representation election because they might be opposed to unionization in general or representation by this union. Or these potential supervisors may have improperly questioned other employees or threatened them for their union support, and the union wants to hold the employer responsible for their actions. Thus, the scope of supervisory status does not always cut in a pro-union or pro-employer direction.

3. Managerial Employees

Managerial employees are non-supervisory personnel who are impliedly excluded from the Act because they function as part of management when they formulate, determine, and effectuate management policies. In *NLRB v. Bell Aerospace Co.*,[39] the Supreme Court rejected the agency's attempt to narrow the implied exclusion of managerial employees to those who are involved in the employer's personnel and labor relations functions (the so-called "labor nexus"). Justice Powell, writing for the Court, explained that Congress intended to exclude supervisors, executives, and others who function as policy-makers or policy-implementers for the company whether or not they supervise employees. Under *Bell Aerospace*, non-supervisory managers are excluded from NLRA coverage; supervisors are already excluded under § 2(11).

In the higher-education context, the question arose whether faculty involved in important policy decisions for the university, such as curriculum, admissions, hiring, and promotion, were excluded managerial employees under *Bell Aerospace*. In *NLRB v. Yeshiva University*,[40] the Court held that one university's set of professors were managerial:

> [The faculty's] authority in academic matters is absolute. They decide what courses will be offered, when they will be scheduled, and to whom they will be taught. They debate and determine teaching methods, grading policies, and matriculation standards. They effectively decide which students will be admitted, retained, and graduated. On occasion their views have determined the size of the student body, the tuition to be charged, and the location of a school.

---

[39] 416 U.S. 267 (1974).

[40] 444 U.S. 672 (1980).

When one considers the function of a university, it is difficult to imagine decisions more managerial than these.[41]

The Board generally has found university faculty to be managerial employees.[42] In a 2014 decision, the Board adopted a framework that asks whether faculty "actually control or make effective recommendations" in five specific areas: academic programs, enrollment management, finances, academic policies, and personnel policies and decisions.[43] Although two Board members disagreed with aspects of the majority's new approach, all five members agreed that the nontenure-track faculty members in the specific case were insufficiently involved in key area of governance to be managerial.[44] Reviewing the Board's new standard, the D.C. Circuit ruled that the Board had erred by focusing on whether the faculty subgroup can force through policy changes with their own voting power.[45] Instead, the critical question is whether "that subgroup is structurally included within a collegial faculty body to which the university has delegated managerial authority."[46] Voting power, the court reasoned, is relevant only if the interests of the subgroup diverge substantially from the other members of the overall faculty group. This called for a remand for the Board to consider this factual question.[47]

Confidential employees are those who "assist and act in a confidential capacity to persons who formulate, determine and effectuate management policies in the field of labor relations."[48] The Board has endeavored to keep this category fairly narrow by requiring more than the mere handling of confidential information[49] or typing of confidential memos.[50] In addition, the Board has not entirely excluded "labor nexus" confidential employees from the Act; they are just excluded for purposes of collective bargaining units.[51]

---

[41] Id. at 686.

[42] Ithaca College, 261 NLRB 577 (1982); LeMoyne College, 345 NLRB 1123 (2005).

[43] Pacific Lutheran University, 361 NLRB 1404, 1420 (2014).

[44] Id.

[45] University of Southern California v. NLRB, 918 F.3d 126 (D.C. Cir. 2019).

[46] Id. at 137.

[47] Upon remand the union disclaimed interest in the unit, and the Board disposed of the case. University of Southern California, No. 31–CA–178831, 2019 WL 3183661, at *1 (July 12, 2019).

[48] B.F. Goodrich Co., 115 NLRB 722, 724 (1956).

[49] Lincoln Park Nursing & Convalescent Home, 318 NLRB 1160 (1995).

[50] Ryder Student Transp. Servs., 336 NLRB 882 (2001).

[51] Peavey Co., 249 NLRB 853, 853 n.3 (1980).

The Supreme Court has upheld the Board's demarcation of this category.[52]

4. Students

Students who simply pay tuition to attend classes are clearly not employees. But what if students have their tuition forgiven or are paid an additional stipend for educational-oriented work, such as teaching classes or conducting research? The Board has oscillated in this area. In 1974, the Board held that graduate students were not employees under the Act.[53] The agency reasoned that even when serving as teaching assistants or research assistants, graduate students were still primarily students. The Board later included medical interns and residents in the student category.[54]

The Clinton Board changed course in *Boston Medical Center Corp.*,[55] ruling that medical interns and residents are statutory employees. There is no statutory exclusion for "student" under § 2(3), the Board observed, and § 2(12) specifically defined professional employees as those who had "completed the courses of specialized intellectual instruction and study." The interns and residents had all completed their schooling and, in the case of the residents, were licensed to practice medicine. Given the amount of work required when balanced against the education provided, the Board found the interns and residents to be employees. A year after *Boston Medical*, the Board held that graduate students serving as paid teaching assistants were employees in *New York University*.[56] Once again, the students' responsibilities toward their degree were not enough to render their work as teachers and researchers outside the realm of employment.

Although the Board's *Boston Medical* precedent has remained in place, the status of graduate students has flipped back and forth. Four years after *NYU*, the Bush Board in *Brown University*[57] returned to the Board's earlier position. The agency held that graduate students had a primarily educational, rather than economic, relationship with the university. Thrusting collective bargaining into the teacher-student relationship, maintained the Board, would disrupt the university's mission and threaten academic freedom. With the onset of the Obama Administration, the Board

---

[52] NLRB v. Hendricks Co. Rural Electric Membership Corp., 454 U.S. 170 (1981).

[53] The Leland Stanford Junior Univ., 214 NLRB 621, 623 (1974).

[54] St. Clare's Hospital, 229 NLRB 1000 (1977); Cedars-Sinai Medical Center, 223 NLRB 251 (1976).

[55] 330 NLRB 152 (1999).

[56] 332 NLRB 1205 (2000).

[57] 342 NLRB 483 (2004).

reversed course in *Columbia University*.[58] The Board held that it had "the statutory authority to treat student assistants as statutory employees, where they perform work, at the direction of the university, for which they are compensated."[59] As of 2024, the *Columbia* decision remained Board law.[60]

When offered the opportunity to determine whether college football players at Northwestern University were employees under the Act to be represented in a separate unit the part of a league comprised of public and private university teams, the Obama Administration Board declined to assert jurisdiction.[61] Because public colleges and universities provide a majority of teams and players in the various football conferences—in this instance, the Big 10 Conference—the Board believed it would not promote stability in labor relations to assert jurisdiction over the remaining private colleges, even if statutorily permissible.[62]

5. Union "Salts"

In *NLRB v. Town & Country Electric, Inc.*[63] the Supreme Court unanimously held that paid union organizers—often called "salts," as they salt the workplace for the union—are employees of the employer even if they are also employees of the union. The Court based its decision on the broad statutory definition of "employee" in § 2(3), and the common law rule that a worker could be an employee of two different employers at the same time. Fears that such workers might do a bad job, or even sabotage the company, could be handled, the Court reasoned, through normal workplace discipline. There was no basis for the assumption, said the Court, that the "salt" would work

---

[58] The Trustees of Columbia Univ. in the City of New York & Graduate Workers of Columbia-GWC, UAW, 364 NLRB 1080 (2016).

[59] Id. at 1080. See also id. ("Statutory coverage is permitted by virtue of an employment relationship; it is not foreclosed by the existence of some other, additional relationship that the Act does not reach.").

[60] The Trump Administration endeavored to use rulemaking to exclude graduate student assistants from the employee category. The original Notice of Proposed Rulemaking (NPRM) was published on September 23, 2019, but a final rule never issued, and the Biden Board withdrew the NPRM in March 2021. 84 Fed. Reg. 49,691 (Sept. 23, 2019) (original notice); 86 Fed. Reg. 14,297 (March 15, 2021) (withdrawal of notice).

[61] Northwestern Univ., 362 NLRB 1350, 1352 (2015).

[62] Under the Biden Administration, GC Abruzzo took the position that college athletes met the requirements for employment status. Jennifer A. Abruzzo, Statutory Rights of Players at Academic Institutions (Student-Athletes) Under the National Labor Relations Act, GC Memorandum 21–08, Sept. 29, 2021. One regional director found the Dartmouth men's basketball team to be an appropriate bargaining unit, but the union subsequently withdrew its petition before appeal. Jimmy Golen, Dartmouth Basketball Players End Their Unionization Attempt in Anticipation of Shifting NLRB, Associated Press, Dec. 31, 2024.

[63] 516 U.S. 85 (1995).

against the interest of the employer: seeking collective representation was consistent with the obligations of the employment relationship. The difficult question in this area is whether an employer can enforce a policy against "moonlighting," even if the motive in doing so is to avoid hiring individuals who also work for a union.

6. Undocumented Immigrant Workers

Undocumented aliens come from another country to work in this country without legal authorization to do so. Federal immigration laws prohibit employers from knowingly hiring undocumented workers, but enforcement is limited.[64] The NLRB considers individuals who are otherwise employees to be covered by labor law, even if they lack legal authorization to work in this country. Thus, employers are still prohibited from committing ULPs against such workers, even if not all NLRA remedies would be available. [65]

The question is one of remedy. The Supreme Court ruled in its 1984 *Sure-Tan* decision that an employee who was no longer in the United States at the time of the Board's order was not entitled to reinstatement or back pay.[66] This restriction on relief was extended in *Hoffman Plastic Compounds, Inc. v. NLRB*,[67] which held that an undocumented immigrant who remained in the country was also not entitled to relief. Even though federal immigration law did not expressly bar undocumented workers from working in the country or bar the provision of relief to them for statutory violations, the Court determined that the policy of federal immigration law prevented NLRA backpay relief because the remedy presupposes legal entitlement to work. Critics of *Hoffman Plastic* argue that it permits employers to hire undocumented workers and retaliate against them with impunity if they seek to form a union and insist on collective representation. A number of federal and state court decisions hold that undocumented workers can sue under wage and hour laws to recover compensation for serviced rendered.[68]

---

64 8 U.S.C. § 1324a(a)(1).

65 Sure-Tan, Inc. v. NLRB, 467 U.S. 883 (1984).

66 Id.

67 535 U.S. 137 (2002).

68 For further discussion, see Singh v. Jutla & C.D. & R's Oil, Inc., 214 F. Supp. 2d 1056, 1060–61 (N.D. Cal. 2002) (*Hoffman* does not bar an undocumented employee from recovering unpaid wages for work actually performed); Garcia v. Pasquareto, 11 Misc. 3d 1, 812 N.Y.S.2d 216 (App. Term 2004) (noting that courts construing *Hoffman* have held consistently that it does not apply to claims for unpaid wages already earned); Ayala v. Lee, 81 A.3d 584 (Md. App. 2013); Jarod S. Gonzalez, Employment Law Remedies for Illegal Immigrants, 40 Tex. Tech L. Rev. 987 (2008); Michael J. Wishnie, Emerging Issues for Undocumented Workers, 6 U. Pa. J. Lab. & Emp. L. 497, 499–500 (2004).

C. Joint Employment

Joint employment—two or more companies managing the same group of workers—often arises in the context of a company that hires a subcontractor to provide a specific set of services that relate to the original company's core business. Does the original company become a joint employer of the subcontractor's employees due to the control that the original company exercises over the subcontractor's workers? In *Boire v. Greyhound Corp.*,[69] Greyhound contracted with an outside maintenance company to provide porters, janitors, and maids at four of its bus terminals. A union sought to represent these employees, naming both Greyhound and the maintenance company as "the employer" of the employees it sought to represent. The union argued alternatively that the unit requested was appropriate as a residual unit of all unrepresented Greyhound employees at the four terminals or that those employees were a distinct appropriate unit. Finding a joint employment relationship, the Board concluded that the unit consisting of all employees under the joint employer relationship was an appropriate unit and set an election date. Before the election took place, Greyhound filed suit in federal district court, claiming that the Board was acting outside of its statutory authority. Without reaching the joint-employer issue, the Supreme Court held that the district court lacked jurisdiction under *Leedom v. Kyne*[70] because the Board's determination was not final and did not involve a clear abuse of discretion but rather was "essentially a factual issue."[71]

The facts in *Boire* indicate why the joint-employer issue can be important. A joint-employer determination provides a means for ensuring that a union contract with the subcontractor will be enforceable against the user employer, even if the subcontractor is practically insolvent; collective bargaining will be meaningful since parties with control over labor terms will be at the table. Sometimes some of these benefits can be achieved without a formal joint-employer determination by, say, the union insisting on a guarantor clause. A general question is how much control, and what kind of control, one employer needs to have over another employer's workforce to be considered a joint employer. Usually the control has to be with respect to the terms and conditions of employment of the workers in the other company. In *NLRB v. Browning-Ferris Indus. of Pennsylvania, Inc.*,[72] the Third Circuit stated that "where two or more employers exert significant control over the same employees—

---

[69] 376 U.S. 473 (1964).

[70] 358 U.S. 184 (1958).

[71] *Boire*, 376 U.S. at 481–82.

[72] 691 F.2d 1117 (3d Cir. 1982).

where from the evidence it can be shown that they share or co-determine those matters governing essential terms and conditions of employment—they constitute 'joint employers' within the meaning of the NLRA."[73]

Under the Obama Administration, the Board moved to expand the definition of joint employer substantially. In a subsequent case also involving Browning-Ferris,[74] the Board majority ruled that the putative joint employer did not have to actually exercise control over the labor conditions of joint employees; it was sufficient that it had the contractual right to control those conditions, either directly or indirectly.[75]

This consideration of "indirect control" opened up a new swath of relationships for possible joint-employer designation, including potentially many franchisor-franchisee pairings. Franchisors need to maintain certain controls over franchisees to preserve the integrity of their brand or for regulatory reasons. The Obama Administration General Counsel initiated a NLRB proceeding against McDonald's for the alleged unfair labor practices of one of its franchisees.[76] The General Counsel's theory was that the franchisor exercised more controls over employment terms that went beyond what was needed to protect brand integrity. With the onset of the first Trump Administration, the McDonald's proceeding ended. In 2020, the Trump Board issued a final rule to the effect that an employer would be a joint employer of another employer's employees "only if the two employers share or codetermine the employees' essential terms and conditions of employment."[77]

In 2023, the Biden Administration Board rescinded the joint-employer rule and undertook rulemaking to reinstate the *Browning-Ferris* standard using common-law principles to determine the extent of direct or indirect control.[78] Concerned about the expansion of coverage to include franchisors and other contracting relationships, Congress passed a resolution under the Congressional Review Act[79] overturning the regulation.[80] President Biden vetoed this measure.[81]

---

[73] Id. at 1124.

[74] See Browning-Ferris Industry of California, Inc., 362 NLRB 1599 (2015).

[75] Id. at 1600.

[76] McDonald's USA, LLC, 363 NLRB No. 144 (Mar. 17, 2016).

[77] NLRB, Joint Employer Status under the National Labor Relations Act, 85 Fed. Reg. 11184, 11235 (Feb. 26, 2020).

[78] NLRB, Standard for Determining Joint Employer Status, 88 Fed. Reg. 73,946 (Oct. 27, 2023).

[79] 5 U.S.C. §§ 801–808.

[80] H.J. Res. 98, Jan. 12, 2024.

[81] White House, Message to the House of Representatives—President's Veto of H.J. Res. 98, May 3, 2024.

In the meantime, a federal district court enjoined the rule as inappropriately broad.[82] After initially appealing the decision to the Fifth Circuit, the Board withdrew its appeal, seeking additional time to consider the lower court's ruling and leaving the Trump Board's rule in place.[83]

---

[82] Chamber of Commerce of United States v. NLRB, 723 F.Supp.3d 498 (E.D. Tex. 2024).

[83] Unopposed Motion for Voluntary Dismissal, NLRB v. Chamber of Commerce of United States, Case No. 24–40331 (5th Cir. July 19, 2024).

Chapter 5

EMPLOYEE RIGHTS TO ENGAGE IN CONCERTED ACTIVITY

This Chapter discusses the rights that employees have under the NLRA to engage in concerted activity in an effort to improve their wages and working conditions as well as the ways that employers[1] can commit unfair labor practices (ULPs) infringing those rights.

A. Overview of Concerted Activity

Section 7 is the fountainhead of the Act. Under this provision, employees have to the right to engage in self-organization, to organize, join and assist labor unions, to bargain collectively and to engage in "other concerted activity for the purpose of collective bargaining or other mutual aid or protection." As added by the 1947 Taft-Hartley Act, employees also have "the right to refrain from all such activities."[2]

Section 7 is broadly framed. The right of employees to engage in concerted activities extends not only to involvement with unions and collective bargaining but also to engaging in "self-organization" and "other mutual aid or protection."[3] This provision protects employees when they engage in informal protests even without any union involvement,[4] or when they support employment-related groups that are not considered labor organizations under the Act. In recent times, for instance, worker centers have emerged as a focal point for worker

---

1 Union ULPs, covered under § 8(b), will be discussed at greater length in Chapters 8 (secondary boycotts and picketing) and Chapter 12 (the union's duty of fair representation).

2 29 U.S.C. § 157.

3 The Railway Labor Act (RLA) does not provide a similarly broad right to engage in protected concerted activity. Section 2, Fourth bans employer interference with the employee's decision to engage in union activities: "No carrier . . . shall deny or in any way question the right of its employees to join, organize, or assist in organizing the labor organization of their choice, and it shall be unlawful for any carrier to interfere in any way with the organization of its employees, or to use the funds of the carrier in maintaining or assisting or contributing to any labor organization." 45 U.SC. § 152, Fourth.

Absent a connection with a union or in opposition to a union, the RLA does not protect individual or concerted protest activity. For example, represented employees under the NLRA have a § 7 right to have a union advocate present during an investigatory interview which the employee reasonably believes might result in discipline. See NLRB v. J. Weingarten, Inc., 420 U.S. 251 (1975). Under the RLA, by contrast, employees do not have such a right. See, e.g., Johnson v. Express One Intl., Inc., 944 F.2d 247 (5th Cir. 1991).

4 See NLRB v. Washington Aluminum Co., 370 U.S. 9 (1962).

protests even though these centers do not seek to engage in collective bargaining with employers.[5]

The NLRA sets forth employer ULPs in § 8(a). Under § 8(a)(1), it is an ULP for the employer to "interfere with, restrain, or coerce employees in the exercise of" their § 7 rights. Section 8(a)(1) also plays a residual role; a charge that alleges a violation any of the more specific employer ULPs also includes a § 8(a)(1) allegation. The other four § 8(a) provisions target narrower behavior: dominating, interfering with, or supporting a labor organization (§ 8(a)(2)); encouraging or discouraging union membership by discrimination (§ 8(a)(3)); retaliating against an employee for filing charges or giving testimony in a Board proceeding (§ 8(a)(4)); or refusing to bargain collectively with the employees' representative (§ 8(a)(5)).

B. Motive-Based Violations

1. Employer Discipline

The quintessential ULP is the employer's discharge of an employee because of their activity in support of a union organizing campaign or other § 7 protected activity—a violation of §§ 8(a)(1) & (3). This is a motive-based violation.[6] Violations of § 8(a)(3) require that the employer take adverse action against the employee using a certain means—"by discrimination"—and with a certain purpose—"to encourage or discourage membership in any labor organization."[7] The Board and the courts have interpreted this section to require a pro- or anti-union motive in order to find a ULP. Although the decisions often use the term "animus," the employer's motivation is unlawful if it includes discriminatory treatment of the employee because of the employee's decision to engage or refrain from engaging in § 7 concerted activity; antipathy or other hostility, which the term "animus" might suggest, is not required.

Consider the facts in *Edward G. Budd Mfg. Co. v. NLRB*,[8] where the employer had acquiesced in all manner of misbehavior by its employee Walter Weigand, who came to work drunk, came and left as he pleased, and had brought in a woman (known as the "Duchess") to fraternize with his male co-workers on work time and on company property. As the court noted, "If ever a workman deserved summary

[5] See Kati L. Griffith, Workers Centers and Labor Law Protections: Why Aren't They Having Their Cake?, 36 Berkeley J. Emp. & Lab. L. 331 (2015).

[6] Where the discipline occurs because of union activity, § 8(a)(3) is violated; where it occurs because of protected concerted activity in the absence of a union, § 8(a)(1) is the relevant provision.

[7] 29 U.S.C. § 158(a)(3).

[8] 138 F.2d 86 (3d Cir. 1943).

discharge it was he."[9] The court of appeals, however, upheld the Board's ruling that his termination of employment violated § 8(a)(3), agreeing that Weigand was not fired for his ongoing misconduct until he had been seen talking to a union organizer. Although the company pointed to Weigand's long list of misbehavior in justifying the discharge, the court agreed with the Board that the evidence showed the employer's motivation was based on Weigand's association with a union organizer, not his violations of the employer's policies.

The Weigand case raises the question whether there is a violation when the employer has two motives for its decision: one lawful and other unlawful. There are essentially four alternative ways in which the Board could deal with the dual-motive issue:

(1) *"Taint" as a Complete Violation*: Under this approach, if the General Counsel were to prove that concerted activity plays a motivating role, a violation would be found and traditional NLRB remedies such as reinstatement and backpay would apply.

(2) *Shifting Burden; "Same Decision" as Complete Defense*: If the General Counsel were to prove that concerted activity played a motivating role, the burden of persuasion would shift to the respondent (usually the employer) to prove that it would have reached the same decision in any event. If the employer were to establish this proof, it would be a complete defense.

(3) *Shifting Burden; Remedial Consequence Only*: Here, as in (2), the persuasion burden would shift to the employer but the "same decision" defense, if established, would limit only individualized remedies for the discriminatee; the Board would still be able to order declaratory and prospective relief.[10]

(4) *Board Must Prove Concerted Activity Was "But For" Cause*: This is the position suggested by the First Circuit,[11] which the Supreme Court in *Transportation Management* held that the Board was free in its discretion to reject.[12]

---

[9] Id. at 90.

[10] An example of option (3) can be found in Title VII of the Civil Rights Act of 1964, 42 U.S.C. § 2000e–2(m).

[11] See NLRB v. Wright Line, 662 F.2d 899 (1st Cir. 1981).

[12] In the antidiscrimination context, the Supreme Court has ruled that when a statute prohibits an employment decision "because of" discrimination against a protected status or activity, the plaintiff (or agency suing on plaintiff's behalf) must show that "but for" that status or activity, the plaintiffs would not have been subject to the adverse employment action. See Univ. of Texas SW. Med. Ctr. v. Nassar, 570

In *NLRB v. Transportation Management*,[13] the Supreme Court approved the Board's adoption of option (2), often referred to as "the *Wright Line* test." As the Board has explained, the *Wright Line* framework provides the following:

> To establish his initial burden under *Wright Line*, the General Counsel must establish four elements by a preponderance of the evidence. First, the General Counsel must show the existence of activity protected by the Act. Second, the General Counsel must prove that the respondent was aware that the employee had engaged in such activity. Third, the General Counsel must show that the alleged discriminatee suffered an adverse employment action. Fourth, the General Counsel must establish a motivational link, or nexus, between the employee's protected activity and the adverse employment action.
>
> If, after considering all of the relevant evidence, the General Counsel has sustained his burden of proving each of these four elements by a preponderance of the evidence, such proof warrants at least an inference that the employee's protected conduct was a motivating factor in the adverse employment action and creates a rebuttable presumption that a violation of the Act has occurred. Under *Wright Line* the burden then shifts to the employer to demonstrate that the same action would have taken place even in the absence of the protected conduct.[14]

In the typical discipline or discharge case, the General Counsel (acting through the Board's regional director) must prove that the action was taken against the employee because of her protected activity.[15] When the employer takes an action that adversely affects an employee with respect to terms and conditions of employment, and the intent behind that action is to encourage or discourage the employees' union support or willingness to engage in concerted activity, the employer has violated § 8(a)(3) or § 8(a)(1), respectively. The burden of persuasion then shifts to the employer to show that it

---

U.S. 338, 347 (2013). The 1991 Civil Rights Act amended Title VII to provide that a motivating factor was sufficient to prove an unlawful employment practice. 42 U.S.C. § 2000e-2(m), but remedies are limited if the employer can show it would have made the same employment decision.

13 462 U.S. 393 (1983).

14 American Gardens Mgmt., 338 NLRB 644, 645 (2002).

15 Under § 8(a)(4), it is a ULP for an employer to terminate an employee because of their participation in Board proceedings, such as filing a ULP charge or acting as a witness at a Board hearing.

would have made the same decision irrespective of the employee's § 7 activity.

The General Counsel often relies on both circumstantial and direct evidence in establishing the employer's unlawful motivation. As in *Edward G. Budd Mfg.*, the timing of events may show that the employer based its action on the employee's union activity. Other types of circumstantial evidence include the employer's failure to follow established procedures or to provide at the time a reason for the discipline or discharge. Part of the General Counsel's required showing is that the employer knew of the employee's union activity. Discharging a union supporter may have the effect of discouraging fellow employees from endorsing the union, but there is no ULP if the employer did not know of the employee's union support or other concerted activity.[16]

An employer's general outspokenness against unions is not, however, proof of an employer's discriminatory motive. Because of § 8(c) (a product of the 1947 Taft-Hartley amendments), the statute specifically protects the employer's right to advocate against unionism or the particular union. Section 8(c) prohibits the use of an employer's views, argument, opinion, or other speech as evidence of an unfair labor practice, unless the employer has used force, threats, or promises of benefits.[17]

Section 8(a)(3) speaks in terms of "discrimination" that would "encourage or discourage membership in any labor organization."[18]

---

[16] See Fry Roofing Co., 237 NLRB 1005 (1978). Employer knowledge of union activity can sometimes be presumed based on the circumstances. The Board has invoked the "small plant doctrine" to establish that the employer's facilities were small enough, and in such close quarters, that the employer is presumed to know about particular employee activities. Coral Gables Convalescent Home, 234 NLRB 1198 (1978).

If the employer's discriminatory motive is established, good faith is not a defense. In NLRB v. Burnup & Sims, Inc., 379 U.S. 21 (1964), the employer fired two union activist employees after hearing that they had threatened to use dynamite to help gain recognition for the union. Although the employer honestly believed the claim, it turned out that the employees had actually made no such threats. The Supreme Court agreed with the NLRB that the employer violated § 8(a)(1) because it had targeted two union supporters despite its honest, reasonable belief that that the employees had engaged in unprotected, indeed unlawful, activity. Another view of the case is that employer's violation occurred not when the employer initially terminated the employees but when it refused to reinstate them after learning that they in fact had made no threats.

[17] 29 U.S.C. § 158(c). The evidentiary bar of § 8(c) does not apply to "verbal acts," where words accompany actions—where, for example, while implementing a discharge, the employer says: "I am doing this because you are a union organizer," or where an employer statement is made while communicating a pay increase during the critical period before an NLRB election. See IBEW, Loc. 501 v. NLRB, 181 F.2d 34, 40 (2d Cir. 1950) ("It never has been held, save by the most extreme partisans, if indeed even by them, that the First Amendment protected all verbal acts as such."), aff'd sub nom. IBEW, Loc. 501, A.F. of L. v. NLRB, 341 U.S. 694 (1951).

[18] 29 U.S.C. § 158(a)(3).

As a general matter, the General Counsel must prove that the employer engaged in discriminatory treatment for the purpose of encouraging or discouraging the underlying union or other protected activity. This is usually not an issue where the employer engages in some sort of adverse treatment of union supporters—the discouragement motive is apparent and does not need to be independently established. But in cases where the employer, for example, discriminates against some employees in order to accommodate the union's wishes, it becomes salient whether independent proof of a motive to encourage union activity is required.

Radio Officers' Union v. NLRB[19] was a consolidation of three cases in the Supreme Court where non-members working in a bargaining unit represented by the union were treated worse than union members as to specific terms of employment: one employee was moved to the bottom of a hiring list, another failed to receive a job from a vacancy list, and a third was denied a retroactive wage increase. The Court agreed that these discriminatory employer acts were "inherently conducive to increased union membership."[20] Therefore, there was no need for the Board to establish that the employer intended to encourage union membership.

In a concurrence, Justice Frankfurter noted that the required intent to discourage or encourage union membership could be addressed in two alternative ways:

> (a) On the basis of the employer's disparate treatment of his employees standing alone, or as supplemented by evidence of the particular circumstances under which the employer acted, it is open for the Board to conclude that the conduct of the employer tends to encourage or discourage union membership, thereby establishing a violation of the statute.
>
> (b) Even though the evidence of disparate treatment is sufficient to warrant the Board's conclusion set forth in (a), there must be a specific finding by the Board in all cases that the actual aim of the employer was to encourage or discourage union membership.[21]

Frankfurter thought that (a) was the appropriate interpretation of the statute—in other words, independent proof of a motive to encourage or discourage concerted activity is not required. But the Supreme Court has not resolved this issue definitively.

---

19 347 U.S. 17 (1954).

20 Id. at 38.

21 Id. at 55–56 (Frankfurter, J., concurring).

While the *Wright Line* test generally applies to cases involving employer discipline, the Board has refrained from using *Wright Line* under certain circumstances involving a mix of misconduct and protected activity: employees' misconduct directed at management, such as abusive language, occurring in the midst of otherwise protected activity;[22] activity involving social media posts and conversations among employees in the workplace;[23] and picket-line misconduct.[24] In these circumstances, the Board looks to a broader set of factors in determining whether the activity is protected, such as the place of the discussion, the subject matter of the discussion, the nature of the employee's outburst, and whether the outburst was provoked by an employer's ULP. The Trump Board has downplayed these additional considerations in favor of applying the *Wright Line* framework and allowing the employer to justify the discharge or discipline if the same measures would have been meted out based on the abusive or otherwise inappropriate nature of the conduct.[25]

2. Business Change Decisions

Under § 8(a)(3), an employer commits a violation whenever it makes a decision adversely affecting employees' terms and conditions of employment because they have engaged in union activities. Although there is no exception for business-change decisions, it is more difficult, as a practical matter, to prove antiunion motivation when significant business decisions, other than individual terminations, are involved.

As a general matter, few employers oppose unions for purely ideological reasons. Often the employer associates unionization with certain adverse consequences and assumes those consequences will inevitably occur. These considerations or fears are not entirely irrational. But if they are permitted to be indulged in too early in the game as a basis for adverse treatment of employees engaged in

---

22 Atlantic Steel Co., 245 NLRB 814 (1979).

23 The Board applies a "totality of circumstances" test, explained further in Desert Springs Hospital Medical Center, 363 NLRB 1824, 1839 n. 3 (2016), and Pier Sixty, LLC, 362 NLRB 505, 506 (2015).

24 Clear Pine Mouldings, Inc., 268 NLRB 1044, 1046 (1984), enfd. mem. 765 F.2d 148 (9th Cir. 1985) (considering whether, under all of the circumstances, non-strikers reasonably would have been coerced or intimidated by the picket-line conduct).

25 General Motors, LLC, 369 NLRB No. 127 (July 21, 2020). The Board stated that allowing this defense was necessary in order to avoid "penaliz[ing] employers for declining to tolerate abusive and potentially illegal conduct in the workplace." Id. at *1.

The Biden Board overturned *General Motors* in Lion Elastomers, LLC, 372 NLRB No. 83 (May 1, 2023), enf. denied, Lion Elastomers, LLC v. NLRB (II), 108 F.4th 252, 255 (5th Cir. 2024) (finding that the agency had exceeded the scope of the court's remand).

concerted activity, little would be left as a practical matter of the protections of §§ 7 and 8(a)(3).

In *NLRB v. J.M. Lassing*,[26] the Board and the Sixth Circuit split over whether an employer's expressed concerns about labor costs demonstrated the requisite antiunion motivation. In that case, the employer fired its drivers after the employees voted to join a union. Disagreeing with the Board, the appellate panel concluded that the employer acted for economic, not antiunion, reasons: the employer had decided a month earlier to end the employment of these employees, who transported gas for the employer, at some point in the near future, because it thought it would be cheaper to pay a common carrier to do the same work. Upon receiving the union's demand for recognition, believing that the union would demand higher wages for its covered employees (thus increasing costs), the company fired the drivers.

The Board has never adopted the view that an employer can fire employees who join a union simply because it fears or even has reason to believe that the union will demand higher wages. *Lassing* is an unusual case, since the employer testified (apparently believably) that it had decided to close down its trucking division before it learned of its employees' union activity. Otherwise, a violation would have been indicated.

The NLRB General Counsel's 2011 complaint against the Boeing Company, and the controversy that followed, illustrates the tensions still present in the law.[27] In 2009, Boeing announced its plan to move one of its production lines for the 787 Dreamliner aircraft from its traditional base of operations in Puget Sound, Washington to a new site in South Carolina. The company's executives explained the planned move by referencing the repeated strikes at the Washington plants, which had occurred with some frequency between 1977 and 2008. Boeing CEO Jim McNerney said in an earnings conference call with market advisors that the switch to South Carolina would diversify the company's labor pool and would avoid the "strikes happening every three to four years in Puget Sound." From the General Counsel's perspective, Boeing's actions were straightforward violations of §§ 8(a)(1) and (3), since the company linked the move to the employees' participation in the union and in strikes called by the union. Boeing countered that the move was based on business factors—specifically, that production disruptions from prior strikes had raised costs and that operating the line in South Carolina would not entail these and related costs. Some contended the Board was

---

[26] 284 F.2d 781 (6th Cir. 1960).

[27] NLRB Complaint, Boeing Company, 19–CA–32431, at § 6(a), April 20, 2011.

going after Boeing simply for moving the work from Washington to South Carolina. Boeing and the union had a longstanding collective bargaining relationship. It was conceded that the employer had satisfied any bargaining obligation, and that no Boeing employee in Puget South would lose his or her job as a result of the move. Ultimately, the parties settled their differences and the General Counsel withdrew the agency's complaint.

The Supreme Court has recognized an exception to § 8(a)(3) for a company's decision to shut down its operations entirely. In *Textile Workers Union v. Darlington Manufacturing Co.*,[28] the employer ceased operations and auctioned its assets after its employees voted to unionize. Although the testimony of company executives reflected a concern about the costs likely to ensue from unionization rather than any antipathy to the union itself, the Court accepted the Board's conclusion that the closing was motivated by discriminatory intent. The Court ruled, however, that the decision to close a business in its entirety—to abandon entirely the business of being an employer—was an essential entrepreneurial right that the NLRA left undisturbed. Because closing the business ended all employment relationships between the employer and its workers, the employer likely did not intend to discourage concerted activity by those employees as there could be no "future benefit" for the employer in its dealings with those workers.[29] The Court distinguished an actual closing from a threatened closure, noting that an employer may not merely threaten to close the plant if its employees unionized. In such cases, there would be a prospect of future benefit to the employer from the deterrent effect on § 7 activity from the threat alone. The employer is allowed to close, but the closing must be a management decision already arrived at, not simply a prediction of future adverse consequences.[30]

For partial closings, the *Darlington* Court announced what might be termed a "chill rights elsewhere" test. "[A] partial closing," the Court stated, "is an unfair labor practice under § 8(a)(3) if it is motivated by a purpose to chill unionism in any of the remaining plants of the single employer and if the employer may reasonably have foreseen that such closing would likely have that effect."[31] The Court made clear that the *Darlington* rationale does not apply to "runaway shops," where the plant disclosure is purely strategic because the employer intends to reopen the plant elsewhere. In these situations, a "future benefit" to the employer can be presumed and

---

28 380 U.S. 263 (1965).

29 Id. at 272.

30 Id. at 274 n.20.

31 Id. at 275.

there is no need to prove that the employer's motive was to chill rights among employees at the new plant.

Although the *Darlington* Court spoke in terms of a purpose to chill the rights of employees "in any of the remaining plants of the single employer," the Court emphasized that demonstrating an organizational integration of plants or corporations is not necessary.[32] Rather, antiunion motivation can be shown under the following conditions:

> [T]he persons exercising control over a plant that is being closed for antiunion reasons (1) have an interest in another business, whether or not affiliated with or engaged in the same line of commercial activity as the closed plant, of sufficient substantiality to give promise of their reaping a benefit from the discouragement of unionization in that business; (2) act to close their plant with the purpose of producing such a result; and (3) occupy a relationship to the other business which makes it realistically foreseeable that its employees will fear that such business will also be closed down if they persist in organizational activities.[33]

In the context of a retaliatory closing of a department within a facility or a decision to subcontract unit work, the Board is willing to presume that there was either a "future benefit" to the employer or a motive to chill rights among the existing employees. [34]

C. Impact-Based Violations: Access Issues

There are cases where the focus is not so much on the employer's motivation but on the impact of the employer's policy or practice on the practical ability of employees to engage in concerted activity. In such cases, even where the rule is otherwise neutral on its face and has not been administered in a discriminatory manner, the policy or practice may still violate § 8(a)(1) if the negative impact on § 7 rights is not justified by the employer's legitimate business interests. This issue often arises where the question is whether the employees are permitted to engage in concerted activity on the employer's premises or use the employer's equipment.

---

[32] Id. at 275.

[33] Id. at 275–76. On remand, the Board found that the closed company was in fact part of a group of textile manufacturing companies and awarded backpay to the terminated workers. Ultimately the company settled by providing $5,000,000 in backpay. NLRB Office of the General Counsel, Release No. 1625, Dec. 3, 1980.

[34] See, e.g., George Lithograph Co., 204 NLRB 431 (1973).

1. Workplace Solicitation and Distribution

The NLRB has long established, with Supreme Court approval, that employees have a strong § 7 right to engage in concerted activity on the employer's premises. The Board has drawn a distinction between "solicitation" and "distribution." With respect to solicitation, which includes not only oral communications between employees but also the wearing of union buttons and seeking signatures on authorization cards or petitions—conduct where there is no concern over littering—the employer cannot generally maintain a rule limiting such on-site solicitation to non-working hours or non-work areas. In *Republic Aviation v. NLRB*,[35] three employees were fired for wearing buttons indicating that they were union shop stewards. The Court agreed with the Board that the § 7 right to talk to coworkers at the workplace about their terms and conditions of employment was so strong and the employer's justifications for barring such talk during non-work time so weak that the employer's rule violated § 8(a)(1) without the need for proof of discriminatory motivation.

Because distribution of literature poses a problem of littering and possible interference with machinery, an employer may lawfully restrict this activity to non-work locations. Unlike "the normal conditions" prevailing in "industrial establishments" that informed *Republic Aviation*,[36] employers in other settings might have special justifications for additional restrictions on employee solicitation and distributions. The Board has, for example, permitted broad no-solicitation rules in retail establishments that ban all solicitation in customer-access areas.[37] This is in recognition of the possible negative impact such activity may have on customers. Similarly, hospitals may ban solicitation in patient-access areas like the corridor outside the patient's room.[38] Employers may also require civility or decorum as long as such policies are not reasonably viewed as preventing § 7 activity.[39]

Employers do not have carte blanche to bar solicitation in retail spaces. The "special circumstances" exception to *Republic Aviation* is narrowly construed. For example, in *In-N-Out Burger, Inc v. NLRB*, the court of appeals approved the Board's protection of "Fight for $15"

---

35 324 U.S. 793 (1945).

36 Id. at 804.

37 Gayfers Dep't Store, 324 NLRB 1246, 1250 (1997) (banning solicitation even during working hours in selling areas); J.C. Penney Co., 266 NLRB 1223, 1224 (1983) (same).

38 NLRB v. Baptist Hospital, 442 U.S. 773 (1979); Beth Israel Hospital v. NLRB, 437 U.S. 483 (1978).

39 Martin Luther Memorial Home, Inc., 343 NLRB 1044 (2004).

buttons worn by employees at a fast-food restaurant.[40] It held that the Board properly found that the employer "failed to demonstrate a connection between the 'no pins or stickers' rule and the company's asserted interests in preserving a consistent menu and ownership structure, ensuring excellent customer service, and maintaining a 'sparkling clean' environment' in its restaurants."[41] The buttons in this case did not criticize the employer's business and did not involve an overt union appeal.

Ordinarily, under the *Republic Aviation* standard, employers may not bar solicitation during non-work time or distribution in non-work areas even if the employer provides alternatives for on-site solicitation and distribution activities. The Board will recognize exceptions only where "special circumstances make the rule necessary in order to maintain production or discipline."[42] When reviewing an employer's claim for such an exception, the Board considers it highly relevant whether the employer provides alternative opportunities for on-site solicitation and distribution.[43]

2. Facial Review of Company Policies and Rules

The Board judges neutral workplace rules under a "reasonably construe" standard: if employees would reasonably construe the rule to prohibit protected concerted activity, then it violates § 8(a)(1).[44] The Board has been concerned that certain types of employer policies, such as civility rules, prohibitions on intemperate language, and workplace confidentiality mandates can have a significant effect on employees' ability to exercise their § 7 rights.[45] Under the agency's 2023 *Stericycle, Inc.* decision,[46] employer policies violate § 8(a)(1) if they have a reasonable tendency to chill employees from exercising their § 7 rights. The rule is interpreted from the perspective of an employee who is subject to the rule and economically dependent on the employer, and who also contemplates engaging in protected concerted activity.[47] *Stericycle* overturned the Trump Board's

---

[40] 894 F.3d 707, 711 (5th Cir. 2018).

[41] Id. at 716.

[42] Peyton Packing Company, Inc., 49 NLRB 828, 843 (1943).

[43] See, e.g., NLRB v. Baptist Hospital, Inc. 442 U.S. 773, 784–85 (1979).

[44] Lutheran Heritage Village-Livonia, 343 NLRB 646 (2004); Stericycle, Inc., 372 NLRB No. 113 (2023).

[45] Lutheran Heritage Village-Livonia, 343 NLRB 646 (2004).

[46] Stericycle, Inc., 372 NLRB No. 113 (Aug. 2, 2023).

[47] To the Board, the employer's intent in maintaining a rule is immaterial. If employee could reasonably interpret the rule to have a coercive meaning, the General Counsel will carry her burden, even if a contrary, non-coercive interpretation of the rule is also reasonable. Id. at *3.

approach in *Boeing Co.*,[48] which involved a balancing test for facially neutral workplace policies.

3. Access Rights of Nonemployees

The access rights recognized in *Republic Aviation* are rights of employees, not rights of non-employee union organizers. Non-employee organizers can claim only derivative rights in limited circumstances, such as where the employees live and work in remote locations and are not reachable by conventional means of communication. This basic principle was set forth in *NLRB v. Babcock & Wilcox, Co.*,[49] in an opinion authored by Justice Reed, who authored the Court's opinion in *Republic Aviation* and had been President Franklin D. Roosevelt's Solicitor General. In order to have access to the employer's property, union organizers had to show that the employees were "beyond the reach of reasonable union efforts to communicate with them."[50]

Prior to *Lechmere, Inc. v. NLRB*,[51] the Board approached the issue of non-employee access through a multifactor balancing test that focused on whether there were reasonably effective alternative means of reaching the employees.[52] The Supreme Court rejected this test in *Lechmere*, stating that under *Babcock & Wilcox* union organizers and other nonemployees are presumed to have no rights of their own under § 7. Rather, they only have derivative rights to be able to access the employer's property when other means of reaching employees are infeasible, rather than merely costly. The retail-store employees in *Lechmere* worked in a shopping center and were not inaccessible. The Court held that neither the employer nor the owner of the shopping center had an obligation under the NLRA to allow union organizers onto the premises to distribute their literature.[53]

In *UPMC & Its Subsidiary, UPMC Presbyterian Shadyside*,[54] the Board extended *Lechmere* to employer property where outsiders are, in fact, generally allowed on the property. In that case, the hospital cafeteria was open to the public, but solicitation was not

---

[48] 365 NLRB 1494 (2017).

[49] 351 U.S. 105 (1956).

[50] Id. at 113.

[51] 502 U.S. 527 (1992).

[52] Jean Country, 291 NLRB 11, 14 (1988).

[53] The union in *Lechmere* was able, with the cooperation of the state department of motor vehicles, to obtain the names and addresses of employees through an inspection of their license plates while parked in the shopping center area. The Court did not, however, limit the reach of its holding to such circumstances. State motor vehicles departments may be barred from providing such information by the Drivers' Privacy Protection Act, 18 U.S.C. § 2721 et seq.; see generally Maracich v. Spears, 570 U.S. 48 (2013).

[54] 368 NLRB No. 2 (June 14, 2019).

permitted. Union representatives were sitting at a table with pro-union literature on it and eating with employees when the employer told them to leave. The Board held that an employer did not commit a ULP in enforcing its non-solicitation and non-distribution policy against the union representatives if it applied such rules without discriminating against union organizers.[55] Citing past court of appeals authority, the Board made clear that an employer had the right to regulate the type of permitted activities on its property, including promotional and organizational activity.[56]

What about employee protests on property that their employer regularly uses but does not own—can the property owner exclude them? In *New York New York, LLC,*[57] the Board held that a property owner may exclude a contractor's employees "who are regularly employed on the property" and who seek to engage in Section 7 organizational activity but "only where the owner is able to demonstrate that [employees'] activity significantly interferes with his use of the property or where exclusion is justified by another legitimate business reason."[58] These third-party property owners might ask: what basis is there in imposing this duty on the owner, if the owner is not acting as an agent for the employer?[59] Critics contend that *Lechmere* and its progeny privileges state property law over federal labor law and does not recognize the practical difficulties unions face in reaching employees at their workplace, even if they do not live and work in remote communities.

One open issue is whether union agents obtain greater access to the employer's property under the NLRA if state law requires some

---

55 Id. at *8 ("[W]e overrule Board precedent holding that discrimination can be established merely by showing that nonemployee union representatives were denied access to a public area within private property, without the Board considering the kind of 'nondisruptive' activity they were engaged in and whether the employer had permitted similar activity by other nonemployees.").

56 Id. The Board approvingly cited the Sixth Circuit's opinion in *Oakwood Hospital v. NLRB*: "If the owner of an outdoor parking lot can bar nonemployee union organizers [as in *Lechmere*], it follows *a fortiori* that the owner of an indoor cafeteria can do so." 983 F.2d 698, 703 (6th Cir. 1993).

During the Biden Administration, the General Counsel issued an Advice Memo stating that the case was wrongly decided. NLRB General Counsel Division of Advice, Memorandum on LAZ Parking Mid Atlantic, LLC, d/b/a LT Transportation, Case 05–CA–281089, Jan. 4, 2022.

57 356 NLRB 907 (2011).

58 Id. at 918–19.

59 The first Trump Administration took a different approach in Bexar County Performing Arts Ctr. Found., 372 NLRB No. 28 (Dec. 16, 2022) (*Bexar II*), holding that contractor employees can be excluded unless they worked regularly and exclusively on property and there were no other reasonable alternatives for spreading their message. The D.C. Circuit denied enforcement, and on remand the Board returned to the *New York New York* standard. Local 23, Am. Fed'n of Musicians v. NLRB, 12 F.4th 778 (D.C. Cir. 2021).

degree of public access. State-law definitions of property rights would seem relevant, but are they determinative?[60] In *Cedar Point Nursery v. Hassid*,[61] the Supreme Court held that a California state regulation requiring agricultural employers to allow union organizers onto their property for up to three hours per day, 120 days per year to solicit support for unionization was a *per se* physical taking, requiring just compensation under the Constitution's Takings Clause.[62]

4. Discriminatory Application of Company Policies and Rules

Discriminatory application of an otherwise lawful no-solicitation rule may impeach the employer's legitimate interests in enforcing the rule. Thus, for example, if an employer allows employees to post buy and sell offers to each other on company bulletin boards, a rule barring bulletin-board access to employees proposing union activity or giving notice of a union meeting would likely violate § 8(a)(1). What if the employer allows certain outsiders onto its property (for charity drives or to hawk their wares) but refuses to afford similar access to union organizers? The Board has met judicial resistance for its decisions finding a violation of § 8(a)(1) for applying a no-solicitation rule to bar access to unions while allowing access to charitable groups. Some courts distinguish between "nonorganizational activity" or sporadic charitable solicitations and an ongoing union organizing drive.[63] Perhaps any disruptive effect can be more easily contained in the case of the former than the latter. The employer's discriminatory application may have a different import where the employer is not asserting operational concerns (which may be undermined by such application) but rather the property owner's right to exclude.

5. Access to Email and Other Company Equipment

The controversy over an employer's control over its physical locations has spilled over to its electronic "space" as well. Employers often establish policies regarding employees' use of the employer's computers, web servers, and email which prohibit use for "personal"

---

[60] See, e.g., Jeffrey M. Hirsch, Taking State Property Rights Out of Federal Labor Law, 47 B.C. L. Rev. 891, 894–95 (2006); Cynthia L. Estlund, Labor, Property, and Sovereignty after *Lechmere*, 46 Stan. L. Rev. 305, 308 (1994).

[61] 594 U.S. 139 (2021).

[62] Id. at 152. See Cal. Code Regs., tit. 8, § 20900(e)(1)(C) (2020).

[63] See, e.g., Be-Lo Stores v. NLRB, 126 F.3d 268 (4th Cir. 1997) (expressing "serious[ ] doubt" that the non-discrimination requirement applies where non-organizational activity is at issue); Cleveland Real Estate Partners v. NLRB, 95 F.3d 457, 465 (6th Cir. 1996). But see Sandusky Mall Co., 329 NLRB 618 (1999) (ordering access for area-standards handbilling when other solicitation was permitted).

purposes. As a general matter, the Board has long held that employees have *no* § 7 right to use employer equipment, whether the telephone or Xerox machines, to conduct concerted activity (absent proof of discriminatory application of the employer's no-personal use rule). Are email systems different because they are analogous to the employer-provided water cooler, break room, or cafeteria—which are viewed as locations where concerted activity may be engaged in consistent with *Republic Aviation*?

In *Guard Publishing Co.* (known also as *Register-Guard*),[64] the Board's first stab at this issue, the employer prohibited employees from using its email system for "nonjob-related solicitations." When it disciplined an employee who had sent out union-related emails on the employer's system to fellow employees, the NLRB's General Counsel filed a complaint alleging that the disciplinary warnings violated § 8(a)(1). The Board, however, disagreed. The warnings did not constitute a violation of § 8(a)(1) because the email system was no different than other employer-provided equipment. In addition, the majority explained, the employer did not discriminate against union activity by allowing some non-work-related emails while prohibiting union-related solicitation. As long as the employer was not discriminating against § 7 activity *per se*, it was permitted to draw distinctions between organizational and non-organizational types of non-work activity.

In the 2014 case *Purple Communications, Inc.*,[65] the Obama Board overruled *Register-Guard*. The Board majority held that "employee use of email for statutorily protected communications on nonworking time must presumptively be permitted by employers who have chosen to give employees access to their email systems."[66] Under *Purple Communications*, employers may justify a total ban on non-work use of email by demonstrating that special circumstances make the ban necessary to maintain production or discipline. "Absent justification for a total ban, the employer may apply uniform and consistently enforced controls over its email system to the extent such controls are necessary to maintain production and discipline."[67]

The first Trump Administration Board returned to the *Register Guard* approach in the 2019 *Caesars Entertainment* decision, overruling *Purple Communications*.[68] The *Caesars Entertainment* majority centered on the argument that the employer's traditional control over the use of its property and premises extended to email

---

[64] 351 NLRB 1110 (2007).

[65] 361 NLRB 1050 (2014).

[66] Id. at 1050.

[67] Id.

[68] Caesars Entertainment, 368 NLRB No. 143 (Dec. 16, 2019).

systems. The decision is consistent with longstanding NLRB decisions that the employer is not required to provide access to its equipment, although it is required under *Republic Aviation* and its progeny to provide employee access to breakrooms and other non-work areas for union solicitation activity.

D. The Scope of Concerted Activity

Along with rights to self-organization, union activity, and collective bargaining, section 7 of the Act protects the right to "engage in other concerted activities for the purpose of collective bargaining or other mutual aid or protection."[69] The Board and the courts have identified three elements in determining whether certain employee activity fits within this protection: (1) the activity must be "concerted," in that it involves two or more employees or is a prelude to such activity; (2) the activity must be for the purpose of bargaining or mutual aid and protection regarding employment terms and conditions; and (3) the activity must use protected means for achieving these ends. The "protected means" requirement is not expressly stated in the statute but is an implied condition under longstanding Board and court decisions.

1. The "Concerted" Nature of the Activity

Activity is "concerted" if it involves two or more employees. But can activity in support of collective employment rights be concerted even if only one person engages in it? Yes—but only in very limited circumstances.

a. *Assertion of Rights Under Collective Bargaining Agreements.* In *NLRB v. City Disposal Systems, Inc.,*[70] the employer discharged a truck driver for refusing to drive a vehicle that he believed had faulty brakes. A clause in the collective bargaining agreement (CBA) governing his employment provided that employees were not in violation of work rules if they refused to operate an unsafe vehicle. Under the Board's *Interboro* doctrine,[71] an individual's assertion of a right grounded in a CBA is concerted activity under § 7 because the CBA is a product of concerted activity and the assertion of a right under the agreement will likely redound to the benefit of coworkers. Although the driver in *City Disposal* did not refer specifically to the CBA in refusing to operate the truck, that was not dispositive. The grievant's activity was concerted because he was acting to enforce a collective right under the CBA, itself an instrument originating from collective activity. Having found the

---

[69] 29 U.S.C. § 157.

[70] 465 U.S. 822 (1984).

[71] See Interboro Contractors, Inc., 157 NLRB 1295, 1298 (1966).

activity to be concerted, the Court remanded for a determination as to whether it was protected.[72]

City Disposal is a limited ruling protecting an employee's invocation of the collectively-negotiated grievance adjustment process even where the union does not believe the grievance has merit and refuses to process it.[73] *City Disposal* does not apply to nonunion workplaces where there is no CBA. The Board has in the past extended protections for safety complaints involving other employment laws under the *Alleluia Cushion*[74] doctrine. In that case, an employee had acted individually in reporting safety violations to a state agency. The Board found the behavior concerted because it would redound to the benefit of all the employees.[75] However, the Board reversed this policy in *Meyers Industries, Inc.*,[76] requiring proof that the employee had engaged in the activity "with or on the authority of other employees."[77] Although these individual complaints are not protected under the Act, they will often be protected under the federal Occupational Safety and Health Act of 1970, state workplace safety law, or whistleblower protections under state statutory and tort law.[78]

b. *Prelude to or Logical Outgrowth of Collective Action.* Individual actions are also protected under the Act if they are a prelude to or logical outgrowth of collective action. Under the Board's *Mushroom Transportation* doctrine, concerted activity includes efforts by individual employees "to initiate or to induce or to prepare for group action, as well as individual employees bringing truly group complaints to the attention of management."[79] Criticizing a new management policy in a group meeting of employees was held to be concerted,[80] as was sending an email to fellow employees complaining

---

[72] The Court noted that the court of appeals would have to determine whether the employee acted in good faith and had reasonable concerns about the vehicle's safety even though it was actually safe.

[73] Under most CBAs, the union has the authority to decide whether or not to bring a represented employee's grievance to arbitration. The duty of unions to fairly represent their bargaining-unit employees in grievance proceedings is discussed further in Chapter 12.

[74] 221 NLRB 999 (1975).

[75] Id. at 1000.

[76] 268 NLRB 493 (1984).

[77] Id. at 497.

[78] See ALI, Restatement of Employment Law ch. 5 (2015) (discussing common-law protections).

[79] Meyers Industries, Inc., 281 NLRB 882, 887 (1986) (citing Mushroom Transp. Co. v. NLRB, 330 F.2d 683 (3d Cir. 1964)). The Board recently reaffirmed this doctrine in Miller Plastic Prod., Inc., 372 NLRB No. 134 (Aug. 25, 2023) (overruling Alstate Maintenance, 367 NLRB No. 68 (Jan. 11, 2019)).

[80] NLRB v. Caval Tool Division, Chromalloy Gas Turbine Corp., 262 F.3d 184, 190 (2d Cir. 2000).

about a change in vacation leave.[81] The circumstances have to indicate that the individual's action contemplated a response from other employees.[82] Individual action stemming from group complaints may be considered concerted.[83] The employer must know about the concerted nature of the activity in order to be liable for an unfair labor practice.[84]

Under *NLRB v. J. Weingarten, Inc.*,[85] employees who are represented by a union in collective bargaining have a § 7 right to request and have a union representative present during an investigatory interview that the employee reasonably believes might result in discipline. Although this protection seems to operate in support of an individual employee, "[t]he union representative . . . is safeguarding not only the particular employee's interest, but also the interests of the entire bargaining unit by exercising vigilance to make certain that the employer does not initiate or continue a practice of imposing punishment unjustly."[86] The employer can simply refuse to interview the employee instead, and it has no duty to engage with the union representative in this context (but would when a grievance is filed). Failure to allow a representative to attend the interview, however, is a violation of § 8(a)(1).

The Board has gone back and forth on whether *Weingarten* rights extend to non-union employees; most recently, the answer has been in the negative.[87] One problem with extending *Weingarten* to non-union settings is that there is no obvious collective right to enforce in the absence of a CBA; nor is there a framework for selecting a representative and determining what that person's role might be.

The right to engage in concerted activity includes the right to resort to available judicial and administrative fora for workplace disputes. It does not include a right to have a particular forum created or a right to depart from the procedures provided for in that forum. The Obama Board had held in *D.H. Horton*[88] that § 7 protected the right of employees—in that case, those not represented by a union—to bring class actions against their employers for

---

81 Timekeeping Systems, Inc. 323 NLRB 244 (1997).

82 Adelphi Inst., Inc., 287 NLRB 1073 (1988); Parke Care of Finneytown, Inc., 287 NLRB 710 (1987).

83 Salisbury Hotel, Inc., 283 NLRB 685 (1987); Every Woman's Place, Inc., 282 NLRB 413 (1986).

84 Meyers Industries, Inc., 268 NLRB 493 (1984).

85 420 U.S. 251 (1975).

86 Id. at 260–61.

87 IBM Corp., 341 NLRB 1288 (2004).

88 357 NLRB 2277 (2012).

workplace-related claims, even if they had agreed to an otherwise valid arbitration clause which prohibited class actions. The Board reasoned that employees did not necessarily have a right to pursue class actions but did have a right to be free of employer insistence as a condition of employment that they forgo collective remedies that otherwise would be available but for the arbitration clause. But absent a § 9 exclusive bargaining representative, an employer can directly negotiate employment terms with its employees, and the clause in question was otherwise enforceable under the Federal Arbitration Act (FAA).[89]

In *Epic Systems Corp v. Lewis*,[90] the Supreme Court rejected the Board's position. Relying on its strong pro-arbitration precedent under the FAA,[91] along with earlier decisions sustaining class action waivers, the Court found no conflict between § 7 and the FAA. The Court questioned whether the right to engage in class actions even fell within the NLRA provision: "[T]he term 'other concerted activities' should, like the terms that precede it, serve to protect things employees 'just do' for themselves in the course of exercising their right to free association in the workplace, rather than the highly regulated, courtroom-bound 'activities' of class and joint litigation."[92] Even after *Epic Systems*, employees should be free of employer discipline for attempting to resort to available non-NLRA remedies, whether a lawsuit or administrative proceeding, to redress workplace grievances; any adverse consequences might also be addressed under federal and state antiretaliation laws.

The Board has ruled that employers cannot condition severance payments on the waiver of labor law rights, such as the ability to communicate with coworkers on terms and conditions of employment. In *McLaren Macomb*,[93] the employer had offered a severance agreement that prohibited furloughed employees from making disparaging statements and from disclosing the terms of the agreement. The Board concluded that the agreement prohibited workers from discussing labor issues, disputes, or even illegal employer behavior, while the confidentiality provision prevented workers from providing information to the Board concerning the employer's unlawful interference with other employees' statutory rights.[94] It remains subject to contest how far the Board can regulate,

---

89 9 U.S.C. § 1 et seq.

90 584 U.S. 497 (2018).

91 9 U.S.C. § 1 et seq.

92 584 U.S. at 512 (some quotations omitted).

93 372 NLRB No. 58 (Feb. 21, 2023).

94 Id. at *8.

especially through review of facial challenges to employer policies, the terms of employment contracts in the non-union sector.[95]

2. Unprotected Objectives

To be protected under § 7, the concerted activity must be engaged in "for the purpose of collective bargaining or other mutual aid or protection."[96] The union or employees' objective has to have some bearing on the wages, hours, and working conditions of employees. What if employees, or a union acting on their behalf, seek to distribute a newsletter on the employer's property in non-working areas? Normally, such a distribution would seem to fit easily within § 7's protection. But what if the newsletter contains political commentary, such as calls to oppose a "right-to-work" statute and to support an increase in the minimum wage (when all the employees in question earn more than the minimum wage)? Such was the situation in *Eastex, Inc. v. NLRB*.[97] The company denied the union permission to distribute the newsletter, and the union filed a charge alleging a ULP under § 8(a)(1). The Board found a violation, and the Court upheld the decision. Although the Court acknowledged that the political messages had "a less immediate relationship" to the employees' collective interests, it agreed that these political issues were linked to employee and union concerns and that "mutual aid or protection" among different groups of employees fostering solidarity are part of the labor tradition embodied in § 7. The Court noted that "[there may well be types of conduct or speech that are so purely political or so remotely connected to the concerns of employees as employees as to be beyond the protection of the clause."[98]

In *Home Depot USA, Inc.*,[99] the Board addressed the extent to which § 7 protects political expression that does not directly relate to wages, working conditions, and workplace issues. A worker had written "BLM" in large letters on their orange Home Depot apron and had been disciplined allegedly because it violated a company ban on "displaying [on an apron] causes or political messages unrelated to workplace matters."[100] The Board ruled that the apron message was intended as a reference to the "Black Lives Matter" movement and was pertinent to employee concerns at this particular store about a

---

[95] The *McLaren Macomb* rule replaced two Trump Board decisions that had fashioned a more lenient standard for such employer clauses. See Baylor University Medical Center, 369 NLRB No. 43 (2020); IGT d/b/a International Game Technology, 370 NLRB No. 50 (2020).

[96] 29 U.S.C. § 157.

[97] 437 U.S. 556 (1978).

[98] *Eastex*, 437 U.S. at 570 n.20.

[99] 373 NLRB No. 25 (Feb. 21, 2024).

[100] Id. at 5.

supervisor's allegedly discriminatory speech and actions. According to the factual findings, the BLM message here clearly related to concerns specific to this workplace.[101] The Board left undecided whether a message unrelated to any particular supervisor's conduct would be similarly protected.[102]

3. Unprotected Means

Although the NLRA does not expressly require that employees use lawful means in conducting their protest activity, it is a likely background assumption of the Act, confirmed in numerous Supreme Court decisions, that the use of violence or mass picketing is not protected by the NLRA. This was evidenced early in the history of the NLRA when the Court held that a sit-down strike resulting in the employees' occupation of a plant was not protected concerted activity even though the sit-down was provoked by employer ULPs.[103] Conduct violative of the Act or other federal laws is also unprotected. But not all violations of state law are unprotected; some state laws may be partially or entirely preempted by the NLRA. For example, to create some room for hot-tempered language in labor disputes, the Court has held that use of defamatory statements in the course of a dispute may be protected but only if the speakers do not knowingly or recklessly act without regard to the truth or falsity of their statements.[104]

Some activity may be unprotected because it is in breach of contract. Breach of contract covers those instances in which the union has waived its employees' rights to engage in certain kinds of protected activity. A no-strike clause, for example, renders a strike during the contract term unprotected.[105] But no-strike clauses do not without clear language render unprotected employees' refusal to cross another union's picket line, or strikes protesting significant employer ULPs, as that would go beyond the likely reach of such clauses.[106]

The more difficult question is when concerted activity is unprotected even if violence is not used and there is no violation of federal or (nonpreempted) state law. The Supreme Court has categorized certain acts as "disloyal" when they harm the employer's brand without making clear the connection to an underlying labor

---

[101] Id. at 9–10.

[102] Id. at 9 n.23 ("[W]e express no view as to whether, in a future appropriate case, we would find protests of workplace racial discrimination to be inherently concerted.").

[103] NLRB v. Fansteel Metallurgical Corp., 306 U.S. 243 (1939).

[104] Linn v. United Plant Guard Workers, 383 U.S. 53 (1966).

[105] NLRB v. Rockaway News Supply Co., 345 U.S. 71 (1953).

[106] Mastro Plastics Corp. v. NLRB, 350 U.S. 270 (1956).

dispute. Striking employees in *NLRB v. Local 1229, IBEW (Jefferson Standard)*[107] distributed flyers to the public criticizing the television station's programming choices without making clear they were engaged in a labor dispute with their employer.[108] The Court held that there was no connection between the strike and the product disparagement leveled in the flyers. Members of the general public, the Court reasoned, would have no means of evaluating the motive behind the flyers and might permanently quit their patronage of the station. *Jefferson Standard* held such "naked" product disparagement to be unprotected. If the employees can make clear the connection to a labor dispute, however, the narrow "disloyalty" rationale generally does not apply.[109]

Physically leaving one's job might be considered an improper means of asserting one' collective rights, but the Act specifically protects the right to strike.[110] A balance must therefore be struck in the regulation of collective activity that disrupts the workplace. In *NLRB v. Washington Aluminum Co.*,[111] non-unionized machine shop employees found themselves on a bitterly cold day with an unheated facility, as the oil furnace had broken down. The employees collectively decided to walk out in protest, even though the manager urged them to wait while the furnace was being fixed. The Court held that the employees' action was protected because it was concerted activity in protest of their working conditions.

The employees' walkout in *Washington Aluminum* was protected even though the employer was trying to deal with the problem and there was no danger to the health of the workers. This is in keeping with the general principle that neither the Board nor the courts should evaluate the reasonableness of the workers' demands in a labor dispute. But there can be questions as to the reasonableness of the timing or the means used. In *Bob Evans Farms, Inc. v. NLRB*,[112] restaurant employees walked off at the start of a busy Friday evening shift after their supervisor had been fired. The Board found the activity to be protected, but the Seventh Circuit denied enforcement. In the court's view, while the purpose of the

---

[107] 346 U.S. 464 (1953).

[108] The flyer called out the station for not having more local and live programming, such as sporting events. It also questioned whether the station considered Charlotte to be a "second class city."

[109] But cf. MikLin Enters., Inc. v. NLRB, 861 F.3d 812, 822 (8th Cir. 2017) (finding that posters implying that sandwich makers might be sick, and asking for support for paid sick leave, were not protected activity because they "indefensibly disparaged the quality of the employer's product or services").

[110] See 29 U.S.C. § 163.

[111] 370 U.S. 9 (1962).

[112] 163 F.3d 1012 (7th Cir. 1998).

walkout was protected because the identity of the supervisor implicated working conditions, that concern did not justify the disruption of a walkout. The court may have been influenced by the fact that the walkout was in protest of a change in supervisors rather than of specific working conditions.

The Board draws a line between an outright strike and a slowdown—where the workers stay on the job but slow their work pace—finding the latter to be unprotected.[113] Slowdowns (sometimes termed "partial strikes") are not protected because they involve a refusal to perform work assignments while remaining at the job. Employers can more readily respond to an all-out strike, by use of management or replacements, than they can to slowdowns. Intermittent strikes (in which the employees engage in short, repeated walkouts) are generally unprotected because like slowdowns they prevent the employer from trying to maintain operations.[114]

Many of these "unprotected means" decisions can be explained as an attempt by the Board and the courts to advance a "bounded conflict" conception of concerted activity.[115] Employees have a right to engage in collective protest action and even impose costs on the employer by their protests, but what they cannot do is to act inconsistently with the continuation of the employment relationship at the resolution of the dispute. Thus, the naked product disparagement in *Jefferson Standard* is unprotected because it could entail lasting damage to the employer. Walking off the job without making provision for the shutoff of equipment which, left unattended, would be damaged irreparably, is another example. The slowdown cases reflect the Board's view, confirmed by Supreme Court decisions dating back to 1938,[116] that employers should be able to try to maintain operations during a strike, which slowdowns and intermittent strikes make difficult.

---

[113] Elk Lumber Co., 91 NLRB 333 (1950).

[114] In October 2012, a non-union group of Walmart workers went out on strikes lasting one to three days in duration. On Black Friday (a busy shopping day) in November 2012, the group called a purportedly nationwide strike lasting one or two days in which about 100 employees participated. In May and early June 2013, 130 employees staged a third strike lasting five to six days so they could travel to Walmart's annual shareholders' meeting in Arkansas to demonstrate. Walmart disciplined or discharged the employees for violating the company's attendance policy. The Board held the walkouts to be unprotected intermittent strikes in Walmart Stores, 368 NLRB No. 24 (July 25, 2019). For further discussion on short and intermittent strikes, see Michael C. Duff, Labor Viscerality? Work Stoppages in the "New Work" Non-Union Economy, 65 St. Louis U. L.J. 115 (2020); Michael M. Oswalt, Short Strikes, 95 Chi.-Kent L. Rev. 67 (2020).

[115] See Samuel Estreicher, Strikers and Replacements, 3 Lab. Lawyer 897 (1987).

[116] See NLRB v. Mackay Radio & Telegraph Co., 304 U.S. 333 (1938).

E. Union Waiver of Employees' § 7 Rights

Employees cannot waive their individual statutory rights. This is the general rule under the NLRA as well as under other protective workplace legislation. Employers once sought to get employees to waive their ability to join a union through so-called "yellow-dog" contracts before such contracts were outlawed by the Norris-LaGuardia Act. But to what extent can the collective bargaining representative waive the collective rights of represented employees? No-strike clauses are common in CBAs; they represent a waiver of the employees' collective right to engage in strikes during the term of a CBA. Typically, the parties have negotiated a grievance and arbitration process to deal with disputes arising during the term of the collective agreement, as a substitute for the right to engage in midterm strikes over such disputes (sometimes termed "rights" disputes as opposed to "interest" disputes, which are over the content of renewal agreements).

Does the standard no-strike clause include a waiver of the employees' right to engage in a strike in protest of the employer's ULPs? In *Mastro Plastics Corp. v. NLRB*,[117] the Supreme Court agreed with the Board that the employees had not waived their right to strike against employer ULPs in a standard no-strike clause that prohibited "any strike."[118] The standard no-strike clause excludes only strikes based on "serious" unfair labor practices.[119] In entering into a standard no-strike agreement, reasoned the Board, the parties do not intend to disable the employees from protesting serious ULPs that undermine the union's ability to represent them.

In *Metropolitan Edison Co. v. NLRB*,[120] the employer had punished union officials more severely than other striking workers for striking in violation of the CBA on the grounds that the union officials had an affirmative duty to uphold the agreement. The Court upheld the Board's determination that the company's selective discipline of the union officials violated § 8(a)(3). The Court rejected the company's argument that the CBA condoned the selective discipline. The union did have the authority to waive the rights of its own employees to challenge harsher sanctions; "a union's decision to bind its officials to take affirmative steps to end an unlawful work

---

[117] 350 U.S. 270 (1956).

[118] Id. at 282–83.

[119] Compare Arlan's Department Store, 133 NLRB 802 (1961) (termination of shop steward for filing a decertification petition was a serious ULP over which the employees had not waived their right to strike), with Dow Chemical Co., 244 NLRB 1060 (1979) (unilateral change in scheduled work was not a serious charge excluded from the reach of the no-strike clause).

[120] 460 U.S. 693 (1983).

stoppage is consistent with the premise of fair representation."[121] Such waivers, however, had to be made "clearly and unmistakably," which had not happened in that case.[122]

In contrast, unions cannot waive organizational rights of represented employees, even if those employees support the union's position. When a union acquiesced in a company's rule barring distribution of literature in the employer's parking lot even when employees were off-duty, the Court agreed with the Board that any purported waiver by the union was legally ineffective.[123] Unions could not waive their members' right to distribute literature supportive of the union, the Court reasoned, because such a waiver would also lead to a restriction of employee rights to read and disseminate at the workplace literature critical of the union; the employees should be able to interact in "a place uniquely appropriate for dissemination of views concerning the bargaining representative."[124]

F. § 8(a)(2): Employer Domination or Support

Section 8(a)(2) makes it an unfair labor practice to "to dominate or interfere with the formation or administration of any labor organization or contribute financial or other support to it."[125] The framers of the NLRA intended § 8(a)(2) to inhibit companies from forming their own employer-dominated unions. Such organizations mushroomed across the country between the passage of § 7(a) of the National Industrial Recovery Act (NIRA) of 1933[126] and the Supreme Court's 1935 decision declaring the NIRA unconstitutional.[127] Senator Robert Wagner and other supporters of the NLRA maintained that employer-dominated organizations could not achieve lasting gains for the employees. Moreover, employers invoked the existence of these organizations as a means of stymieing the holding of fair representation elections and the emergence of legitimate labor organizations.

Section 8(a)(2)'s breadth has raised a number of difficult boundary questions. To what extent may companies establish a consultative process for working out workplace disputes between management and employees? If the employees are represented by an exclusive bargaining agent, such a process would have to be

121 Id. at 706.

122 Id. at 709.

123 NLRB v. Magnavox Co. of Tennessee, 415 U.S. 322 (1974).

124 Id. at 325.

125 29 U.S.C. § 158(a)(2).

126 Pub. L. No. 73–67, 48 Stat. 195 (June 16, 1933).

127 Schechter Poultry Corp. v. United States, 295 U.S. 495 (1935).

negotiated with the union. Where the employees are not represented, however, is the only legal alternative unilateral management? What intra-firm organizational structures can a company use to facilitate employee input on shop practices or terms of employment? What legitimate concerns of the Act are undermined when employees and employers seek to find ways in which workplace issues can be discussed, considered, and even in some sense negotiated, where a union is not present and the consultative mechanism is not used to block independent union organizing?

There are two elements to a § 8(a)(2) violation: determining (1) whether the group, policy, or practice at issue is a "labor organization" under § 2(5) of the NLRA; and if so, (2) whether the employer has dominated, interfered, or provided financial support to it. In the case of the NIRA-era company unions, step one was fairly easily met. But the reach of § 8(a)(2) extends significantly beyond unions or bargaining agents in the traditional sense. The Act defines labor organization as "any organization of any kind, or any agency or employee representation committee or plan, in which employees participate and which exists for the purpose, in whole or in part, of dealing with employers concerning grievances, labor disputes, wages, rates of pay, hours of employment, or conditions of work."[128] The Supreme Court has made clear that the critical "dealing with" element does not require collective bargaining or any sort of formal bargaining process or organization.[129]

The breadth of the "labor organization" definition is illustrated in the Board's 1992 decision in *Electromation, Inc.*[130] The employer in *Electromation* had gotten "blowback" from employees after it had decided to reduce employee benefits. Sixty-eight of the employer's 200 employees had signed a petition complaining of the changes, and the employer's president met with employees to discuss issues such as wages, bonuses, and attendance and leave policies.[131] Concluding that the company had serious morale issues, the president established a set of five "action committees" designed to engage with employees on their concerns.[132] Each committee would have six employees and one or two members of management as well as the benefits manager, who served as coordinator. Employees were to sign up for a maximum of one committee per employee, and the employer posted the final memberships. The committees—dealing with absenteeism, no-smoking policies, the communication network, pay

---

[128] 29 U.S.C. § 152(5).

[129] NLRB v. Cabot Carbon Co., 360 U.S. 203, 212–13 (1959).

[130] 309 NLRB 990 (1992), enforced, 35 F.3d 1148 (7th Cir. 1994).

[131] 309 NLRB at 990.

[132] Id. at 991.

progression for "premium" positions, and the attendance bonus program—were to meet on a weekly basis during working hours to develop proposals for management to consider.[133] The employees on the attendance bonus committee did, in fact, develop a policy, but the management member of the committee rejected it as too costly; they then developed a second policy which was never presented to the president.[134] About two weeks after the committees began to meet, a Teamsters union local made a demand for recognition, and a month later the employer suspended the committees until after the scheduled NLRB representation election.[135]

The Board held that Electromation's action committees violated § 8(a)(2). To reach that conclusion, the Board first had to determine that the committees were statutory labor organizations, despite seeming more akin to a set of employer staffing assignments. The Board noted that: "[a]ny group, including an employee representation committee, may meet the statutory definition of 'labor organization' even if it lacks a formal structure, has no elected officers, constitution or bylaws, does not meet regularly, and does not require the payment of initiation fees or dues."[136] The action committees met the other two statutory requirements as they included employees and they had the purpose of "dealing with" terms and conditions of employment. The "dealing with" element was held satisfied by the design of the committees to elicit employee proposals which would then be responded to by management in a back-and-forth manner. The Board ruled that the "action committees" were employer-supported labor organizations in violation of § 8(a)(2) because they were created by the employer, staffed according to the employer's specifications, and required to meet on work time at the employer's premises.[137]

If we remove the § 8(a)(2) lens, the employer's actions may seem laudable, particularly in contrast with traditional unilateral management in non-union shops. But the Board characterized the employer's actions as presenting employees with a "Hobson's choice of accepting the status quo, which they disliked, or undertaking a bilateral 'exchange of ideas' within the framework of the Action Committees."[138] Perhaps a choice is better than no choice. The employer was using the committees to obtain employee input and feedback on issues that they cared about. The process was controlled by the employer, but there was no basis for believing the employees

[133] Id.

[134] Electromation, 309 NLRB at 991–92.

[135] Id. at 992.

[136] Id. at 994.

[137] Id. at 997–98.

[138] Id. at 998.

thought the committees were an independent union representing their interests.[139]

There are two approaches for avoiding the prohibitory sweep of § 8(a)(2). First, employers may avoid the "dealing with" prong of the "labor organization" definition by delegating certain managerial tasks completely to employees or employee groups. In *Crown Cork & Seal Co.*,[140] the employer utilized four production teams and three administrative committees to manage a variety of workplace issues. The teams had the authority to stop production lines, allocate training assignments, and even administer the employee absentee program.[141] And even though upper-level management did reserve authority to review these decisions, it deferred to the teams in almost every instance.[142] *Crown Cork* was an important decision for management, sending a green light that so-called "self-directed" production work teams were lawful under the NLRA. In *Keeler Brass Co.*,[143] by contrast, the Board did find an employee-grievance committee to be a labor organization, because the committee's grievance decision was rejected by management and sent back for further proceedings. The Board held that the committee was "dealing with" management because they "went back and forth explaining themselves until an acceptable result was achieved."[144]

A second way around § 8(a)(2) is for management to steer employee committees away from § 2(5)'s terms and conditions of employment. As Member Devaney noted in his *Electromation* concurrence, "[t]he statute does not forbid direct communication between the employer and its employees to address and solve significant productivity and efficiency problems in the workplace."[145] If the employee committee is not dealing with the employer on § 2(5) subjects, there would be no violation of the Act. It may be difficult as a practical matter, however, for a committee to discuss productivity or product quality without dealing with compensation and working conditions.

One final note on § 8(a)(2) remedies: the traditional remedy is for the Board to order the unlawfully dominated labor organization

---

139 See Samuel Estreicher, Employee Involvement and the "Company Union" Prohibition: The Case for Partial Repeal of § 8(a)(2) of the NLRA, 69 N.Y.U. L. Rev. 125 (1994).

140 334 NLRB 699 (2001).

141 Id.

142 Id.

143 317 NLRB 1110 (1995).

144 Id. at 1114.

145 Electromation, 309 NLRB at 1005 (Devaney, Mem., concurring).

to disband.[146] Situations involving only interference and support, rather than domination, merely require the employer to cease any dealings with the organization until it becomes certified as the employees' representative under § 9 of the NLRA.

G. Remedies for Unfair Labor Practices

The NLRA gives the Board the authority to provide "make-whole" relief to employees who have suffered an unfair labor practice. Section 10(c) of the Act provides that the Board can "take such affirmative action including reinstatement of employees with or without back pay, as will effectuate the policies of this subchapter."[147] Back pay and reinstatement are the typical remedies for any employee who has been discharged or suffered other discipline from an employer ULP.

The Board's remedies are supposed to be compensatory, rather than punitive: they are to create "a restoration of the situation, as nearly as possible, to that which would have obtained but for the illegal discrimination."[148] Unlike the remedies available under Title VII of the Civil Rights Act of 1964 after the 1991 Civil Rights Act amendments,[149] the Board has no authority to award punitive damages under the Act.[150]

In *Thryv, Inc.*,[151] the Biden Board expanded the definition of "make-whole" relief to include all "direct or foreseeable pecuniary harm" that workers suffer as a result of ULPs. This expansion of scope was designed to make workers whole for the consequences of the illegal adverse employment actions beyond the direct loss of income and benefits. Such potential expenses include credit card fees, penalties for withdrawing money from retirement accounts, and medical costs. In order to secure such damages, the General Counsel would need to demonstrate the "amount of pecuniary harm, the direct

---

146 Id. at 998 (ordering the employer to "[i]mmediately disestablish and cease giving assistance or any other support to the Action Committees").

147 29 U.S.C. § 160(c).

148 Phelps Dodge Corp. v. NLRB, 313 U.S. 177, 194 (1941).

149 Civil Rights Act of 1991, Pub. L. 102–166, Nov. 21, 1991, 105 Stat. 107, 42 U.S.C. § 1981A.

150 42 U.S.C. § 1981A(a)(1).

151 372 NLRB No. 22 (Dec. 13, 2022). The Fifth Circuit denied enforcement of the Board's order, finding that the employer had not committed the alleged ULPs (and thus no remedies were in order). Thryv, Inc. v. NLRB, 102 F.4th 727, 737 (5th Cir. 2024). However, the court did not specifically consider the Board's new approach to remedies. The Ninth Circuit has upheld the Board's new approach to remedies, IUOE Local 39 v. NLRB, 127 F.4th 58 (9th Cir. 2025), while the Third Circuit has found that the Board exceeded its authority in awarding expenses beyond lost wages. NLRB. v. Starbucks Corp., 125 F.4th 78, 97 (3d Cir. 2024) ("While the Board can certainly award some monetary relief to the employees, that relief cannot exceed what the employer unlawfully withheld.").

or foreseeable nature of that harm, and why that harm is due to the respondent's unfair labor practice."[152] In response, the employer would have a chance to challenge the claimed sums, arguing that the harm was not direct or foreseeable, or that it would have occurred regardless of the ULP.[153]

The *Thryv* decision could have important ramifications for ULP claims by raising the potential for remedies beyond simple reinstatement and backpay. The decision also raises the question whether this broadened definition of "make-whole" remedies is a form of punitive damages that the Supreme Court has held to be outside the Board's authority,[154] and whether a damages award triggers Seventh Amendment rights to a civil jury.[155] In backpay determinations under the NLRA, employees must try to mitigate their damages by making reasonable efforts to find substantially equivalent employment.[156] The employer has the burden of persuasion to show that the employee has failed to mitigate.[157] The Board in 2007 changed the burden of production in mitigation hearings. If the employer demonstrates that there existed "substantially equivalent jobs" in the area for the employee(s) to obtain, the General Counsel and the discriminatee must then come forward with evidence that the discriminatee made a reasonable effort to find one of those available jobs.[158] Moreover, terminated discriminatees must start looking for alternative work within two weeks of their discharge; otherwise, back pay is tolled until a reasonable effort at a search begins.[159]

Even if employees have found work elsewhere and are no longer "employees" of the particular employer, they may be reinstated to their original employment.[160] However, employees who are not legally authorized to work in the United States are not entitled to reinstatement or back pay. The Supreme Court held in *Hoffman*

---

152 Id. at *6.

153 Id. at *6.

154 See Republic Steel Corp. v. NLRB, 311 U.S. 7, 12 (1940) (holding that damages are to "restore and make whole employees who have been discharged in violation of the Act").

155 See SEC v. Jarkesy, 603 U.S. 109, 127 (2024) (holding that "matters concerning private rights may not be removed from Article III courts").

156 See, e.g., Allegheny Graphics, Inc., 320 NLRB 1141, 1144 (1996).

157 St. George Warehouse, 351 NLRB 961, 961 (2007).

158 Id.

159 Grosvenor Resort, 350 NLRB 1197, 1200 (2007) ("[W]e find that reasonably diligent discriminatees should at least have begun searching for interim work at sometime within the initial 2-week period, whether or not they continued to engage in picketing activities to regain their former jobs.").

160 Phelps Dodge Corp. v. NLRB, 313 U.S. 177, 196 (1941).

Plastic Compounds, Inc. v. NLRB[161] that federal immigration law prevented the Board from awarding reinstatement or back pay to employees who could not lawfully work in this country. The Court observed that that the Board had other remedial tools at its disposal, including a "cease and desist" order and a notice-posting.[162] The dissent cautioned that the absence of a back pay remedy would actually encourage employers to hire such workers.[163]

The Board has authority under § 10(j) of the NLRA to seek preliminary injunctive relief in the federal courts, which it has used in cases where union supporters are discharged in order to stymie organizing efforts.[164]

---

161 535 U.S. 137 (2002).

162 Id. at 152.

163 Id. at 156 (Breyer, J., dissenting).

164 29 U.S.C. § 160(j). See Samuel Estreicher, Improving the Administration of the National Labor Relations Act Without Statutory Change, 25 ABA J. Lab. & Emp. L. 1, 17–20 (2009).

Chapter 6

CHOOSING AN EXCLUSIVE BARGAINING REPRESENTATIVE

The primary purpose of § 9 of the NLRA is to facilitate the selection of an exclusive bargaining representative to engage in collective bargaining with the employer regarding terms and conditions of employment. If designated as the bargaining representative, a union negotiates on behalf of all employees in the unit as their exclusive bargaining agent. There are essentially three routes to exclusive bargaining status: (1) voluntary recognition by the employer of a union that has the support of a majority of employees in an appropriate unit; (2) certification by the NLRB after the union has won a majority vote in a secret-ballot election run by the Board; or (3) a remedial bargaining order based on a showing of majority support (via means other than an NLRB election) and an employer's unfair labor practices (ULPs) committed during the representation campaign.[1] Increasingly, unions have sought exclusive bargaining authority outside of the NLRA election process by placing economic and regulatory pressures on employers to agree to recognize the union on the basis of a showing of authorization cards alone or a private secret-ballot process. Recognition arising out of such agreement is another form of voluntary recognition. Negotiation of the framework agreement for such arrangements, even in a pre-hire context, has been held by the Board to be lawful.[2]

The § 9 process is irrelevant if the union does not seek exclusive bargaining authority over the entire bargaining unit. Members-only unionism, where the union represents only those employees wishing to join the union, is lawful and does not require NLRB certification, but the employer is under no duty to bargain with a minority union or an uncertified union under the NLRA.[3] Even though members' only unionism is commonplace in Germany, France, and other countries, few American unions pursued a members-only strategy because they prefer the advantages of exclusive bargaining status

---

[1] NLRB v. Gissel Packing Co., 395 U.S. 575 (1969); Cemex Construction Materials Pacific, LLC, 372 NLRB No. 130 (Aug. 25, 2023).

[2] Dana Corp., 356 NLRB No. 49 (2010), pet. for review den. sub nom. Montague v. NLRB, 698 F.3d 307 (6th Cir. 2012).

[3] Retail Clerks Int'l Ass'n v. Lion Dry Goods, 369 U.S. 17, 29 (1962); Consol. Edison Co. v. NLRB, 305 U.S. 197, 237 (1938); Dana Corp., 356 NLRB No. 49, at 4 (Dec. 6, 2010) (dictum); see also Charles J. Morris, The Blue Eagle at Work: Reclaiming Democratic Rights in the American Workplace (Cornell Univ. Press 2005) (advocating for stronger rights for members-only unions).

and the right to enforce a bargaining obligation against the employer, and there no provision in U.S. law, as there is in Germany, for administrative extension of collective bargaining agreements to the non-union sector.

A. "Designated or Selected"

The NLRA does not expressly provide that a union's status as exclusive bargaining depends on winning a majority of votes in a secret-ballot election. Section 9(a) provides: "Representatives designated or selected for the purposes of collective bargaining by the majority of the employees in a unit appropriate for such purposes, shall be the exclusive representatives of all the employees in such unit for the purposes of collective bargaining in respect to rates of pay, wages, hours of employment, or other conditions of employment."[4] In principle, the "designated or selected" language could be interpreted to include a situation in which the union presents signed authorization cards from the majority of employees in an appropriate unit.

Under the *Joy Silk* doctrine,[5] the Board held that absent a good faith doubt as the union's majority support, the employer had a duty to recognize and bargain with the union in the absence of an NLRB election win. During this time, Democrat and Republican administration boards disagreed over the extent and gravity of ULPs that would derogate from good-faith doubt, and whether the employer or the Board would have the burden of persuasion on the issue.[6]

In *NLRB v. Gissel Packing Co.*,[7] the Board (through its appellate counsel) moved away from the "good faith doubt" test and instead adopted an "election preference" policy whereby it would issue a bargaining order only (i) where a union demonstrated a prior majority and (ii) an employer's serious ULPs undermined that majority and precluded fair rerun conditions.[8] The Court upheld this policy as a reasonable exercise of agency discretion which it reaffirmed in *Linden Lumber Div., Summer &Co. v. NLRB*,[9] holding

---

4 29 U.S.C. § 159(a) .

5 Joy Silk Mills Inc., 85 NLRB 1263 (1949), enf'd, 185 F.2d 732, 741 (D.C. Cir 1950).

6 See discussion of Joy Silk and Aaron Bros., 158 NLRB 1077 (1966), in NLRB v. Gissel Packing Co., 395 U.S. 575, 592–94 (1969).

7 395 U.S. 575 (1969).

8 Brandon R. Magner, The Good-Faith Doubt Test and the Revival of *Joy Silk* Bargaining Orders, 56 U. Mich. J.L. Reform 151, 178–83 (2022).

9 419 U.S. 301 (1974).

than an employer had no duty to petition for an election even where it had "independent knowledge" of the union's majority.[10]

In its 2023 ruling in *Cemex Construction,*[11] the Biden Administration Board sought to revive the *Joy Silk* doctrine, although it did not carry forward the "good faith doubt" test or the doctrine's requirement of employer ULPs inconsistent with such doubt. Under *Cemex*, the employer can no longer simply refuse to recognize a union with majority support and await a possible election, should the union choose to file. Instead, the employer must either recognize the union or file a petition itself promptly—generally within two weeks.[12] If the employer does neither of these, the Board will deem the employer to have recognized the union and will find that the employer has committed a ULP if it fails to bargain. The employer could still demand an election, even in the presence of a card majority, but must petition for one.[13] Employers can likely circumvent this new policy by filing its petition proposing a different unit, the resolution of which would require a hearing not unlike a conventional representation-case hearing. Otherwise, the Board would presumably hold the election unless employer ULPs triggered its blocking-charge policy.[14]

B. Determining the Appropriate Bargaining Unit

A petition for an NLRB election or a demand for employer recognition without an election must identify which employees the union wishes to represent. The group of employees to be represented is known as the "bargaining unit," although technically the term refers to the jobs in the unit because in some employment settings there may be considerable turnover. Before an election can be held, the Board must determine that the proposed unit is an "appropriate bargaining unit." If the employer challenges the union's proposed unit, the Board's regional office will hold a hearing to determine whether it is an appropriate unit under Board precedent.

1. "Community of Interest" Standard

In the Board's longstanding view, the unit proposed by the petitioner need not be the "most" appropriate unit of employees for

---

[10] The employer had knowledge of the union's support because the employees had been engaged in a recognitional strike.

[11] Cemex Construction Materials Pacific, LLC, 372 NLRB No. 130 (Aug. 25, 2023).

[12] Id. at *25 n.139 ("Allowing for unforeseen circumstances that may be presented in a particular case, we will normally interpret 'promptly' to require an employer to file its RM petition within 2 weeks of the union's demand for recognition.").

[13] Id. at *25.

[14] For a discussion of the Board's blocking charge policy, see Part C.1.

collective bargaining purposes. The inquiry is whether the unit as described in the petition is *an* appropriate unit for bargaining. In order to be appropriate, the proposed unit's employees must share a "community of interest" with each other. This test is context-specific and examines whether the employees share common interests in the aspects of their employment that would be subject to collective bargaining. The Board has identified the following factors in determining a community of interest:

> [W]hether the employees are organized into a separate department, have distinct skills and training; have distinct job functions and perform distinct work, including inquiry into the amount and type of job overlap between classifications; are functionally integrated with the Employer's other employees; have frequent contact with other employees; interchange with other employees; have distinct terms and conditions of employment; and are separately supervised.[15]

Because petitioning labor organizations need only choose an appropriate unit, rather than the most appropriate unit, the Board will defer to the petitioner organization's unit if it is otherwise appropriate.[16] The petitioner labor organization's wishes are given weight in part because the purpose of the Act is to facilitate collective bargaining, and the union has chosen a unit that it believes will demonstrate its majority support. Section 9(c)(5) of the Act, as amended by the 1947 Taft-Hartley amendments, specifies that "the extent to which the employees have organized shall not be controlling" in the unit determination process. The Board's view is that if the petition's proposed unit is otherwise appropriate, the extent of organization is not in fact "controlling."[17]

Employers may challenge a proposed unit if they believe the employees in the unit do not, in fact, share a community of interest. The Board and courts have recognized an employer's interest in avoiding crazy-quilt units that hamper its ability to maintain a uniform personnel/labor-relations policy.[18] A frequent employer

---

15 United Operations, Inc., 338 NLRB 123, 123 (2002).

16 See Boeing Co., 337 NLRB 152, 153 (2001) ("The Board's procedure for determining an appropriate unit under Section 9(b) is to examine first the petitioned-for unit. If that unit is appropriate, then the inquiry into the appropriate unit ends.").

17 Country Ford Trucks, Inc. v. NLRB, 229 F.3d 1184, 1191 (D.C. Cir. 2000) ("[T]he NLRB may simply look at the Union's proposed unit and, if it is an appropriate unit, accept that unit determination without any further inquiry.").

18 See NLRB v. Solis Theater Corp., 403 F.2d 381, 382 (2d Cir. 1968) (noting that the Board "must respect the interest of an integrated multi-unit employer in maintaining enterprise-wide labor relations"); see also Friendly Ice Cream Corp. v. NLRB, 705 F.2d 570 (1st Cir. 1983).

objection concerns the exclusion of employees who should otherwise be included in the unit because they share a community of interest with the union's proposed unit. The Board has held the union's proposed unit is appropriate unless the employer could show that the excluded employees shared an "overwhelming" community of interest with employees in the proposed unit.[19] This issue remains in contention, as Republican administrations favor a stronger push to include employees left out of the union-proposed unit.[20]

2. Craft vs. Industrial Units

In the Board's early years, one axis of controversy was whether craft workers should be included within larger "industrial" (i.e., company-wide or "wall-to-wall") units. The American Federation of Labor (AFL) tended to favor craft units and its newly-formed competitor the Congress of Industrial Organizations (CIO) favored more inclusive industrial units. (The rivalry between the two federations did not end until their merger in 1954 as the AFL-CIO.) The Board was accused of leaning towards the CIO's position, and this criticism is reflected in § 9(b)(2), also a product of the Taft-Hartley amendments, which provides that the Board cannot find a proposed craft unit inappropriate because another more inclusive unit previously had been established by the agency "unless a majority of employees in the proposed craft unit vote against separate representation."[21] When competing unions offer alternative units involving at least some of the same employees, the Board's so-called "*Globe*" election procedure gives employees a chance to select whether they want a separate craft unit or a larger "industrial" unit.[22] In theory, under § 9(b)(2), craft workers would seem to have a right to sever, or seek a vote to sever, themselves from a broader industrial unit. The Board presently uses a multifactor analysis that makes it difficult, as practical matter, for a craft severance bid to succeed absent proof that the interests of the craft group are systematically ignored.[23]

---

19 Specialty Health Care and Rehabilitation Center of Mobile, 357 NLRB 934 (2011).

20 The Trump Administration Board held that any excluded employees needed to be "sufficiently distinct" in order to be excluded from the unit. PCC Structurals, Inc., 365 NLRB No. 160, at *9 (Dec. 15, 2017). The Biden Administration Board returned to the earlier standard, finding that employees inside and outside a proposed unit would have an overwhelming community of interest if "there are only minimal differences, from the perspective of collective bargaining." American Steel Construction, Inc., 372 NLRB No. 23, at *17 (Dec. 14, 2022).

21 29 U.S.C. § 159(b)(2).

22 See Globe Machine & Stamping Co., 3 NLRB 294 (1937).

23 See Mallinckrodt Chemical Works, 162 NLRB 387, 397 (1966) (using a six-factor test that looks at the separateness of the trade, the history of collective

3. Single-Location Presumption

A recurring question for the Board is whether employees at a particular location of a multifacility employer—say, employees at one particular Walmart store—constitute an appropriate unit for bargaining. The Board maintains a presumption that employees at a single store in a retail chain form an appropriate unit for bargaining.[24] This presumption can be overcome, however, if two or more stores are near each other, there is a high degree of employee interchange among stores, and management sets labor and personnel policies at the multistore or broader level. Whether the presumption is overcome in a particular case is a question of fact to be determined in the representation proceeding.[25] In 1995, the Board proposed a regulation that would have made single-location units nearly conclusively appropriate if at the location there were fifteen or more employees, at least one supervisor, no other unit was located within a mile, and there were no mitigating "extraordinary circumstances."[26] The proposed rule drew fierce opposition from Congress, which attached riders to the Board's appropriations prohibiting the Board from expending any funds to create or enforce the rule. Three years after proposing the rule, the Board officially withdrew it.[27]

4. Acute Health-Care Facility Units

One successful example of Board rulemaking involves its bargaining-unit rule for acute care hospitals. The rule designated eight presumptive bargaining units based on the following job categories: registered nurses, physicians, other professionals, technical employees, skilled maintenance employees, business office clerical employees, guards, and other non-professional employees.[28] The Supreme Court unanimously recognized the Board's authority to promulgate substantive regulations under § 6 of the Act and upheld

---

bargaining at the plant, the existence of a separate identity for these employees, the pattern of collective bargaining within the industry, the degree of integration of the production processes, and the qualifications of the petitioning union).

[24] See Haag Drug Co., Inc., 169 NLRB 877, 878 (1968). The Biden Administration Board recently confirmed this presumption in Starbucks Corp., 371 NLRB No. 71 (Feb. 23, 2022).

[25] See, e.g., NLRB v. Chicago Health & Tennis Clubs, Inc., 567 F.2d 331 (7th Cir. 1977).

[26] 60 Fed. Reg. 50146 (1995).

[27] 63 Fed. Reg. 8890 (1998). See generally William B. Gould IV, Labored Relations 168–75 (2000).

[28] 29 C.F.R. § 103.30. Groups of five or fewer employees, however, would not be considered appropriate units.

the eight-unit rule.[29] In non-acute-care facilities, the agency applies its traditional "community of interest" approach.[30]

5. Accretion

What if the employer has an existing group of employees with union representation, but then adds a new facility in which workers are doing work similar to those in the bargaining unit? Should these employees be automatically absorbed into the existing unit, even if they would not fit the definition of the unit that was certified by the Board? Because the employees in an accreted unit are not polled on their preferences, the Board in general will not recognize an "accretion" of the new group to the preexisting unit. The agency will do so "only when the additional employees have little or no separate group identity. . . and when the additional employees share an overwhelming community of interest with the preexisting unit to which they are accreted."[31]

6. "Bargaining Unit" vs. Bargaining Structure

The employer and union cannot change the scope of the Board's appropriate unit determination, but they can by agreement bargain on a broader basis than the unit of initial certification or recognition. For example, a particular union obtaining separate certification at five different stores of a multi-store grocery chain can bargain with the employer on a five-store basis, as long as the union has bargaining authority at each of the stores.[32]

Similarly, two or more separate employers can agree to bargain with a union representing their employees. Such a unit requires consent from all parties, and the union must be the majority representative for each of the constituent employers.[33] The Board will not hold an election on a multiemployer basis.[34] In some industries, such as the automobile industry, the employer and the union have at times engaged in "pattern" bargaining in which employers indicate

---

29 American Hospital Ass'n v. NLRB, 499 U.S. 606 (1991).

30 The Board applies a modified burden-shifting approach to non-acute care units in Specialty Health Care and Rehabilitation Center of Mobile, 357 NLRB 934 (2011).

31 Super Valu Stores, Inc., 283 NLRB 134, 136 (1987).

32 See, e.g., Almacs, Inc., 176 NLRB 671 (1969).

33 Charles D. Bonanno Linen Service, Inc. v. NLRB, 454 U.S. 404 (1982); Brown v. Pro Football, Inc., 518 U.S. 231, 240 (1996). For an overview of the prevalence of multiemployer bargaining, see id. at 251 (Appendices A & B).

34 There is some question whether the agency even has statutory authority to certify a multiemployer unit without the consent of each of the employers. See NLRA § 9(b), 29 U.S.C. § 159(b) ("The Board shall decide in each case whether [the appropriate unit] shall be the employer unit, craft unit, plant unit, or other subdivision thereof.").

they will follow the pattern of what has been achieved in bargaining with the lead employer. This grouping is simply a series of individual employer-union agreements, however, rather than a formal multi-employer bargaining structure.

7. Mixed Units of Single and Joint Employment

As discussed in Chapter 4, two or more companies may be in a "joint employment" relationship with a group of employees. This happens when they each have significant authority over aspects of the employees' wages and working conditions.[35] If all of the bargaining unit employees are jointly employed, then both employers would have a duty to bargain in good faith with the union. What about those cases, however, where a bargaining unit is split: some employees are jointly employed, while others are employed by just one of the employers?

Such situations may arise in the temporary employment context. In the typical case, a contracting agency supplies temporary employees ("supplier employer") to another employer ("user employer") for certain projects or positions. Although such jobs are denominated as temporary, they may in fact continue over many years. In some cases, the employees are hired, fired, and paid by the supplying firm but directed and supervised by the user firm. These employees would likely be considered jointly-employed employees; a union could seek to represent the supplier employer's employees separately or seek to bargain with both employers as joint employers.[36] If the supplied employees work side-by-side with employees of the user firm who are not supplied or supervised by the supplier employer, the union may seek a combined unit of the supplied employees with those other employees.

The Board traditionally recognized a multi-employer unit in such split circumstances only if both supplier-employer and user-employer consented.[37] But in the 2000 *Sturgis* case, the Board changed the rule and allowed employees of a supplier employer that were supervised in part by the user employer to be in the same bargaining unit with employees who were solely employed by the user employer—even without the consent of both employers.[38] The

[35] See Boire v. Greyhound Corp., 376 U.S. 473 (1964).

[36] See, e.g., NLRB v. Browning-Ferris Indus., 691 F.2d 1117, 1123 (3d Cir. 1982); Riverdale Nursing Home, 317 NLRB 881, 882 (1995).

[37] H.S. Care, Inc. d/b/a Oakwood Care Center, 343 NLRB 659 (2004); Lee Hospital, 300 NLRB 947 (1990).

[38] M.B. Sturgis, Inc., 331 NLRB 1298 (2000). The Board required each employer to bargain over the terms and conditions that it controlled as to the separate sets of employees.

Board briefly returned to its consent policy in 2004,[39] but reverted to the *Sturgis* approach in 2016.[40]

C. Grounds for Not Entertaining a Question Concerning Representation (QCR)

Even where a unit is otherwise appropriate and the petitioning labor organization has filed authorization cards signed by at least 30% of the employees in the unit, there are number of grounds where the Board will refuse to consider the representation question.

1. "Blocking Charge"

Under its traditional "blocking charge" policy, if an ULP charge has been filed regarding acts by the employer or union involved in the election, the Board will defer the election until after the charge has been resolved.[41] The policy stems from the concern that the unresolved charge will likely taint the outcome of the election. Blocking charges can play an important strategic role in delaying an election until a time-consuming ULP proceeding can be concluded. In its 2020 rulemaking regarding election procedures, the Trump Administration Board altered the blocking charge policy by allowing elections to go forward while holding off counting the ballots until the ULP charges had been resolved.[42] Under this policy, if the charging party prevailed in the election, the ULP issue would be moot; if the charging party did not prevail, the Board would have election results in place and could consider whether the ULP charges had merit and were of sufficient severity to unfairly affect the election conditions. The Biden Administration Board reverted to its prior approach;[43] this potentially delays the effective date of election results until time-consuming ULP charges are resolved.[44]

---

[39] Oakwood Care Center, 343 NLRB 659 (2004).

[40] Miller & Anderson, Inc., 364 NLRB 428 (2016).

[41] NLRB Casehandling Manual, Pt. 2, Representation Proceedings, §§ 11730–11734 (1999).

[42] NLRB, Representation—Case Procedures: Election Bars; Proof of Majority Support in Construction-Industry Collective-Bargaining Relationships, 85 Fed. Reg. 18366 (April 1, 2020).

[43] See NLRB, Representation—Case Procedures: Election Bars; Proof of Majority Support in Construction Industry Collective-Bargaining Relationships, 89 Fed. Reg. 62,952 (Aug. 1, 2024) (amending 29 C.F.R. Part 103). The Board declined to allow the election to proceed rather than embargoing results until ULP proceedings are concluded.

[44] See Samuel Estreicher, Improving the Administration of the National Labor Relations Act Without Statutory Change, 25 ABA J. Lab. & Emp. L.1, 9–10 & Table 2 (2009).

2. Election and Certification Bars

The Act itself prohibits elections within a year of a "valid" election in the same bargaining unit.[45] The so-called "election bar," added by the Taft-Hartley amendments, was extended by the Board's "certification bar." Under the certification-bar doctrine, the Board will not order an election, nor may the employer lawfully withdraw recognition, for a reasonable time after a union has been certified as the exclusive representative for the unit.[46] The presumption provides a one-year bar from the date of certification. The certification bar is important despite the statutory election bar, as (1) certification comes after the election—sometimes much later if the employer challenges the results; and (2) the certification bar can be tolled if the employer's misconduct, such as an improper refusal to bargain, denies the union a year's fair opportunity to bargain.[47]

3. Voluntary-Recognition Bar

The Board also maintains a "voluntary recognition" bar to an election where the employer recognizes the union as collective bargaining representative based on a showing of majority support.[48] That bar is also for a "reasonable time" but is more flexible than the certification bar (although generally not less than six months). In 2007, the Board announced a new process which required that employees have forty-five days after the employer's recognition of a union to file an election petition with the Board to remove the union or select a different union.[49] The 45-day period did not begin until the employees had received adequate notice of their right to file a petition within that period. The Board has oscillated back and forth on this proposal, most recently returning to the traditional recognition bar through rulemaking.[50]

4. Contract Bar

The Board's "contract bar" doctrine bars an election during the period of a written, definite-term CBA for up to three years.[51] No election will be held during the period of the agreement, save for a

---

[45] 29 U.S.C. § 159(c)(3).

[46] Brooks v. NLRB, 348 U.S. 96 (1954).

[47] See Mar-Jac Poultry, 136 NLRB 785 (1962); Lamar Hotel, 137 NLRB 1271 (1962).

[48] Keller Plastics Eastern, 157 NLRB 583, 587 (1966).

[49] Dana Corp., 351 NLRB 434 (2007).

[50] Representation—Case Procedures: Election Bars; Proof of Majority Support in Construction Industry Collective-Bargaining Relationships, 89 Fed. Reg. 62,952, 62,959–60 (Aug. 1, 2024) (amending 29 C.F.R. Part 103).

[51] Auciello Iron Works, Inc. v. NLRB, 517 U.S. 781 (1996). The Board reaffirmed the contract-bar doctrine in Mountaire Farms, Inc., 370 NLRB No. 110 (Apr. 21, 2021).

thirty-day window between 90 days and 60 days prior to the end of the agreement.[52] The bar lasts as long as the term of the CBA, except that it has a maximum of three years.[53] If the union and the employer agree to a new three-year agreement at the close of the previous one, the bar will go into effect again.[54]

The contract bar erects a significant hurdle to employees looking to decertify their representative in the midst of employer-union harmony, or to bring in an outside union to negotiate a new agreement. The bar also insulates the union from employer challenges to its majority, because the Board, with Supreme Court approval, irrebuttably presumes continuing majority support for the union during the contract-bar period.[55] The Board will lift the contract bar only under very limited circumstances: if there is a fundamental schism within the union, the union has become defunct, or the union affirmatively disclaims interest in representing the employees.[56]

The contract bar does not apply in the first place, however, if the union did not legally have the authority to exclusively represent the bargaining unit employees. For example, if an employer closes a facility for a sustained period of time and then opens the facility with new employees, the prior contract will not bar an election.[57] In *General Extrusion*,[58] the Board formulated a rule to deal with premature recognition that would also apply to new operations: "[A] contract does not bar an election if executed (1) before any employees

---

[52] The sixty-day period following the election window is referred to as the "insulated period," and it is designed to give the parties two months to negotiate "free from the threat of overhanging rivalry and uncertainty." Deluxe Metal Furn. Co., 121 NLRB 995, 1001 (1958). Health-care institutions have the same thirty-day window, but the insulated period is ninety days, rather than sixty, so the window is from 120 days to 90 days. Trinity Lutheran Hosp., 218 NLRB 199 (1975).

[53] General Cable Corp., 139 NLRB 1123 (1962).

[54] If the agreement is executed before the thirty-day election window, however, that window will still remain open despite the new agreement, in order to prevent the elimination of any chance to challenge the relationship.

[55] See NLRB v. Burns Int'l Security Servs., Inc., 406 U.S. 272, 290 n.12 (1972); Auciello Iron Works, Inc. v. NLRB, 517 U.S. 781 (1996).

[56] Hershey Chocolate Corp., 121 NLRB 901 (1958); American Sunroof Corp., 243 NLRB 1128 (1979).

[57] See also General Extrusion Co., 121 NLRB 1165, 1167 (1958) (explaining that "a contract does not bar an election after an indefinite period of closing" after which an employer resumes operations with new employees); Slater System Md., Inc., 134 NLRB 865, 866 (1961) (noting that an amended contract which makes it applicable to a new location does not bar an election where the original location closed for 26 months and the company hired none of the employees from the original cafeteria at the new location); NLRB v. Dominick's Finer Foods, Inc., 28 F.3d 678, 684 (7th Cir. 1994) (recognizing an exception to the contract-bar rule where an employer resumes operation with new employees after an extended period of closing).

[58] 121 NLRB 1165 (1958).

had been hired or (2) prior to a substantial increase in personnel. When the question of a substantial increase in personnel is in issue, a contract will bar an election only if at least 30 percent of the complement employed at the time of the hearing had been employed at the time the contract was executed, *and* 50 percent of the job classifications in existence at the time of the hearing were in existence at the time the contract was executed."[59]

D. Regulation of Campaign Propaganda and Other Conduct

1. *General Shoe* Doctrine

The Board has essentially two avenues for regulating the conduct of an election: (1) the § 8 or ULP route or (2) the § 9 route. Under the ULP route, a party that commits significant ULPs risks the usual remedies for such violations as well as having an election win overturned. In addition, the filing of a ULP charge may have the effect of holding an election in abeyance under the Board's blocking-charge policy. Under the § 9 route, the Board has authority to refuse to certify election results even if ULPs have not been committed. The latter is termed the "laboratory conditions" or *General Shoe* doctrine.

In *General Shoe Corp.*,[60] the Board established that "[i]n election proceedings, it is the Board's duty to provide a laboratory in which an experiment may be conducted, under conditions as nearly ideal as possible, to determine the uninhibited desires of employees."[61] Under the "laboratory conditions" doctrine, conduct constituting a ULP is considered a *per se* infringement upon required campaign conditions.[62] In addition, some conduct may adversely affect fair election conditions even if there is no violation of § 8.

2. § 8(c) Free Speech Provision

To the extent § 8(c) of the NLRA protects the expression or activity in question, the Board cannot use its ULP authority to reach such expression or activity (even as evidence of a ULP).[63] Under *General Shoe*, however, the Board has considerable leeway in deciding the grounds for certifying or setting aside election results

---

[59] Id. at 1167.

[60] 77 NLRB 124, 127 (1948).

[61] General Shoe Corp., 77 NLRB 124, 127 (1948).

[62] Dal-Tex Optical Corp., 137 NLRB 1782, 1786–87 (1962).

[63] Under § 8(c), "the expression of any views, argument, or opinion" could not be deemed to an unfair labor practice "if such expression contain[ed] no threat of reprisal or force or promise of benefit." 29 U.S.C. § 158(c) (2000). There is also a potential First Amendment issue which is usually not reached because § 8(c) applies. See *Gissel*, 395 U.S. at 616–17 (noting that "§ 8(c) merely implements the First Amendment"); NLRB v. Golub Corp., 388 F.2d 921 (2d Cir. 1967) (per Friendly, J.).

without implicating § 8(c) strictures because it is not adjudicating a ULP charge.[64]

Over time, the Board has endeavored to flesh out the line between permissible campaigning and improper influence. The agency has developed specific rules regarding threats, promises, inflammatory appeals, and misrepresentations.

3. Threats

The Board's prohibitions against employer coercion in the election context build on § 8(a)(1) of the Act, which makes it an unfair labor practice for employers "to interfere with, restrain, or coerce employees in the exercise of [their collective bargaining] rights."[65] Any effort to compel or threaten the employee to vote a certain way is deemed not only an infringement of laboratory conditions but also a ULP. Although threats of physical violence are certainly prohibited, the more common concerns are threats of unfavorable economic treatment, including discontinuance of benefits or closing of a plant, because of support of the union.

A difficult line is maintained between threats, which are prohibited, and predictions of adverse consequences of unionization, which are protected by § 8(c) and may hold information employees would find relevant to their decision. Employees at other companies may have been organized by the particular union and then met an undesirable fate, such as a long strike or plant closure; the employer is permitted to refer to these events, even if ominous.[66] Such information could be important, perhaps critical, to a reasonable employee's decision whether to be represented by the particular union. But at the same time, an employer can couch its adverse predictions in such a way as to convey the message that it is willing to take adverse action against the employees simply because they choose union representation. Because the employer has the ultimate control over the fate of the plant, the employer's prediction may be perceived by employees as more akin to a threat than in other contexts.[67]

---

[64] The D.C. Circuit ruled differently in dealing with an analogous question under the Railway Labor Act. See US Airways, Inc. v. NMB, 177 F.3d 985 (D.C. Cir. 1999) (entertaining free-speech objections as a basis for overturning the results of a representation election). See Shawn J. Larsen-Bright, Free Speech and the NLRB's Laboratory Conditions Doctrine, 77 N.Y.U. L. Rev. 204 (2002).

[65] Id. § 158(a)(1).

[66] See, e.g., NLRB v. Golub Corp., 388 F.2d 921 (2d Cir. 1967) (holding that employer predictions based on past experiences at other companies did not violate § 8(a)(1)).

[67] Is the following tweet from Tesla CEO Elon Musk a threat to Tesla employees about the futility of unionization? "Nothing stopping Tesla team at our car plant from

The Supreme Court broadly delineated the boundaries of threat and prediction in *NLRB v. Gissel Packing Co.*[68] The Court requires that adverse predictions about unionization must be "carefully phrased on the basis of objective fact to convey an employer's belief as to demonstrably probable consequences beyond his control or to convey a management decision already arrived at to close the plant in case of unionization."[69] Any suggestion that the "prediction" is instead a statement about what an employer could do solely on its own initiative would render such a prediction a threat of reprisal falling outside of § 8(c)'s protection.

In practice, the difference between permissible predictions and unlawful threats is difficult to operationalize because the Court's test appears to turn on phrasing and tone more than anything else.[70] An important factor is whether the employer is stating or suggesting that the adverse consequences are within its control; this would be an assertion the union could not easily rebut. Another factor is the timing of the employer's statement: has the union been given an opportunity to contest the factual content of the employer's prediction?

The lines are indeed difficult to draw. An employer may describe its contractual rights and the limits of NLRA protections even if such descriptions paint a gloomy picture of the prospects of collective bargaining. The employer may tell employees that they are not required to agree to anything when bargaining with the union, and that it has as much a right to ask for wage and benefit reductions as the union has to ask for increases.[71] Similarly, an employer may offer an opinion about the possibility of union-called strikes and may note that it has the right to permanently replace employees who go out on strike. Employers may not, however, threaten unlawful conduct by intimating they will bargain in bad faith or reduce benefits illegally prior to bargaining.[72] And any insistence that they will "bargain from

---

voting union. Could do so [tomorrow] if they wanted. But why pay union dues & give up stock options for nothing? Our safety record is 2X better than when [this] plant was UAW & everybody already gets healthcare." See Elon Musk, Tweet, May 20, 2018, https://twitter.com/elonmusk/status/998454539941367808?lang=en. The Fifth Circuit assumed without deciding that the tweet violated the NLRA but refused to enforce the Board's order that the tweet be deleted because it was considered constitutionally protected speech. Tesla, Inc. v. NLRB, 120 F.4th 433, 438–39 (5th Cir. 2024).

68 395 U.S. 575 (1969).

69 Id. at 618.

70 See, e.g., El Dorado Tool, 325 NLRB 222 (1997) (holding that a graveyard with tombstones of other union-represented plants that had closed, along with a final tombstone for the employer with a question mark, constituted an implicit threat).

71 See Fern Terrace Lodge of Bowling Green, 297 NLRB 8 (1989).

72 See, e.g., Golden Eagle Spotting Co., 319 NLRB 64 (1995); Advo Systems, 297 NLRB 926 (1990).

scratch" even if not a ULP may be deemed an attempt to undermine laboratory conditions by suggesting that collective bargaining will be an entirely futile process.

Ultimately, there is no clear line between impermissible threats and permissible campaign rhetoric. The Board has emphasized the need to look at the totality of the circumstances in figuring out where employer campaign statements and other conduct falls. If the overall campaign has had a tendency to threaten employees with possible violations of their collective rights, then the Board will find a § 8(a)(1) violation and may overturn the election. These determinations, based as they are on a multifactor contextual test, will be subject to indeterminacy and uncertainty. As such, they threaten either to under-deter coercive threats or discourage the provision of information that may be helpful to the employees' decision.

An employer is limited in its ability to ascertain union support among its employees. Questioning an employee to determine the employee's support for the union is generally unlawful under § 8(a)(1). Factors that might support a contrary determination are (1) the background (i.e., the prior actions of the employer, especially ULPs, in the context of concerted activity); (2) the nature of the information sought; (3) the identity of the questioner; and (4) the place and method of interrogation.[73] Where the employer is questioning an open union supporter, this will be viewed as less coercive.[74]

Systematic polling of employees about their union support, although also a form of interrogation, is given a somewhat wider berth. In the Board's view, polling is inherently coercive. The employer must have a legitimate reason for engaging in the polling: the employer may poll if it has a reasonable, good-faith doubt of the union's continuing majority[75] or, in an initial-recognition context, to test the union's majority support before extending recognition.[76] In addition, the polling must satisfy the so-called *Struksnes* safeguards: (1) the poll is intended to determine whether a union's claim of majority support is true; (2) this purpose is communicated to employees; (3) the employer gives assurances against reprisals; (4) the poll is conducted by secret ballot; and (5) the employer has not otherwise engaged in unfair labor practices or created a coercive

---

[73] See, e.g., Timsco Inc. v. NLRB, 819 F.2d 1173 (D.C. Cir. 1972).

[74] Rossmore House, Inc., 269 NLRB 1176, 1178 n.20 (1984).

[75] Allentown Mack Sales & Service, Inc. v. NLRB, 522 U.S. 359 (1999).

[76] ILGWU v. NLRB, 366 U.S. 731 (1961).

atmosphere.[77] The Board views employer surreptitious surveillance as a ULP even if the employees are unaware of it at the time.

4. Promises and Grants of Benefit

Like threats, an employer's promise to grant benefits to employees if they vote against union representation fall outside of the protections of § 8(c). Such promises are viewed as a form of employer manipulation because they are artificial lures, akin to promises of bribes, that come into being solely as a result of the union organizing drive. Under the *Exchange Parts* doctrine,[78] the Board, with Supreme Court approval, has extended this prohibition to an employer's actual improvements in terms and conditions of employment when made for the purpose of influencing the employees' vote on representation. Such improvements violate § 8(a)(1) and laboratory conditions.

A ULP under *Exchange Parts* is a motive-based violation. Employers make changes in wages and working conditions all the time; it is only when they do so for the purpose of affecting the outcome of an NLRB election that they violate the law. The Board uses what might be termed a "dynamic status quo" approach. If the employer enacts improvements in wages and other terms that would have occurred in the ordinary course, there is no violation. In fact, the employer commits a ULP if it refuses to implement otherwise promulgated changes because of a pending union organizing campaign or scheduled NLRB election.

Union promises to obtain improvements in wages and working conditions if they secure bargaining authority are generally permissible under § 8(b)(1)(A), since employees, in the Board's view, recognize that such promises are "dependent on contingencies beyond the Union's control."[79] The union ULP provision (§ 8(b)(1)(A)) is narrower than the employer provision (§ 8(a)(1)) in reaching only union restraint or coercion of employees in their § 7 activities, not simply interference with the exercise of these rights. Unions are expected to promise improved wages and working conditions, but they are not permitted to offer tangible, valuable benefits to employees in the context of a representation campaign. Election results have been overturned because of union gifts of life insurance coverage,[80] jackets,[81] hats and shirts,[82] and alcoholic drinks.[83] Union-

---

[77] See Struksnes Construction Co., 165 NLRB 1062 (1967).

[78] NLRB v. Exchange Parts Co., 375 U.S. 405 (1964).

[79] Smith Co., 192 NLRB 1098, 1101 (1971).

[80] Wagner Elec. Corp., 167 NLRB 532 (1967).

[81] Owens-Illinois, Inc., 271 NLRB 1235 (1984).

[82] NLRB v. Shrader's, Inc., 928 F.2d 194 (6th Cir. 1991).

[83] Revco D.S. v. NLRB, 830 F.2d 70 (6th Cir. 1987).

supported lawsuits against employers on behalf of employees in the midst of a representation campaign may also violate laboratory conditions.[84]

The Supreme Court in *NLRB v. Savair Manufacturing Co.*[85] held that unions cannot offer to waive initiation fees for employees who sign authorization cards before an election.[86] The Court explained that such a practice would allow the union to "buy endorsements and paint a false portrait of employee support during its election campaign."[87] The Court did not explain why the union's offer was a basis for overturning an election when the cards were used only to obtain an election. A waiver of initiation fees, the *Savair* Court noted, would not disturb election results if the waiver had been open "not only to those who have signed up with the union before an election but also those who join after the election."[88]

5. Racial and Ethnic Inflammatory Appeals

Applying its laboratory-conditions doctrine, the Board will overturn the results of elections involving appeals to racial prejudice or pride that it deems too "inflammatory" for the campaign. The foundational case is *Sewell Manufacturing Co.*,[89] in which the employer appealed to racial prejudice in its campaign against the union. The employer linked the union to unrelated desegregation efforts and used a picture of a white union official dancing with a black woman in its campaign literature. The Board found such conduct to be grounds for a new election. According to the Board, racial appeals were only permissible if they were truthful, germane to the election, and not overly inflammatory

Under the *Sewell* standard, the Board has generally applied a more lenient standard to appeals to racial pride and solidarity.[90] However, the U.S. Courts of Appeals have at times clashed with the Board about its allowance of such campaign tactics.[91] The Board's

---

[84] See, e.g., Nestle Ice Cream v. NLRB, 46 F.3d 578, 584 (6th Cir. 1995) (concluding that union lawsuit on behalf of employees for overtime pay was an impermissible union grant of benefit).

[85] 414 U.S. 270 (1973).

[86] Id. at 277.

[87] Id.

[88] Id. at 272 n.4.

[89] 138 NLRB 66 (1962).

[90] See, e.g., Baltimore Luggage Co., 162 NLRB 1230 (1967).

[91] See, e.g., NLRB v. Schapiro & Whitehouse, 356 F.2d 675 (4th Cir. 1966) (refusing to enforce bargaining order because of appeals to racial pride); KI (USA) Corp. v. NLRB, 35 F.3d 256, 260 (6th Cir. 1994) (denying enforcement of a bargaining order based on the union's use of a letter by a Japanese businessman which allegedly inflamed racial tensions); Case Farms v. NLRB, 128 F.3d 841, 850 (4th Cir. 1991)

view is that appeals to racial pride or solidarity must be repeatedly uttered to meet the "inflammatory" threshold. Here, too, there has been some judicial resistance, as courts have found that a one-time use of epithets can be sufficiently inflammatory to warrant a new election.[92]

6. Misrepresentation

Under the Board's laboratory-conditions doctrine, factual misrepresentations *per se* are not prohibited during the election campaign. The overall policy is that "exaggeration, inaccuracies, half-truths, and name calling, though not condoned, will not be grounds for setting aside an election" presumably because such statements will be swiftly rebutted by the other side in the contest.[93] As the Board noted: "absolute precision of statement and complete honesty are not always attainable in an election campaign, nor are they expected by employees."[94] Despite this baseline policy, however, the Board has oscillated fairly significantly in this area. From 1962 to 1977, the Board prohibited a subset of misrepresentations that it felt had a particularly deleterious effect on fair-election conditions. The rule established in *Hollywood Ceramics Co.*[95] stated:

> [A]n election should be set aside only where there has been a misrepresentation or other campaign trickery, which involves a substantial departure from the truth, at a time which prevents the other party or parties from making an effective reply, so that the misrepresentation, whether deliberate or not, may reasonably be expected to have a significant impact on the election.[96]

The Board overruled *Hollywood Ceramics* in its 1977 *Shopping Kart* decision.[97] Noting that the *Hollywood Ceramics* rule had been criticized for vagueness and indeterminacy, the Board maintained that its rules "must be based on a view of employees as mature individuals who are capable of recognizing campaign propaganda for

(Williams, J., concurring in judgment) (expressing "concern with the Board's apparent disregard for the decisions of the Circuit Courts" as to inflammatory racial appeals).

92 See, e.g., M & M Supermarkets v. NLRB, 818 F.2d 1567 (11th Cir. 1987); NLRB v. Eurodrive, 724 F.2d 556 (6th Cir. 1984); NLRB v. Triplex Mfg. Co., 701 F.2d 703 (7th Cir. 1983). Cf. Clearwater Transport, Inc. v. NLRB, 133 F.3d 1004, 1010 (7th Cir. 1998) (voicing a "strong objection" to the NLRB's "seemingly casual reading" of past precedent in such cases).

93 Hollywood Ceramics Co., 140 NLRB 221, 226 n.6 (1962).

94 Id. at 223.

95 140 NLRB 221 (1962).

96 Id. at 224.

97 Shopping Kart Food Market, 228 NLRB 1311 (1977).

what it is and discounting it."[98] A year later, the Board reversed course, and a three-member majority in *General Knit of California* returned to the *Hollywood Ceramics* standard.[99] Four years after that, however, the hands-off policy of *Shopping Kart* was yet again reinstated by a three-member Board majority in *Midland National Life Insurance Co.*[100]

The hands-off approach in *Midland* has remained Board law. Although settled law, it is not clear why material misrepresentations of fact made at a time soon before a scheduled election—when the other side does not have an opportunity to reply—do not affect laboratory conditions.[101] Some courts of appeals have resisted *Midland* and suggest that "pervasive" misrepresentations should be a basis for overturning election results.[102]

7. Access to Employee Electorate

Despite the fine-grained regulation of what cannot be said during the representation campaign, the Board has done little to require information disclosure from the parties. For example, in *Florida Mining & Materials Corp.*,[103] the Board refused to overturn a union win on the grounds that the union failed to reveal to the employees that the day before the election it had been placed under temporary trusteeship by the international union.

One instance of required disclosure is *Excelsior Underwear, Inc.*[104] In that case, invoking its *General Shoe* authority, the Board required employers to provide the union with the names and addresses of employees in the unit. This information is required within seven days of the approval of an election agreement; the union need not request it. The *Excelsior* requirement gives the union the ability to send materials and other communications to the employees at their home address. The Board's election rules now require employers to provide personal email addresses and cell phone numbers as well, if in the employer's records.[105]

---

98 Id. at 1313.

99 General Knit of California, 239 NLRB 619 (1978).

100 Midland Nat'l Life Ins. Co., 263 NLRB 127 (1982).

101 Matthew T. Bodie, Information and the Market for Union Representation, 94 Va. L. Rev. 1, 19–22, 66–67 (2008).

102 NLRB v. New Columbus Nursing Home, 720 F.2d 726 (1st Cir. 1983); Van Dorn Plastics Machinery Co. v. NLRB, 736 F.2d 343, 348 (6th Cir. 1984).

103 198 NLRB 601, enforced, 481 F.2d 65 (5th Cir. 1973).

104 Excelsior Underwear, Inc., 156 NLRB 1236 (1966).

105 79 Fed. Reg. 74308, 74336 (Dec. 14, 2014). Overturning a Trump administration rule, the Biden Administration Board reinstated the 2014 rules. Representation-Case Procedures, 88 Fed. Reg. 58,076 (Aug. 25, 2023) (amending 29 C.F.R. § 102.63 et seq.).

Unions are otherwise restricted in their access to the employee electorate. There is no requirement that employers offer access to employees equal to or commensurate with the interactions they have with employees on the election issue.[106] Under the Board's 1948 decision in *Babcock & Wilcox Co.*,[107] employers could require that employees attend meetings on company time in which the employer presents its views on the union representation question. As long as the employer had not otherwise violated laboratory conditions, such "captive audience" meetings were permissible.[108] The only restriction had been that mass-audience meetings by either side violated laboratory conditions when held within 24 hours of the election.[109] In a change in policy, the Biden Administration Board ruled that an employer's mandatory campaign meeting on company time, without more, is a ULP.[110] Although recognizing the employer's right to free speech, the Board concluded that "Section 8(c) does not license employers to compel employees, on pain of discipline or discharge, to attend meetings where they are forced to listen to the employer's views."[111]

The Board could do more to provide greater union access to the employee electorate. By extension of its reasoning in *Excelsior*, the Board could rule that once the union demonstrates sufficient employee interest to warrant the scheduling of an NLRB representation election, there is a strong § 7 interest in providing employee access to the union campaign even on the employer's property. Such access would require appropriate security measures and could be limited to non-working areas such as break rooms and cafeterias for scheduled periods.[112]

E. Conducting the Election

NLRB elections are generally held in a very traditional style: the board agent sets up a voting booth and provides paper ballots which

---

106 See NLRB v. United Steelworkers of America (Nutone and Avondale), 357 U.S. 357 (1958).

107 77 NLRB 577 (1948).

108 See Livingston Shirt Corp., 107 NLRB 400, 409 (1953). Prior to *Livingston*, the Board had briefly required employers to give unions a chance to respond to captive-audience meetings. See Bonwit-Teller, Inc., 96 NLRB 608 (1951). The Supreme Court seemingly upheld this approach in NLRB v. United Steelworkers of America, 357 U.S. 357 (1958).

109 Peerless Plywood Co., 107 NLRB 427 (1953). See also Guardsmark, LLC, 363 NLRB 931 (2016) (holding that in elections involving mail ballots, the mass-meeting prohibition begins 24 hours before the ballots are scheduled to be mailed).

110 Amazon.com Services, LLC, 373 NLRB No. 136 (2024).

111 Id. at *12.

112 See Samuel Estreicher, "Easy In, Easy Out": A Future for U.S. Workplace Representation, 98 Minn. L. Rev. 1615, 1632–33 (2014); Bodie, Information, supra, at 35.

are placed in a box and counted after the election. (As mentioned, the union must get a majority in order to win; a tie means no representation.) The local regional office is charged with conducting the representation election on behalf of the Board. The Board agent who runs the balloting is tasked with complete neutrality, both in action and in appearance. The election is generally held at the employer's work site to obtain maximum voter turnout. Prior to the COVID-19 pandemic, the Board had allowed for mail balloting only if the employees were dispersed and would find it difficult to travel.[113] In the face of national and regional lockdowns in spring 2020, many NLRB regions moved to voting by mail. In *Aspirus Keweenaw*,[114] the Board identified six situations in which mail-ballot elections would be appropriate based on circumstances associated with the ongoing COVID-19 pandemic.[115] The Board subsequently modified one of these factors but largely adheres to the same instructions to the regions.[116]

F. Representation Authority Without an Election

1. Voluntary Employer Recognition and Card Check

The NLRA provides for the Board-run election as the exclusive process through which a union becomes certified as the collective bargaining representative for an appropriate unit of employees. Section 9(a) of the Act, however, states that: "Representatives *designated or selected* for the purposes of collective bargaining *by the majority of the employees* in a unit appropriate for such purposes, shall be the exclusive representatives of all the employees in such unit for the purposes of collective bargaining. . . ."[117] Thus, the Act does not require an election for the union to be recognized as the exclusive bargaining representative. But nor does the Act require the employer to acquiesce to a showing of majority support outside of the election. Even if the union presents a verifiable showing of support from 100% of the bargaining unit, the employer can refuse to bargain

---

[113] NLRB Representation Casehandling Manual § 1130. The National Mediation Board, which administers the Railway Labor Act, has long used mail balloting and has begun using electronic balloting as well. National Mediation Board Representation Manual 14.02 (2009); In re Continental Airlines, 35 N.M.B. 42 (2008).

[114] 370 NLRB No. 45 (2020).

[115] Id. at *6–*11 (discussing NLRB mandatory telework status, increases in regional COVID-19 rates, local or state health ordinances, employer failure to institute safety protocols for the election, a COVID outbreak at the employer's facility, or other compelling situations).

[116] Starbucks Corp., 371 NLRB No. 154 (Sept. 29, 2022).

[117] 29 U.S.C. § 159(a).

until the union has been selected through the Board's secret-ballot election procedure.[118]

Prior to the Taft-Hartley amendments, the Board was willing to require an employer to recognize a union based on a demonstration of majority support outside the election process, as the 1935 law provided that the Board "may take a secret ballot of employees, or utilize any other suitable method to ascertain such representatives."[119] And even after Taft-Hartley, the Board continued to hold that an employer could refuse to recognize a *bona fide* showing of majority support only if it had a good faith doubt as to the union's actual majority support.[120] This *Joy Silk* doctrine eventually gave way to the Board's "election preference" policy—in essence, a recognition of the employer's prerogative to require an election before recognizing the union.[121] That policy, referenced in the Court's decision in *Gissel*, is in effect to this day, albeit with more responsibility on employers to file for such an election.[122]

An employer may voluntarily recognize the union as long as the union does in fact have majority support. If an employer recognizes a union that does not have the support of the majority of employees in the unit, the employer violates §§ 8(a)(1) & (2), and the union violates § 8(b)(1)(A). The only exception is in the construction industry, where pre-hire agreements are permitted under § 8(f) of the Act.[123] A good-faith belief in the union's majority support is no defense. In *International Ladies' Garment Workers Union (Bernhard-Altmann) v. NLRB*,[124] the employer began negotiating with the union after the union asserted that it represented a majority of employees according to its own calculations. The employer made no effort to check whether the signatures matched up with an actual majority of the unit. The parties initially negotiated a memorandum of understanding, and then reached a full collective bargaining agreement a month and a half later. By the time the CBA was agreed upon, the union did in fact obtain authorization cards from a majority of the unit. Both the Board and the Supreme Court held the subsequent acquisition of a majority was irrelevant, however, since the majority was obtained after the employer had already recognized the union as the employees' exclusive bargaining agent. The premature recognition

118 See Linden Lumber Div. Summer & Co. v. NLRB, 419 U.S. 301 (1974).

119 National Labor Relations Act of 1935, § 9(c), Pub. L. No. 74–198, 49 Stat. 449, 453 (amended 1947).

120 Joy Silk Mills, Inc., 85 NLRB 1263 (1949).

121 *Gissel,* 395 U.S. at 594.

122 See Cemex Construction Materials Pacific, LLC, 372 NLRB No. 130, at *25 (Aug. 25, 2023).

123 29 U.S.C. § 158(f).

124 366 U.S. 731 (1961).

afforded the union "a deceptive cloak of authority" that facilitated its subsequent organizational efforts.[125]

Under the Board's *Majestic Weaving* doctrine, the employer and the union cannot negotiate a CBA conditioned on the subsequent demonstration of majority support.[126] The employer's bargaining with a union that did not, at that moment, represent a majority was "similar to formal recognition with respect to the deleterious effect upon employee rights."[127]

If a union and employer have a preexisting collective bargaining relationship culminating in a CBA as to a certain unit of employees, to what extent can the agreement be extended to new groups of employees at other facilities? Under the Board's *Kroger* "after acquired facility" doctrine, the employer and union may agree to extend an existing CBA to the employees at a new facility acquired after the agreement, on the assumption that union has majority support at the new location.[128]

In *Dana Corp.* ("*Dana II*"),[129] the Board was confronted with a situation falling between *Majestic Weaving* and *Kroger*: the employer and union, already having an established collective bargaining relationship, negotiated a "letter of agreement" (LOA) as a framework for future relations at the employer's non-union plants.[130] Along with card-check and neutrality provisions, the LOA provided "principles" that would guide negotiations between the two sides, in the event the union would obtain majority support. The Board held that the LOA did not amount to pre-majority support recognition or bargaining and therefore did not contravene *Bernhard-Altmann* or *Majestic Weaving*. There was nothing in the LOA, the majority noted, that "would reasonably have led employees to believe that recognition of the [union] was a foregone conclusion or, by the same token, that rejection of [union] representation was futile."[131] The

---

[125] Id. at 736.

[126] 147 NLRB 859, 859–60 (1964), enforcement denied on other grounds, 355 F.2d 854 (2d Cir. 1966).

[127] 29 NLRB Ann. Rep. 69 (1964).

[128] Kroger Co., 219 NLRB 388 (1978); see also Haarte & Co., 278 NLRB 947 (1986) (employer may recognize union at new factory where employees were likely to relocate from the unionized plant to the new facility).

[129] 356 NLRB 256 (2010), enforced, Montague v. NLRB, 698 F.3d 307 (6th Cir. 2012).

[130] *Dana II*, 356 NLRB at 256.

[131] Id. For open issues after *Dana II*, see Andrew M. Kramer & Samuel Estreicher, NLRB Allows Pre-Recognition Framework Agreements Between Employer and Labor Union, N.Y.L.J., Feb. 23, 2011, at 4:

> First, the Board will need to decide in a future case whether the pre-recognition framework agreement should be made readily available to the

dissent urged, however, that *Dana II* "threaten[ed] to reinstate . . . the establishment of collective-bargaining relationships based on self-interested union-employer agreements that preempt employee choice and input as to their representation and desired terms and conditions of employment."[132]

As the *Dana II* majority made clear, the employer is not required under the NLRA to maintain a position of neutrality with respect to unionization or any particular union. Just as the employer can advocate zealously against union representation, it is allowed to indicate its preference for unionization or for a particular union as well. Section 8(a)(1) prohibits employer interference with employee choice, and § 8(a)(2) prohibits domination of or interference with a labor organization. But the employer can use its § 8(c) speech rights to oppose or support a union bid and can agree to be neutral during the campaign, whether or not the union can demonstrate majority support at the time of the neutrality agreement. An employer can also waive its right to insist upon a Board election prior to recognizing majority support. A "card-check" agreement sets up an alternative to the certification election whereby the union collects authorization cards from employees, generally with a set time limitation for the collection. The parties are free to negotiate whatever terms they like provided the union at least has a majority before it is recognized by the employer.

Card-check and neutrality agreements are often negotiated after a union "corporate campaign" has been mounted to wrest such terms. In some instances, the union works with the employer to secure benefits for both parties, such as increased governmental funding for the industry. In other instances, the union puts pressure on a set of employers in a particular industry or region, using media, student, clergy, and political and regulatory pressure to get the employers to agree to such a system. The Board has enforced card-check neutrality agreements against parties that try to breach them after the fact.[133]

---

affected employees before they are asked to vote on unionization or solicited by the union to sign authorization cards. We believe . . . transparency and an informed vote by the employees are especially important in this context. A second issue is whether the union can enter into such a framework agreement with an employer with whom it has no prior relationship. Because the *Dana* [*II*] majority did not rely on the *Kroger* doctrine, the absence of a preexisting relationship should not make a legal difference.

[132] *Dana II*, 356 NLRB at 265 (Hayes, M., dissenting).

[133] See Sullivan Elec. Co., 199 NLRB 809 (1972), enforced, 479 F.2d 1270 (6th Cir. 1973) (employer violates § 8(a)(5) by refusing to bargain with union subsequent to majority showing through card-check agreement); Verizon Information Systems, 335 NLRB 558 (2001) (union cannot file election petition after agreeing to card-check system); Lexington House, 328 NLRB 894 (1999) (dismissing union petition to represent employees after union agreed not to attempt to organize those employees as part of a larger card-check-neutrality agreement).

These agreements may sometimes contain their own arbitration mechanism.

What are an employer's obligations with regard to recognition when more than one union seeks to represent a particular bargaining unit? Under the Board's *Midwest Piping*[134] doctrine, an employer violated § 8(a)(2) by recognizing one of two competing unions when both had filed election petitions. The Board's objective was to prevent the employer from determining the outcome of a representation struggle between two unions when a Board election was likely. The agency extended the doctrine for a time, however, to prevent an employer from recognizing a union with majority support so long as the other union had a "colorable claim" to employee support. The effect was to allow a minority union to forestall recognition without even requiring it to muster the support necessary to petition for an election. In *Bruckner Nursing Home*,[135] the Board changed course and allowed employers to recognize a union with majority support as long as an election petition had not been filed by another union; once a valid petition has been filed, the employer has to wait until the results of the election.[136]

2. Bargaining Orders Under *Gissel* and *Cemex*

In Chapter 5, we discussed the standard remedies for employer ULPs: notice positing, orders to refrain from the conduct, reinstatement, back pay, and orders to bargain in good faith. Where an election has been held and lost by the union because of employer ULPs, the Board can order a rerun election; the one-year election bar in § 9(c)(3) does not apply if the prior election was invalid. In *NLRB v. Gissel Packing Co.*, the Supreme Court upheld the Board's authority to issue a bargaining order for a union that previously demonstrated a card majority when a fair rerun election could not be held because of the employer's serious ULPs. The Court recognized the possibility there might be extreme circumstances where employer ULPs so polluted the possibility of a fair election that as a remedial matter the Board could issue a bargaining order in favor of a union that had not previously obtained a majority. The Board presently has eschewed minority-union bargaining order authority.[137] It has issued *Gissel* bargaining orders only where the union enjoyed majority support at one point but then suffered a sustained campaign of employer ULPs.

---

[134] Midwest Piping & Supply Co., 63 NLRB 1060 (1945).

[135] Bruckner Nursing Home, 262 NLRB 955, 956 (1982).

[136] See Samuel Estreicher & Suzanne Telsay, A Recast *Midwest Piping* Doctrine: The Case for Judicial Acceptance, 36 Lab. L.J. 14 (1985).

[137] Gourmet Foods Inc., 270 NLRB 578 (1984).

The effectiveness of the *Gissel* bargaining order is an open question. The Board's ULP route is a lengthy process that can require two years or more in heavily-contested cases. By the time the case gets to the court of appeals, the agency is questioned on its premise that a fair rerun election cannot be held because of illegality that occurred years before. Courts have demanded that the Board provide a more detailed and analytical justification for orders in particular circumstances, with an emphasis on showing the ineffectiveness of traditional Board remedies.[138] They have also been more likely to take into account evidence of changed circumstances, such as employee turnover or change in managerial leadership.[139] A study of *Gissel* orders issued between 1986 and 1993 found that thirty-eight percent of bargaining orders issued by the Board were reversed.[140] Another study found that only twenty percent of bargaining orders resulted in a first contract.[141] Given the chilly reception in the courts and the difficulty of cultivating a bargaining relationship on such rocky terrain, the Board has tended to use *Gissel* orders sparingly.

The Board signaled two new potential grounds for bargaining orders without elections in *Cemex Construction*.[142] Overruling the Board's approach in *Linden Lumber*,[143] the *Cemex* majority first held that employers can no longer reject a union's majority support and wait for the union to file an election petition, instead requiring the employer to promptly file an election petition itself to avoid a ULP.[144] In addition, going beyond existing *Gissel* bargaining orders for sustained and severe employer ULPs, the Biden Board ruled that almost any ULP during the campaign period can block an election

---

138 The D.C. Circuit has been particularly interested in such justifications. See, e.g., Douglas Foods Corp. v. NLRB, 251 F.3d 1056, 1065–67 (D.C. Cir. 2001).

139 See NLRB v. U.S.A. Polymer Corp., 272 F.3d 289, 293 (5th Cir. 2001); NLRB v. Cell Agricultural Mfg. Co., 41 F.3d 389, 398 (8th Cir. 1994).

140 James J. Brudney, A Famous Victory: Collective Bargaining Protections and the Statutory Aging Process, 74 N.C. L. Rev. 939, 1003–05 (1996). A later study found a similar reversal rate. Arthur Leff, Failing to Give the Board Its Due: The Lack of Deference Afforded by the Appellate Courts in *Gissel* Bargaining Order Cases, 18 Lab. & Emp. Law. 1 (2002) (finding a 36 percent reversal rate between 1994 and 1996). For an early assessment, see Samuel Estreicher, The Second Circuit and the NLRB 1980–1981: A Case Study in Judicial Review of Agency Action, 48 Brook. L. Rev. 1063 (1982).

141 Terry A. Bethel & Catherine Melfi, The Failure of *Gissel* Bargaining Orders, 14 Hofstra Lab. L.J. 423, 437–38 (1997) (study of bargaining orders issued between 1979 and 1982).

142 Cemex Construction Materials Pacific, LLC, 372 NLRB No. 130 (Aug. 25, 2023).

143 Linden Lumber Division, Summer & Co., 190 NLRB 718 (1971), rev'd. sub nom Truck Drivers Union Local No. 413, 487 F.2d 1099 (D.C. Cir. 1973), aff'd. 419 U.S. 301 (1974).

144 Cemex Construction, supra, at *25. As noted earlier, employers may have a readily accessible means of mitigating the effect of this innovation by filing its petition in a significantly different unit, the resolution of which would require a hearing not unlike a conventional representation-case hearing.

"unless it is virtually impossible to conclude that the misconduct has affected the outcome of the election."[145]

G. Ousting an Incumbent Union

Just as an election is the Board's standard route for choosing union representation, the Board also provides for an election when employees choose to drop their union representation. Employees can file a timely decertification petition—a petition to decertify the union as their representative—if at least thirty percent of the unit signs cards indicating an interest in a decertification election. Recall the various bars to entertaining a petition, including the Board's blocking-charge policy. Perhaps for these reasons, there is a general pattern that close to half of the decertification petitions filed never culminate in an election.[146]

What if an employer has reason to believe that its employees no longer wish to be represented by the union? The employer essentially has three choices: file an election petition, poll its employees regarding their support, or withdraw recognition. Prior to 2001, the Board permitted the employer to choose between these three options as long as it had "good faith reasonable doubt" of the union's continuing majority status. The Board's application of its doctrine came in for heavy criticism from the Supreme Court in *Allentown Mack Sales & Service, Inc. v. NLRB.*[147] The case involved an employer's decision to poll its employees in the face of several pieces of evidence that the employees no longer wanted the union. The union lost the secret ballot poll (conducted by a priest), and the employer withdrew recognition. The Board ruled that the poll was unlawful because the employer did not have a good-faith, reasonable doubt of the union's loss of majority before polling. In his opinion for the Court, Justice Scalia (joined by Justices Breyer, Stevens, Souter, and Ginsburg) upheld the Board's "good faith reasonable doubt" standard for polling as well as withdrawal of recognition, noting the Board had found polling to be disruptive and unsettling to employees. In the second part of the opinion, however, Justice Scalia—this time writing for himself, Chief Justice Rehnquist, and Justices Kennedy, O'Connor, and Thomas—held that the Board had improperly applied its own standard, because it had in fact required much more than reasonable doubt to justify the polling.

In the 2001 case *Levitz Furniture Co. of the Pacific,*[148] the Board changed the requirements for the various employer responses to

---

145 Id. at *11.

146 60–64 NLRB Annual Rep. Table 10 (1995–1999).

147 522 U.S. 359 (1998).

148 333 NLRB 717 (2001).

potential loss of a union's majority. Under the new rule, an employer need only have "reasonable uncertainty" as to majority status in order to file a decertification petition. In contrast, the employer would need proof of loss of majority in fact in order to withdraw recognition from the union. Although not speaking directly to the matter, the Board retained the "good faith reasonable doubt" standard for polling.[149] Despite arguments that the employer should not be permitted to withdraw recognition prior to an actual election under any circumstances, the Board believed that it cabined the requirements sufficiently such that employers would only act on the basis of clear evidence. After *Levitz,* the employer needs only reasonable, good-faith doubt to obtain an election that is not otherwise barred, but it needs proof of actual loss of majority to withdraw recognition unilaterally.

Once an employer has obtained proof of loss of majority in fact, consistent with *Levitz,* and has stated that it withdraws recognition from the union at the expiration of the collective bargaining agreement (to avoid a breach of contract claim), the union cannot subsequently rebut the loss-of-majority evidence with later proof that it reobtained majority support.[150] Instead, the union must file an election petition within 45 days from the date of the announced withdrawal in order to avoid loss of recognition. Such anticipatory withdrawals by the employer cannot be made in the 90 days before the CBA expires.

---

[149] Struksnes Construction Co., 165 NLRB 1062 (1967).

[150] Johnson Controls, Inc., 368 NLRB No. 20 (July 3, 2019). The Board distinguished *Johnson Controls* in Nexstar Broad., Inc. d/b/a Koin-TV & Nat'l Ass'n of Broadcast Emps. & Technicians, the Broadcast & Cable Television Workers Sector of the Commc'ns Workers of Am., Loc. 51, AFL-CIO, 371 NLRB No. 118 (July 27, 2022), affirming an ALJ decision that *Johnson Controls* did not apply when the employer "withdrew recognition from the Union after the CBA expired, and thus could not have given notice that [the employer] intended to withdraw recognition after the CBA expired." Id. at *36.

Chapter 7

THE COLLECTIVE BARGAINING PROCESS

In this Chapter, we address the guts, the engine of the NLRA—the duty to bargain collectively. It is the legal requirement that drives everything else. Without the legal requirement of a duty to bargain, even if employees were to elect a union representative, they could simply encounter a continuation of the struggle over recognition. Of course, under § 8(d)—another product of the Taft-Hartley amendments—good-faith bargaining does not require the parties to reach agreement. But the employer cannot refuse to deal with the exclusive representative of its employees and instead must meet and confer at reasonable times in a sincere effort to reach agreement.

The NLRA imposes a duty to bargain on both employer, through § 8(a)(5), and union, through § 8(b)(3). The contours of these duties are discussed further below. First, however, we begin with the principle of exclusivity—that the union acts as the exclusive representative for the employees in the unit.

A. Exclusive Representation

Section 8(a)(5) makes it a ULP for the employer "to refuse to bargain collectively with the representative of its employees, subject to the provisions of section 9(a)." In turn, § 9(a) provides that "[r]epresentatives designated or selected for the purposes of collective bargaining by the majority of the employees in a unit appropriate for such purposes, shall be the exclusive representatives of all the employees in such unit for the purposes of collective bargaining in respect to rates of pay, wages, hours of employment, or other conditions of employment."[1]

1. Impact on Individual Employment Agreements

In most settings, before any union enters the scene, employees have preexisting relationships with their employers which are governed by employer rules subject to the state common law of contracts.[2] In *J.I. Case Co. v. NLRB*,[3] the employer entered into written employment agreements with its employees and invoked those agreements as a bar to any collective bargaining with the exclusive representative selected by the employees. The Supreme

---

1 29 U.S.C. § 159(a).

2 See Restatement of Employment Law chs. 2–3 (2015).

3 321 U.S. 332, 338 (1944).

Court held that the individual agreements provided no bar to the employer's duty to bargain with the employees' exclusive representative. "The very purpose of providing by statute for the collective agreement is to supersede the terms of separate agreements of employees with terms which reflect the strength and bargaining power and serve the welfare of the group."[4]

Because unions can negotiate arrangements allowing for individual agreements, as in the sports and entertainment industries,[5] *J.I. Case* is best seen as establishing a presumption that can be overcome by clear evidence of the union's waiver of its right to insist on exclusive dealing. One reason for the presumption in favor of a unitary agreement is that individual contracts could dissipate the strength of the collective agent. As the Court noted, "advantages to individuals may provide as disruptive of industrial peace as disadvantages."[6]

2. Impact on Employee Protests

The Supreme Court reaffirmed the exclusivity principle in *Emporium Capwell Co. v. Western Addition Community Organization*.[7] In that case, employees at a unionized company believed that the employer was discriminating on the basis of race in making job assignments and promotions. The union urged the affected employees to utilize the CBA's grievance-arbitration process. Two of these employees began picketing the store advocating for a consumer boycott and demanded repeatedly—including at a press conference—to deal directly with the company's president. Fired after receiving written warnings, the employees filed ULP charges maintaining that the employer violated § 8(a)(1). The Supreme Court sustained the Board's determination that there was no NLRA violation because the employees had engaged in unprotected activity by attempting to pressure the employer to deal directly with them rather than through the exclusive bargaining representative. The proviso to § 9(a) would have protected the employer from any ULPs for dealing with the group, but the proviso did not require the employer to engage in such direct dealing.[8]

---

[4] Id. at 338.

[5] In unionized U.S. professional sports leagues, collective agreements set minimum terms, but it is expected by all parties that individual talent will negotiate above that minimum.

[6] Id.

[7] 420 U.S. 50 (1975).

[8] The Court did not explain why the employees' activity was unprotected when they were seeking an opportunity to meet directly with the employer over their grievances. A request to meet with the employer would not be problematic but

Given the history that some unions tolerated, or even engaged in, racial and ethnic discrimination, the result in *Emporium Capwell* may seem harsh. In the case itself, the union had a strong civil rights record, opposed discrimination, and appeared willing to address the complaints through the grievance process. If the union had been hostile to the employees' discrimination claims, the employees could have claimed a breach of the union's duty of fair representation to all employees in the unit under § 8(b)(1)(A) of the Act. The employees could also have filed charges and pursued an action against the union under Title VII of the Civil Rights Act of 1964 for discriminatory handling of their grievances and against the employer for possible retaliation.[9]

Even though the NLRA specifically protects the right to strike (§ 13), employees cannot go out on strike to demand that their employer bargain with them separately from the union, as in *Emporium Capwell*. When employees go out on an unauthorized (sometimes called a "wildcat") strike, such conduct is usually considered unprotected because it is in derogation of the employees' choice to negotiate through an exclusive representative.[10] A few decisions, however, extend protection to a limited set of unauthorized walkouts that are in support of the union's position at the bargaining table.[11]

3. Impact on Employer Communications with Employees

In keeping with the requirements of exclusive representation, the employer must carefully cabin its communications with its employees so as not to deal directly with them with respect to terms and conditions of employment. The employer's obligation here is in some tension with its rights under § 8(c) to communicate its views to its workforce. The employer can inform the workers of positions it has taken at the bargaining table but may not present proposals to employees for ratification or engage in a back-and-forth with employees that constitutes de facto bargaining with them rather than the exclusive representative.

---

employee concerted activity to pressure the employer into doing so, the Court implied, could undermine the exclusive bargaining agent's position.

[9] See Hughes Tool Co., 147 NLRB 1573 (1964); cf. Steele v. Louisville & Nashville R. Co., 323 U.S. 192 (1944) (recognizing exclusive representative's implied duty of fair representation under the Railway Labor Act). For possible Title VII claims, see Goodman v. Lukens Steel Co., 482 U.S. 669 (1987).

[10] NLRB v. Shop Rite Foods, Inc., 430 F.2d 786 (5th Cir. 1970). For further discussion, see Michael C. Harper, Union Waiver of Employee Rights under the NLRA: Part I, 4 Indus. Rel. L.J. 335, 368–71 (1981).

[11] East Chicago Rehabilitation Center v. NLRB, 710 F.2d 397 (7th Cir. 1983).

4. Dealing with Minority or Members-Only Unions

In the absence of a § 9(a) representative, the employer has no duty to bargain with any group of employees, including minority or "members-only" unions, but neither does the NLRA prohibit such bargaining. Some commentators have argued that the NLRA requires employers to bargain with minority unions, as long as no majority representative has been selected,[12] but the Board has never taken this view.[13] From a practical standpoint, a duty to bargain with minority unions poses a substantial risk of non-uniformity for employees performing the same or similar work, as deals struck with one group would not necessarily extended to other groups; employer opportunism (where the employer picks the weaker labor group to impose an employer-wide agreement, as occurs in some Continental European countries); and employee opportunism (where employees exit members-only terms to seek better terms by forming a new group). Despite *Emporium Capwell*, the Act may protect employee concerted activity in support of their minority representative, at least where there is no § 9(a) exclusive representative.[14]

B. Bargaining in Good Faith

The duty to bargain under §§ 8(a)(5) and 8(b)(3) is generally characterized as the "duty to bargain in good faith," thanks to § 8(d). Added by the Taft-Hartley Act in 1947, § 8(d) was intended to cabin the Board's authority to infer a breach of the duty from the mere failure of either party to reach agreement.[15] The proviso to § 8(d) states that the obligation to bargain in good faith "does not compel either party to agree to a proposal or require the making of a concession."

1. The *Insurance Agents* Principle

Economic pressure is consistent with the duty to bargain. In *NLRB v. Insurance Agents' International Union*,[16] while engaging in what was concededly good-faith bargaining at the table, the union authorized an in-plant, by-the-book "slowdown." The tactic included having the employees refuse to solicit new business, refuse to comply

---

12 Charles J. Morris, The Blue Eagle at Work: Reclaiming Democratic Rights in the American Workplace (2005).

13 See, e.g., Mooresville Cotton Mills, 2 NLRB 952, 955 (1937).

14 See Union-Buffalo Mills Co., 58 NLRB 384 (1944) (workers who strike in support of minority union's demands protected by the Act against termination); Pennypower Shopping News, Inc., 244 NLRB 536 (1979) (same).

15 H.R. Rep. No. 245, 80th Cong., 1st Sess. 19 (1947) (stating that the Board had been "setting itself up as the judge of what concessions an employer must make and of the proposals and counterproposals that he may or may not make").

16 361 U.S. 477 (1960).

with reporting structures, report late for certain activities and meetings, and enlist the support of customers against the company. The Board and the Court assumed that such activities were unprotected because, as discussed in Chapter 5, they are akin to "partial strikes" that are inconsistent with the employees' duties while at work. However, the Court held that, even if unprotected,[17] the union had not violated § 8(b)(3). The Court viewed the Board's finding of a violation as an inappropriate attempt to regulate bargaining tactics in an effort to equalize the bargaining position of the parties, which was inconsistent with the hands-off theme of § 8(d).

There are two readings of *Insurance Agents*. The broader interpretation, which the Court often adverts to, is that the statutory duty to bargain in good faith does not authorize the NLRB to regulate the weapons of economic conflict. Under this view, conflict is inherent in the statute,[18] and the regulation of economic tactics provides an indirect means of regulating the substantive terms of any deal. Otherwise, "the Board in the guise of determining good or bad faith in negotiations could regulate what economic weapons a party might summon to its aid, . . . [and] it would be in a position to exercise considerable influence upon the substantive terms on which the parties contract."[19] As long as the parties are engaged in good-faith bargaining at the table, the statutory duty is satisfied. Only discriminatory weapons that violate §§ 8(a)(3) or 8(b)(2) are within the Board's regulatory ambit.

A narrower reading is also tenable. Under this view, the Board erred in *Insurance Agents* because it did not present a justification for claiming the slowdown evidenced bad-faith bargaining given the agency's acknowledgement that the union's conduct in the actual bargaining was in good faith. The slowdown may be an effective tactic and, in some circumstances, may be more useful to the union than a traditional strike, but the employer is not without recourse as these employees could be discharged or otherwise disciplined. It is not a

---

[17] The Court would later rule that states could not prohibit a peaceful slowdown, even if such activity was unprotected by the NLRA. See Lodge 76, Machinists v. Wisconsin Employment Relations Comm'n, 427 U.S. 132 (1976).

[18] "[A]t the present statutory stage of our national labor relations policy, the two factors—necessity for good-faith bargaining between parties, and the availability of economic pressure devices to each to make the other party incline to agree on one's terms—exist side by side." *Insurance Agents*, 361 U.S. at 489.

[19] Id. at 490.

tactic inconsistent with good-faith bargaining under the Act or what one of us has termed the Act's model of "bounded conflict."[20]

2. "Surface Bargaining" and Substantive Rigidity

What is the minimum that the parties need to agree to, in terms of substance, to avoid a charge of bad-faith bargaining? For example, can the employer take certain aspects of wages and working conditions off the table by insisting on a "management rights" clause that would render those aspects subject to unilateral management determination? In *NLRB v. American National Insurance Co.*,[21] the Board had found the employer to be in violation of § 8(a)(5) for proposing and insisting on a "management functions" clause that would give it complete authority over hiring, firing, promotions, work schedules, and employee discipline. The clause would essentially have allowed the employer unreviewable discretion over these critical terms of the employment relationship. Despite its breadth, however, the Board had to acknowledge that such a clause could lawfully be agreed to. This put the Board in a difficult position: it had to say that it was not a ULP for the employer to simply propose the clause, but that it was a ULP to insist on the clause to impasse. The Supreme Court held that the employer's insistence on the management-rights clause did not violate its good-faith bargaining obligation, stating the Board lacked authority to "pass upon the desirability of substantive terms of labor agreements."[22]

Because of the § 8(d) restriction, the Board is wary of review of the substantive rigidity of bargaining proposals. Consider a case where, unlike the clause in *American National Insurance*, the employer insists on a provision that renders *all* significant aspects of the employment relationship the subject of unreviewable employer discretion. The employer would be, in effect, saying: "We know you have won an NLRB representation election, but all we can agree to is a contract that does not restrict us in any way." Is this consistent with a bona-fide desire in good faith to reach an agreement with the employee's representative?[23] Judge Calvert Magruder, a former NLRB general counsel among other distinguished public service, perhaps put it best:

---

[20] See Samuel Estreicher, Strikers and Replacements, 3 Lab. Lawyer 897 (1987); Samuel Estreicher, Collective Bargaining or "Collective Begging"?: Reflections on Antistrikebreaker Legislation, 93 Mich. L. Rev. 577 (1994).

[21] 343 U.S. 395 (1952).

[22] Id. at 408–09.

[23] Some courts have considered an employer's insistence on unilateral authority over the resolution of grievances to violate § 8(a)(5). See Continental Ins. Co. v. NLRB, 495 F.2d 44 (2d Cir. 1974); Vanderbilt Prods., Inc. v. NLRB, 297 F.2d 833 (2d Cir. 1961); White v. NLRB, 255 F.2d 564 (5th Cir. 1958).

> [W]hile the Board cannot force an employer to make a 'concession' on any specific issue or to adopt any particular position, the employer is obliged to make *some* reasonable effort in *some* direction to compose his differences with the union, if § 8(a)(5) is to be read as imposing any substantial obligation at all.[24]

A rare example of a successful surface bargaining challenge is *NLRB v. A-1 King Size Sandwiches, Inc.*[25] In that case, the employer had met with the union at reasonable times and places, and there was no evidence of animus towards the union. However, throughout the bargaining process, the employer insisted upon the following: total control over wages; a "zipper" clause waiving all bargaining rights during the term of the agreement; a no-strike clause that included ULP strikes; unfettered control over discharge and discipline; and sole discretion over layoff and recall. The employer also rejected the union's request for a dues check-off clause and—perhaps the *coup de grace*—proposed an even broader management rights clause after the union failed to agree to the first one. Agreeing with the Board that § 8(a)(5) had been violated, the court of appeals noted that the union would have been worse off if it agreed to the employer's proposals than if it had simply relied solely on its right to strike.[26]

The § 8(d) conundrum raises the question as to the role of the Act when the employer has no interest in coming to any likely agreement with the union. Of course, where the union has the ability to impose economic or other pressure on the employer, the employer has some incentive to reach agreement in order to be free of the strike or other pressure. But where union does not have any leverage, the most the Act can do is force a process of discussion—essentially an educative process—where the parties are in a sense compelled to explore areas of possible common interest.

Do at least first-contract situations require a substantive boost not presently available under the law? For example, the proposed "Employee Free Choice Act" would have provided for interest arbitration where the parties could not reach an initial agreement on their own.[27] In interest arbitration, the parties select a third-party neutral to decide the substantive content of the agreement; as in baseball's salary arbitration, interest arbitration can be limited to particular subjects. How would interest arbitrators determine the substantive terms of an agreement? Moreover, what happens when

---

[24] NLRB v. Reed & Prince Mfg., Co., 205 F.2d 131, 134–35 (1st Cir. 1953).

[25] 732 F.2d 872 (11th Cir. 1984).

[26] Id. at 877.

[27] S. 560, H.R. 1409, 111th Cong. (2009).

the first contract expires and there is no provision for renewal arbitration? It is not clear that the mere existence of a prior contract necessarily alters the relationship between the parties and thereby obviates recourse to conflict or repeated interest arbitration.

3. Procedural Rigidity

Given the focus of § 8(d), the Board has greater leeway in regulating the procedural aspects of bargaining. The Board has found bargaining ULPs where the employer fails to release employees serving as union representatives to negotiate during working hours;[28] when one party records bargaining sessions over the other party's objection;[29] when the employer refuses to bargain because the union team includes representatives from other unions;[30] and when one party unreasonably fails to agree to a sufficient number of bargaining sessions.[31]

Can parties cut through all the bargaining back-and-forth and present their final proposals at the very outset, or would such an approach undercut the very notion of bargaining, which requires openness, listening, and a willingness to engage in the process? This dilemma was addressed in the case of Lemuel R. Boulware, who adopted a "take-it-or-leave-it" approach as vice-president of labor relations for General Electric Co. (GE) in the early 1960s. His strategy, which came to be known as "Boulwarism," consisted of one "firm, fair, final" offer from which the company would not budge. GE polled its employees to ascertain their desires before making its proposal, and then after the proposal was made, the company deployed a "veritable avalanche of publicity" to "sell" the terms to them.[32] In upholding the Board's § 8(a)(5) charge, the Second Circuit noted that these communications to employees, heralding the firmness of its position, essentially prevented GE from genuinely considering the union's alternative proposals—even in one instance where the union proposal would not have increased costs. Arguably, the problem with "Boulwarism," as practiced, was not necessarily the "firm, fair, final offer" format but the employer's inability to entertain any cost-neutral variation from that position because of its communication campaign.

---

28 Borg-Warner Controls, 198 NLRB 726 (1972).

29 Bartlett-Collins Co., 237 NLRB 770 (1978).

30 General Elec. Co. v. NLRB, 412 F.2d 512 (2d Cir. 1969).

31 Garden Ridge Management, Inc., 347 NLRB 131 (2006).

32 NLRB v. General Electric Co., 418 F.2d 736, 740–41 (2d Cir. 1969).

4. Disclosure Obligations

The duty to bargain in good faith requires each party to disclose information that is "relevant" to bargaining objectives or positions[33] or to the union's other statutory duties, including grievance processing.[34] Most of the time, the disclosure requests are directed to the employer rather than the union.[35] In order to assist the parties in determining the scope of the obligation, the Board has labeled information related to the terms and conditions of represented employees, such as wages, benefits, and job classifications, as presumptively relevant; and information related to employees outside the bargaining unit or third-party vendors of services, as presumptively irrelevant. These presumptions are rebuttable; the employer may defeat the disclosure request by proving irrelevance or some other strong factor, such as past union misuse of such information, while the union may prove relevance of extra-unit information when, for example, the claim is that employees outside the unit are performing bargaining-unit work. In between these two presumptions lies material that may be relevant in certain situations, but its relevance must be proven as to the individual case.

An employer's financial records or other business-related information are generally not considered relevant to negotiations, even though such information could assist the union in formulating its own position and evaluating the employer's. Public companies file annual reports, but often results are not reported for subsidiaries, corporate divisions, or individual plants where the bargaining unit is usually located. For private companies, the audited financial reports are generally not public and thus unavailable to the union.

If the employer places its financial condition in issue during the negotiations, its financial records may become relevant. In *NLRB v. Truitt Manufacturing Co.*,[36] the employer asserted that it could not afford to pay the union's requested pay increase, as it was undercapitalized and would be put out of business by such a raise. The union requested access to the company's financial records. The

---

[33] NLRB v. Truitt Manufacturing Co., 351 U.S. 149 (1956).

[34] Detroit Edison Co. v. NLRB, 440 U.S. 301 (1979).

[35] Unions have disclosure obligations to their members under the Landrum-Griffin Act of 1959 (also known as the Labor-Management Reporting and Disclosure Act, 29 U.S.C. §§ 401 et seq.); reports filed with the Department of Labor under Landrum Griffin are generally publicly available. The Board has largely resisted any requirements for union disclosure of internal governance matters under the NLRA. See Fla. Mining & Materials Corp., 198 NLRB 601, 601 (1972), enforced, 481 F.2d 65 (5th Cir. 1973) (holding that the union had no duty to disclose an imminent takeover by the international union prior to the election); Matthew T. Bodie, Information and the Market for Union Representation, 94 Va. L. Rev. 1, 45–69 (2008) (discussing informational asymmetries in union elections).

[36] 351 U.S. 149 (1956).

employer refused. The Board held, and the Supreme Court agreed, that that the employer violated § 8(a)(5) in refusing access to its financial records which were relevant to the employers' inability-to-pay plea. As the Court stated, "If such an argument [about inability to pay] is important enough to present in the give-and-take of bargaining, it is important enough to require some sort of proof of its accuracy."[37]

The *Truitt* test is in some ways a trap for the unwary; the employer can bring the obligation down upon itself by making claims during bargaining about its dire financial condition. However, well-advised companies can avoid the trap by referring merely to competitive disadvantage or general market conditions in turning down disclosure requests. At one point, the Board held that the disclosure requirement was triggered even by claims of "competitive disadvantage," but it has stepped back from that position because of judicial resistance.[38] Under its *Nielsen II* test, the Board requires disclosure only when the employer claims an "inability to pay."[39] In enforcing the Board's order, Judge Posner wrote for the Seventh Circuit that an employer has an unfair advantage in bargaining only when it claims it cannot afford to pay a certain wage, as this is akin to an express or implied threat of bankruptcy.[40] However, claims about loss of business or the need to scale back on staffing if the union's proposals were granted require no such verification, presumably because the union could check them out without the employer's assistance. If the employer, however, "makes claims of poverty, or any other substantiable factual claim, it must substantiate the claims if the union so demands."[41]

The Court also made clear in *Truitt* that the employer had made no claims that the disclosure would be "unduly burdensome or injurious," and left those situations for future Board development.[42] One area that has been litigated involves the countervailing interests in employer confidentiality and employee privacy. The employer in *Detroit Edison Co. v. NLRB*[43] had administered a battery of aptitude

---

[37] Id. at 152–53.

[38] Nielsen Lithographing Co., 305 NLRB 697 (1991), enforced sub nom. Graphic Communications Int'l Union Local 508 v. NLRB, 977 F.2d 1168 (7th Cir. 1992) ("*Nielsen II*").

[39] *Nielsen II*, 305 NLRB at 700 ("[A]n employer's obligation to open its books does not arise unless the employer has predicated its bargaining stance on assertions about its inability to pay during the term of the bargaining agreement under negotiation.").

[40] Graphic Communications Int'l Union Local 508 v. NLRB, 977 F.2d 1168, 1170–71 (7th Cir. 1992).

[41] Id. at 1171.

[42] *Truitt*, 351 U.S. at 151.

[43] 440 U.S. 301 (1979).

tests to fill a particular position; none of the incumbent employees received scores sufficient to qualify them for the job. The union sought to grieve these denials of promotion and requested the testing materials. The employer refused to provide any of the actual tests, the applicants' test papers, or their scores, on grounds of confidentiality and in order to preserve the future efficacy of the tests. It did, however, offer to provide the tests and answer sheets to an industrial psychologist selected by the union for review. The Board found the employer's refusal was a ULP and ordered the employer to turn over the tests and answer sheets to the union; the union was only required to restrict its use of the materials to the grievances. The Supreme Court disagreed and held there was no violation. As to the tests themselves, the Court ruled that the Board had failed to make adequate provision to protect confidentiality. And as to the applicants' test scores, the Court specified that the union could not obtain access without the applicants' individual consent. *Detroit Edison* stands for the proposition that even where the requested materials are relevant to the union's grievance-adjustment function, the Board must make adequate provision for maintaining confidentiality or, in some cases, simply obviate the need for one party to provide relevant material due to privacy concerns.

The Board, responding to the Court's suggestion in *Detroit Edison*, increasingly makes provision for preserving confidentiality of sensitive materials, whether employer trade secrets or employee personnel files, by restricting access to union-selected intermediaries who will respect the relevant professional norms and either evaluate the materials on their own or release to the unions only redacted information.[44] Sometimes unions are required to execute trade secret agreements as other contractors are required to do.[45]

The existing disclosure jurisprudence is problematic for a number of reasons. One problem is that under *Truitt*, candor is penalized and subterfuge rewarded. When employers have a good relationship with unions, information will be shared without the law's intervention.[46] But where the relationship is new, i.e., a first-contract situation, or has been damaged by prior conduct generating mistrust, the educative force of the process is undermined by incentives to flatly state "unwillingness to pay" when there may be concrete economic evidence that, if shared with the union, perhaps through an intermediary, would foster better bargaining outcomes.

---

[44] New Jersey Bell Tel. Co., 289 NLRB 318 (1988).

[45] Hercules, Inc. v. NLRB, 833 F.2d 426 (2d Cir. 1987).

[46] See Art. XVII, § 5, National Agreement between General Electric and IUE-CWA (2011–2015), reprinted in Labor Law: Selected Statutes, Forms, and Agreements 213–16 (Michael C. Harper, Samuel Estreicher & Kati Griffith eds. 2015).

A second problem stems from the collateral consequences of a disclosure dispute. From the union's standpoint, if the thrust of the employer's position is to seek bargaining concessions, the union may have a strong interest merely in delaying the point at which the employer is able to implement its final proposal. Also, the union has a strategic interest in provoking or sustaining disclosure disputes if they help convert an economic strike into a protest over employer ULPs. An employer cannot permanently replace ULP strikers[47] but can hire permanent replacements for jobs opened up by economic strikers.[48] Because a dispute over an information request could potentially transform an economic strike into a ULP strike, the stakes for such ULP charges could rise considerably.

5. The *Katz* Doctrine and Impasse

As § 8(d) makes clear, the parties are not required to bargain until agreement or to make any particular concession.[49] However, under longstanding NLRB decisions, the parties must continue to bargain until "impasse." The parties are at an impasse when they have exhausted their avenues for bargaining and genuinely cannot reach an agreement.[50] Once an impasse has been reached, the duty to bargain further is suspended until the parties' positions or other circumstances have changed.[51] In addition, at impasse the employer is free to implement its own terms consistent with its final offer to the union. (Where relevant, unions can implement changes in work rules under their control consistent with their bargaining position.)

Unlike the Railway Labor Act where the parties cannot resort to self-help until after the National Mediation Board has offered voluntary arbitration,[52] in the NLRA context the parties can declare impasse on their own, and the Board weighs in after the fact as to whether a bona-fide impasse was reached. Under the NLRA, employers cannot implement their final offer until a bona-fide impasse has occurred. Premature implementation violates § 8(a)(5) and can convert an economic strike into a ULP strike. If reductions

---

47 Mastro Plastics v. NLRB, 350 U.S. 270 (1950).

48 NLRB v. Mackay Radio & Telegraph Co., 304 U.S. 333 (1938).

49 29 U.S.C. § 158(d).

50 See Hi-Way Billboards, Inc., 206 NLRB 22, 23 (1973) ("A genuine impasse in negotiations is synonymous with deadlock: the parties have discussed a subject or subjects in good faith, and, despite their best efforts to achieve agreement with respect to such, neither party is willing to move from its respective positions.").

51 See Charles D. Bonanno Linen Service, Inc. v. NLRB, 454 U.S. 404, 412 (1982) (noting that deadlock is only temporary until it is broken through "a change of mind or the application of economic force").

52 Railway Lab. Act §§ 6–7, 45 U.S.C. §§ 156–157.

in prior wages or benefits are implemented, significant backpay liability may be incurred.

In addition to the timing issue, under *NLRB v. Katz*[53] the employer may not implement terms and conditions that are more favorable than those it offered to the union at the bargaining table. The justification for this rule is that implementing terms more generous than the final offer would be a form of direct dealing for the purpose of undermining the union's position. The employer generally can implement less favorable terms than have been offered to the union.[54]

If a preexisting collective bargaining agreement expires during the course of negotiations, it largely continues in effect until a new agreement is reached or the employer implements new terms consistent with *Katz*. The *Katz* principle also requires the "controlling party"—the party that controls the particular term in the absence of a collective agreement, which is typically the employer—not to make changes to any terms and conditions of employment (so-called "mandatory" subjects requiring bargaining under § 8(d))[55] until that party has proposed the change to the other party and has bargained to the point of impasse. The employer may make unilateral changes during the term of the contract if they are a continuation of an established past practice of annual or regular changes, such as yearly changes to a health insurance plan.[56]

This obligation to bargain over changes in terms and conditions of employment during the post-CBA expiration period does not extend to so-called "permissive" subjects; as we shall see, agreements over permissive subjects lawfully may be reached but there is no duty to bargain over them. That includes waivers of statutory rights, such as a no-strike clause.[57] In another example of policy oscillation, the Biden Administration Board, returning to Obama Board precedent, has held that dues checkoff provisions do survive the end of a collective bargaining agreement, and an employer may not terminate

---

[53] 369 U.S. 736 (1962).

[54] Taft Broadcasting Co., 163 NLRB 475, 478 (1967), enforced sub nom. AFTRA v. NLRB, 395 F.2d 622 (D.C. Cir. 1968).

[55] The difference between mandatory and permissive subjects of bargaining is discussed just ahead in Section C infra.

[56] This rule does not apply to a past practice developed before the employees were represented by the union, nor can an employer justify a change based on a past practice under a CBA after expiration of a CBA. See Tecnocap LLC, 372 NLRB No. 136 (Aug. 26, 2023) (holding that employer's past practice of unilateral changes developed under expired CBA's management-rights clause cannot authorize unilateral changes made after CBA's expiration); Wendt Corp., 372 NLRB No. 135 (Aug. 26, 2023) (holding that the narrow past-practice defense does not apply during a CBA hiatus or in the midst of negotiations for a first contract).

[57] See Litton Financial Printing Div. v. NLRB, 501 U.S. 190 (1991).

them without bargaining.[58] Management-rights clauses generally do not survive contract expiration, but "if an employer has frequently engaged in a pattern of unilateral change during the term of the CBA," the employer may continue to do so after the contract has expired.[59] Similarly, a so-called "rights" arbitration clause, where the parties agree to arbitrate disputes they may have under a collective bargaining agreement, does not continue after the expiration of the agreement because arbitration normally requires an agreement. Even in the absence of an agreement, however, the employer must continue to confer with the union over grievances and follow established procedures to resolve them, except for the final step of arbitration.[60]

Section 8(d) of the Act also provides procedures for dealing with the winding down of the agreement. If one of the parties desires to terminate or modify an existing contract, it must provide the other party with written notice within at least 60 days of the termination date or of the proposed change.[61] The party must also notify the Federal Mediation and Conciliation Service (FMCS) and the cognate state agency.[62] The party must then refrain from strikes or lockouts for the next 60 days after notice.[63] More stringent rules apply to health-care institutions and their unions under the 1974 amendments.[64]

C. Mandatory and Permissive Subjects of Bargaining

The duty to bargain under § 8(d) is limited to "mandatory" subjects of bargaining. The idea of mandatory subjects derives from the Act's description of collective bargaining to include the obligation to "confer in good faith with respect to wages, hours, and other terms and conditions of employment."[65]

---

[58] Valley Hospital Medical Center, Inc., 371 NLRB No. 160 (Sept. 30, 2022), enf'd, 93 F.4th 1120 (9th Cir. 2024). The Board returned to its earlier holding in Lincoln Lutheran of Racine, 362 NLRB 1655 (2015), which had overturned the Board's longstanding approach in Bethlehem Steel, 136 NLRB 1500 (1962).

[59] Beverly Health & Rehabilitation Services v. NLRB, 297 F.3d 468, 480–82 (6th Cir. 2002) (upholding the Board's position).

[60] Hilton-Davis Chem. Co., 185 NLRB 241 (1970).

[61] 29 U.S.C. § 158(d)(1).

[62] Id. § 158(d)(3).

[63] Id. § 158(d)(4).

[64] Id. § 158(d)(4)(A)–(C) (providing for ninety, rather than sixty, days advanced notice), 158(g) (requiring unions to provide at least ten days' notice before engaging in any strike, picketing, or other concerted refusal to work).

[65] 29 U.S.C. § 158(d).

1. The *Borg-Warner* Framework

The Supreme Court's *Borg-Warner* decision[66] identifies three categories of subjects with the following consequences:

1. *Mandatory Subjects.* These are the § 8(d) terms over which the parties have a duty to bargain, including disclosure obligations under *Truitt* and its progeny. The controlling party, typically the employer, cannot make changes in these subjects until bargaining with the other party to the point of impasse. The controlling party has the "right to insist" on its position over mandatory subjects in the sense they can be deal-breakers (assuming good-faith bargaining otherwise has transpired). The duty to bargain during the term of the collective agreement (mid-term bargaining) also extends to these subjects.

2. *Permissive Subjects.* These topics are lawful subjects of bargaining, but they fall outside of the scope of § 8(d). Neither side has a duty to bargain over them. The controlling party has the right to implement changes in these subjects (absent contractual restrictions). The non-controlling party cannot treat its position on these subjects as a deal-breaker. There are no statutory disclosure obligations or any duty to engage in mid-term bargaining over these subjects. The only remedy for breach is contractual, not statutory.[67]

3. *Unlawful Subjects.* There is no duty to bargain, and no lawful agreement can be reached, on these subjects.[68]

In *NLRB v. Borg-Warner Corp.*,[69] the Supreme Court addressed an employer's efforts to insist on two terms as a condition to reaching an overall agreement: (1) a "ballot clause" requiring employees to vote on the employer's last offer before ratifying a strike, and (2) a "recognition clause" which listed only the local union, rather than the

---

[66] NLRB v. Wooster Division of Borg-Warner Corp., 356 U.S. 342 (1958).

[67] See Allied Chemical & Alkali Workers v. Pittsburgh Plate Glass Co., 404 U.S. 157 (1971) (retiree benefits).

[68] Such subjects are comparatively rare. One example is a proposal for the union to waive the rights of employees to distribute organizational literature at the work-site during off hours. Because such a proposal would harm the § 7 rights of the employees and any such waiver would be unenforceable, it is illegal to press for such a term. NLRB v. Magnavox, 415 U.S. 322 (1974). See also Penello v. International Union, United Mine Workers, 88 F. Supp. 935 (D.D.C. 1950) (granting § 10(j) injunction against union's efforts to press for closed shop with pension benefits limited to union members).

[69] 356 U.S. 342 (1958).

international parent union, as the collective bargaining representative. The parties reached impasse after the employer refused to back down on these terms, and eventually the union yielded. The Board held that the employer's insistence amounted to a failure to bargain in good faith, as both terms were not within the scope of mandatory bargaining. The Court agreed that both proposals were only permissive subjects of bargaining. The ballot clause was different from a traditional no-strike clause, in the Court's view, because it interfered with the union's relationship with represented employees rather than addressing the employer's relationship with the union.[70] The recognition clause also sought to interfere with the internal structure of the bargaining agency, because the international union, not the local union, had been certified as the exclusive representative.

In a separate opinion, Justice Harlan questioned the logic of preventing parties from bargaining to impasse over permissive bargaining subjects. For Harlan, "[t]he right to bargain becomes illusory if one is not free to press a proposal in good faith to the point of insistence."[71] The right to insist would not be unlimited, Justice Harlan noted, because the parties would still be subject to an overall duty to bargain in good faith.[72]

The *Borg-Warner* framework has been criticized for encouraging subterfuge in the presentation of proposals[73] and preventing creative bargaining solutions. It does have the virtue, however, of simplifying the bargaining agenda and preventing the stronger party from insisting on terms that involve an interference with the internal structure of the other party or are put forward strategically for purposes of delay and harassment because they cause more harm to the other side than benefit to the proposing party.

2. Decisions Concerning the Basic Scope or Direction of the Business

What constitutes a mandatory subject? Impact alone is not sufficient, for a great many managerial decisions have an impact on

---

[70] Id. at 350.

[71] Id. at 352 (Harlan, J., concurring in part and dissenting in part).

[72] *Borg-Warner*, 356 U.S. at 353–54 (Harlan, J., concurring in part and dissenting in part); see also Samuel Estreicher, Labor Law Reform in a World of Competitive Product Markets, 69 Chi.-Kent L. Rev. 3, 39–40 n.134 (1993) (limiting Harlan's approach by placing certain subjects "beyond the reach of either party's insistence").

[73] See, e.g., Theodore J. St. Antoine, Legal Barriers to Worker Participation in Management Decision Making, 58 Tulane L. Rev. 1301, 1306 (1984) ("If a party deeply desires a concession on a permissive subject that may not legally be carried to impasse, it will be tempted to hang the bargaining up on a false issue that happens to enjoy official approbation as a mandatory topic.").

employee wages and working conditions. From the *Borg Warner* standpoint, the question is not whether the parties are willing to discuss a subject but rather whether the non-controlling party can insist on its position, using whatever leverage it can muster, to the point of holding up any agreement on conceded § 8(d) subjects. Should unions be able to strike for greater influence over the company's executive personnel, product, investment and marketing decisions? Those decisions are important, and they undoubtedly affect the welfare of the business and job security, but do they trigger the duty to bargain and corollary right to insist?

In *Fibreboard Paper Products Corp. v. NLRB*,[74] the employer decided to replace its maintenance employees with employees from another firm. The company informed the union of the decision and said that bargaining would be futile as the decision had already been reached. The Board ruled that the employer violated § 8(a)(5) because the subcontracting decision was a mandatory bargaining subject. Even though the employer's motive had been purely economic—to save money—it still needed to negotiate with the union before making the decision. The Supreme Court agreed and upheld the Board's order for the employer to rehire all of the unit employees and commence good-faith bargaining.

Fibreboard was a relatively easy case. The subcontracting involved "the replacement of employees in the existing bargaining unit with those of an independent contractor to do the same work under similar conditions of employment."[75] The case was akin to a situation where "the employer had . . . discharged all its employees and replaced them with other workers willing to work the same job in the same plant without the various fringe benefits so costly to the company."[76] Justice Stewart concurred to emphasize that the case did not involve managerial decisions concerning the "basic scope" or "basic direction" of the enterprise which, in his view, would be permissive subjects only.

The Supreme Court offered a framework for dealing with the bargainability of business decisions in *First National Maintenance Corp. v. NLRB*.[77] Justice Blackmun for the Court suggested three categories of decisions lying across a spectrum. At one end, there are decisions going to "an aspect of the relationship between employer and employee," such as the order of succession of layoffs and recalls, production quotas, and work rules, that are considered mandatory

---

74 379 U.S. 203 (1964).

75 Id. at 215.

76 Id. at 224 (Stewart, J., concurring).

77 452 U.S. 666 (1981).

even if they affect overall business strategy.[78] At the other extreme lie decisions such as advertising, product design, and financial arrangements that are permissive, as they pertain to entrepreneurial control and "have only an indirect and attenuated impact on the employment relationship."[79] Finally, there is an intermediate category in which a management decision "had a direct impact on employment, since jobs were inexorably eliminated" but at the same time "had as its focus only the economic profitability" of the decision "wholly apart from the employment relationship."[80] Since this third category implicated core concerns of employees and management, the inquiry was whether the employer's freedom of action to make such decisions based on economic concerns outweighed the union's interests in participating in the decision.[81] If so, the subject was permissive; if not, then mandatory.

The Court proceeded to balance the costs versus the benefits of mandatory bargaining for the partial closing in that case. Even before the union obtained bargaining authority, the employer had a dispute with one of its customers (a nursing home) over the size of its management fee. That dispute resulted in the termination of that relationship and the discharge of the unit employees engaged in servicing the customer. In the Court's view, this "partial closing" decision was a permissive subject of bargaining as the employer's decision was primarily related to the profitability of the contract, not terms and conditions of employment. The decision to terminate a customer relationship was likened to "opening a new line of business or going out of business entirely."[82] Mandatory bargaining, Justice Blackmun's opinion reasoned, could interfere with needed business flexibility without compensating benefits.[83] If there was a basis for exploring labor-cost concessions with the union, the law was not needed to prod such exploration; it would happen of its own accord. Although bargaining was not required over the partial-closing decision, the employer was under a duty to bargain with the union

---

[78] Id. at 677.

[79] Id.

[80] Id.

[81] Id. at 679.

[82] Id. at 688

[83] The Court feared that: "[l]abeling this type of decision mandatory could afford a union a powerful tool for achieving delay, a power that might be used to thwart management's intentions in a manner unrelated to any feasible solution the union might propose." Id. at 683.

"in a meaningful manner and at a meaningful time" over the effects of its decision on unit employees.[84]

The *First National Maintenance* Court is right that concessionary bargaining generally will occur without the law's prodding. But an implicit purpose of the duty to bargain is to compel the parties to undergo an educative process of dealing with each other. In the particular case before the Court, it was doubtful union concessions could come in time to avert the termination of the customer relationship. The Court, it should be noted, is approaching the bargainability issue not from the standpoint of whether labor concessions were likely but rather from the vantage of whether the union should be able to use its leverage to block the decision. From a right-to-insist perspective, the Court is reasoning, decisions whether to serve or withdraw from certain segments of the market should be made by the company free of pressures from the union or the delay inherent in bargaining.[85]

Plant and work relocations decisions can be different from partial-plant closings because they do not necessarily involve a decision to drop a customer or withdraw from a segment of the market. After *First National Maintenance*, the Board developed a framework for dealing with plant and work relocation decisions in *Dubuque Packing Co.*:

> Initially, the burden is on the General Counsel to establish that the employer's decision involved a relocation of unit work unaccompanied by a basic change in the nature of the employer's operation. If the General Counsel successfully carries his burden in this regard, he will have established prima facie that the employer's relocation decision is a mandatory subject of bargaining. At this juncture, the employer may produce evidence rebutting the prima facie case by establishing that the work performed at the new location varies significantly from the work performed at the former plant, establishing that the work performed at the former plant is to be discontinued entirely and not moved to the new location, or establishing that the employer's decision involves a change in the scope and direction of the enterprise. Alternatively, the employer may proffer a defense to show by a preponderance of the evidence: (1) that

---

[84] Id. at 681–82. Since the effects bargaining need not occur before the decision has been made, the union has limited leverage and the time for serious concessions may have lapsed.

[85] Professor Harper calls this the "product market" principle. See Michael C. Harper, Leveling the Road from *Borg-Warner* to *First National Maintenance*: The Scope of Mandatory Bargaining, 68 Va. L. Rev. 1447 (1982).

labor costs (direct and/or indirect) were not a factor in the decision or (2) that even if labor costs were a factor in the decision, the union could not have offered labor cost concessions that could have changed the employer's decision to relocate.[86]

Under *Dubuque*, the Board must provide evidence to show that the relocation decision does not involve a "basic change" in the operation. Then, the employer has two alternative responses: show that the decision does involve a basic change in its business, or show that there was no basis for labor-cost concessionary bargaining with the union. Most courts have accepted this framework. One exception is the Fourth Circuit, which views "[t]he decision of where to locate a business [as] fundamentally a managerial decision."[87] There is also a dispute over the treatment of subcontracting decisions. The Board's view is that the employer must bargain over most subcontracting decisions absent a showing by the employer that the decisions were part of a basic entrepreneurial design to change the scope of the business.[88] However, the Third Circuit has ruled that subcontracting is a mandatory subject only when the decision is motivated by labor costs or other issues amenable to collective bargaining.[89]

3. WARN Legislation

If the employer shuts down a facility but has committed no bargaining violation, displaced workers can also potentially turn to the Worker Adjustment Retraining and Notification Act of 1988 (WARN),[90] which requires companies with 100 or more employees to provide at least 60-day notice to both the employees and their union (if any) of (1) any facility shutdown causing job loss for at least 50 employees within a 30-day period or (2) any "mass layoff" of

[86] Dubuque Packing Co., 303 NLRB 386, 391 (1991). The Board further specified: "Under the second prong, an employer would have no bargaining obligation if it showed that, although labor costs were a consideration in the decision to relocate unit work, it would not remain at the present plant because, for example, the costs for modernization of equipment or environmental controls were greater than any labor cost concessions the union could offer. On the other hand, an employer would have a bargaining obligation if the union could and would offer concessions that approximate, meet, or exceed the anticipated costs or benefits that prompted the relocation decision, since the decision then would be amenable to resolution through the bargaining process." Id.

[87] Dorsey Trailers v. NLRB, 233 F.3d 831, 845 (4th Cir. 2000).

[88] Torrington Indus., 307 NLRB 809 (1992); Finch, Pruyn & Co., 349 NLRB 270 (2007).

[89] Furniture Rentors of America, Inc. v. NLRB, 36 F.3d 1240, 1248–50 (3d Cir. 1994).

[90] 29 U.S.C. §§ 2101–2109.

employees within a 30-day period.[91] The notice requirement is modified if the employer is actively looking to avoid the shutdown or layoffs by pursuing additional capital or business, as long as the employer reasonably believes that the notice would preclude any chance to obtain such assistance.[92] In such cases, the employer "shall give as much notice as is practicable and at that time shall give a brief statement of the basis for reducing the notification period."[93] Similarly, only practicable notice is required if the shutdown or layoff required quick action and was caused by circumstances that were not reasonably foreseeable.[94] Unions can bring WARN Act enforcement suits, along with affected employees, and the remedies include back pay for each day of violation and benefits, including health expenses that would have been covered by the employer's plan.[95] The Act does not provide for enjoining the shutdown or mass layoff.[96] Some states have passed their own plant-closing notice statutes.[97]

D. Midterm Bargaining

The NLRA in § 8(d) contemplates a continuation of the duty to bargain in good faith even during the term of a CBA unless the terms over which bargaining is sought are "contained in" the CBA. The RLA, by contrast, imposes a duty "to exert every reasonable effort to make and maintain agreements" until the parties have been released to engage in self-help.[98]

In the midterm-bargaining context, the distinction between mandatory and permissive subjects remains important. Even if the parties have reached agreement on a permissive subject and put a term in the contract covering it, the employer does not commit a ULP if it changes that term unilaterally. Section 8(d) reaches only mandatory subjects of bargaining, the Supreme Court held in *Allied Chemical & Alkali Workers v. Pittsburgh Plate Glass Co.*[99] That case involved an employer's midterm change in health benefits for retirees to reflect recent Medicare legislation. An NLRA remedy is not available for modification of an agreement with respect to permissive subjects, but a contractual one may be.

---

[91] See id. § 2102 (providing 60-day notice requirement). "Mass layoff" is defined as a reduction of at least 500 employees, or at least 50 employees if such employees represent at least a third of the workforce. Id. § 2101(a)(3).

[92] Id. § 2102(b)(1).

[93] Id. § 2102(b)(3).

[94] Id. § 2102(b)(2).

[95] Id. § 2104(a)(1).

[96] Id. § 2104(b).

[97] See, e.g., 820 Ill. Comp. State § 65/1–99; Cal. Labor Code §§ 1400–1408.

[98] 45 U.S.C. §§ 152, 156.

[99] 404 U.S. 157 (1971).

When a collective bargaining agreement is in place, an employer's unilateral change of a contract provision concerning a mandatory subject would be a § 8(a)(5) violation, while a union's insistence on a change in such a provision would be a § 8(b)(3) violation. Parties are not required to bargain about mandatory subjects if they are "contained in" the CBA.[100] Thus, neither party may force the other party into bargaining about wages, for example, if the CBA already set the wages in place. Can one party require the other to bargain about a mandatory subject that is not covered at all by the agreement? The Board has said yes.[101] As a practical matter, this issue rarely arises because parties have inserted "zipper clauses" into their CBA which terminate any midterm bargaining obligations.

When is a term or condition "contained in" the CBA, thus triggering the § 8(d) prohibition on unilateral modification? Express terms are plainly contained in the CBA. An employer's established past practices, such as giving a free turkey to employees every Thanksgiving, may also be "contained in" the CBA for § 8(d) purposes. If so, there would be a potential contractual remedy under the CBA for abrogation of such a practice as well as a statutory remedy for violation of § 8(a)(5) (both for the modification and the failure to bargain). The Board's general view is that a "zipper clause" provides only a "shield" against union demands to add to the agreement and does not provide a "sword" to permit the employer to rescind or modify implied terms that have become part of the agreement.[102]

For a party to use the CBA as a shield against further bargaining, the Board requires a fairly tight nexus between the CBA and the proposal at issue. In *Milwaukee Spring Division (Milwaukee Spring II)*,[103] the Board held that an employer could unilaterally relocate a section of its operations to another, nonunion facility after bargaining to impasse with the union. The union argued that the employer needed its permission, even though the CBA did not contain an express work-preservation or no-relocation clause, because the employer indicated during negotiations that it was primarily looking for relief from the CBA's wage level. This evidence, the union argued, indicated that the employer's relocation decision constituted an

---

100 See id.; Jacobs Manufacturing Co., 94 NLRB 1214, 1219 (1951) ("What § 8(d) does is to reject the pronouncements contained in some pre-1947 Board and court decisions . . . to the effect that the duty to bargain continues even as to those matters upon which the parties have reached agreement and which are set forth in the terms of a written contract.").

101 Id.

102 CBS Corp. f/k/a Westinghouse Corp., 326 NLRB 861 (1998).

103 268 NLRB 601 (1984).

attempt to change the wage term.[104] The Board, on remand from the D.C. Circuit, held that the relationship between the topic of bargaining (relocation of unit work) and the CBA term claimed to be modified (the wage provisions) was too attenuated to trigger the § 8(d) prohibition on unilateral modification of terms "contained in" the CBA.

E. Multiemployer Bargaining

Multiemployer bargaining units are consensual; all of the employers must agree to be included in the group and the union must consent to joint bargaining.[105] There are often good reasons for both sides to consent. Employers can rest assured that they will not be undercut by competitors with respect to labor costs, and smaller employers can benefit from the negotiation resources of their larger partners. At the same time, unions can save on bargaining costs as well and benefit from the uniformity of labor terms across competitors; the multiemployer structure ensure labor costs are taken out of competition.

Because multiemployer units are consensual, the Board has made it easy for employers to drop out prior to the beginning of negotiations. But in order to maintain the integrity of a multiemployer unit, the agency strictly limits exit from the unit once bargaining begins. After negotiations commence, employers may leave the group only if there is mutual consent from all parties or there are "unusual circumstances."[106] The Board has defined such circumstances rather narrowly, to include only situations in which the employer is faced with closing down the business, bankruptcy, or plant closure. The Board looks for "extreme economic difficulties."[107]

In *Charles D. Bonanno Linen Service, Inc. v. NLRB*,[108] the Court held that a bargaining impasse does not provide justification for an untimely withdrawal from a multiemployer unit. One employer in a group of laundry companies dropped out of the multiemployer unit after bargaining had reached impasse without consent from the other parties. The Board ruled that the employer's withdrawal was a

---

[104] The employer conceded that the decision to transfer operations was a mandatory subject of bargaining.

[105] Employers can also bind themselves to the results of multiemployer bargaining even if they are not formally in the multiemployer unit or a member of the multiemployer association. See America Piles, Inc., 333 NLRB 1118, 1118–19 (2001) (finding § 8(a)(5) violations when small construction employers refused to execute multiemployer association agreement after agreeing with the union to execute that agreement).

[106] Retail Associates, Inc., 120 NLRB 388 (1958).

[107] Hi-Way Billboards, Inc., 206 NLRB 22, 27–28 (1973).

[108] 454 U.S. 404 (1982).

violation of its bargaining duty, and the Court affirmed. The Board, in the Court's analysis, was exercising its authority to preserve the stability of the multiemployer unit. As elaborated by the Board, impasses are often met with the use of economic weapons, which seek to break the deadlock.[109] Impasse is thus a moment in the bargaining cycle, rather than an end to it.

One way the Board mitigates the effects of a multiemployer bargaining impasse is to allow individual employers in the group to agree to interim agreements with the union. Such agreements allow individual parties to adapt temporarily to current circumstances without the need for group agreement. These interim agreements, however, must give way once the multiemployer group and the union have agreed upon a new contract. If the union negotiates interim agreements that last beyond the results of the group negotiations, the union and the involved employer have violated their bargaining duties and have provided an "unusual circumstance" that justifies other members leaving the group.[110]

F. Remedies for Bargaining Infractions

The Board's principal remedy for bargaining violations is a bargaining order as well as restoration of prior working terms, conditions, or operations if changes were made without good-faith bargaining. The Supreme Court has made clear that § 8(d) prevents the agency from imposing substantive terms as a remedy. In *H.K. Porter Co. v. NLRB,*[111] the Board had ordered the employer to grant the union a dues checkoff provision, after holding that the employer had used its intransigence on that issue to stymie bargaining. The Court overturned the Board's order, however, concluding that the Board "is without power to compel a company or a union to agree to any substantive contractual provision of a collective bargaining agreement."[112] Such a power "would violate the fundamental premise on which the Act is based—private bargaining under governmental supervision of the procedure alone, without any official compulsion over the actual terms of the contract."[113]

The Board can affect substantive terms only in one respect: it is permitted to order restoration of terms that existed prior to when the illegal bargaining actions occurred. This order is common in situations where the employer has unilaterally changed terms after improperly declaring an impasse. As one example, in 1995, the Board

---

109 *Hi-Way Billboards*, 206 NLRB at 23.

110 *Bonanno*, 454 U.S. at 415.

111 397 U.S. 99 (1970).

112 Id. at 102.

113 Id. at 108.

sought injunctive relief against Major League Baseball that included a restoration of the collective bargaining agreement; then-federal district judge Sonia Sotomayor granted the § 10(j) injunction, and the strike was settled quickly thereafter.[114]

The restoration of the status quo remedy for a bargaining violation is particularly dramatic when the employer has made a substantial business change and then later learns it has violated its bargaining duty. For example, in the *Fibreboard* case, the Supreme Court upheld the Board's remedy requiring the employer to retract its subcontracting decision and reinstate the employees who had been laid off with back pay.[115] However, the Board will not order restoration of former operations if such a restoration would be "unduly burdensome."[116] The agency will try to make employees whole by requiring the employer to offer them positions at locations that are still open and even provide travel expenses for significant geographic expanses.[117]

Even when the employer's decision to shut down a plant or relocate its operations is only a permissive subject of bargaining, employers still need to bargain over the effects of the decision. If the employer fails to do so, the Board will order a "*Transmarine* remedy": back pay for employees in the affected unit, starting five days after the Board's decision until the earliest of: (1) the parties' reaching an agreement after bargaining; (2) a bona fide impasse; (3) the union's failure to make a timely request for bargaining; or (4) subsequent bad faith bargaining by the union.[118]

A more controversial possibility for bargaining violations is awarding make-whole relief predicated on bargaining results that would have occurred if there had been good-faith bargaining. In *Ex-Cell-O Corp.*,[119] the Board determined that it was not authorized to award such relief, as it would need to create the terms to which the employer should have agreed. Such presumed terms would violate the no-substantive-term-as-remedy mandate of *H.K. Porter*. Former General Counsel Abruzzo indicated her interest in overturning *Ex-Cell-O* and providing make-whole relief for the hypothetical bargaining result that would have occurred had the parties

---

[114] See Silverman v. Major League Baseball Players Committee, Inc., 880 F. Supp. 246, 261 (S.D.N.Y. 1995).

[115] *Fibreboard*, 379 U.S. at 215.

[116] See, e.g., Owens-Brockway Plastic Products, Inc., 311 NLRB 519 (1993); Atlantic Brands, Inc., 297 NLRB No. 22 (1989).

[117] See *Owens-Brockway*, 311 NLRB at 535.

[118] Transmarine Navigation Corp., 170 NLRB 389 (1968).

[119] 185 NLRB 107 (1970).

bargained in good faith.[120] In 2023 the Biden Board expressly reserved this issue in one case but did not return to it.[121]

The Board has ordered monetary relief in the form of bargaining and litigation expenses. Such relief is reserved for those instances in which the party's behavior is particularly objectionable. Negotiation expenses have been awarded when the Board found that the party's "unusually aggravated misconduct" wasted the other party's resources and dissipated its economic strength.[122] The Board has also awarded litigation expenses when parties have acted in bad faith leading up to litigation, or in the conduct of the litigation itself.[123] However, the D.C. Circuit has held that the Board does not have the authority to impose litigation expenses under § 10(c).[124] It should also be noted that the Equal Access to Justice Act (EAJA) requires that federal agencies, including the Board, reimburse litigation expenses to small companies if the agency cannot show that its position was "substantially justified."[125] Employers have been successful in pursuing such actions against the Board.[126]

120 Jennifer Abruzzo, Memorandum, Seeking Full Remedies, GC 21–06, Sept. 8, 2021. Abruzzo directed the Regions to submit all cases concerning the applicability of the *Ex-Cell-O Corp* decision to consider make-whole remedies that would compensate employees for the losses they sustain because of the employers' failure to bargain

121 In *Hudson Institute of Process Research,* the Board ruled that the employer unlawfully failed to bargain with the union but severed the issue of whether to order the employer to "make its employees whole for the lost opportunity to bargain." 372 NLRB No. 73, at *4 (April 4, 2023). The appeals court denied enforcement of the Board's failure to bargain claim. Hudson Inst. of Process Research. Inc. v. NLRB, 117 F.4th 692, 696 (5th Cir. 2024).

122 Frontier Hotel & Casino, 318 NLRB 857, 859 (1995), enforced in relevant part, 118 F.3d 795 (D.C. Cir.).

123 Alwin Mfg. Co., 326 NLRB 646 (1998); Teamsters Local Union No. 122 (August A. Busch & Co.), 334 NLRB 1190 (2001).

124 Unbelievable, Inc. v. NLRB, 118 F.3d 795 (D.C. Cir. 1997).

125 28 U.S.C. § 2412(d) (covering entities with fewer than 500 employees and less than $7 million in net worth).

126 See, e.g., Hess Mechanical Corp. v. NLRB, 112 F.3d 146 (4th Cir. 1997).

Chapter 8

WEAPONS OF ECONOMIC CONFLICT

Although good-faith bargaining is an important driver within the NLRA's system of collective labor relations, another critical component is the parties' use of "economic weapons," such as strikes, lockouts, boycotts, and informational picketing. Use of these weapons, such as the calling of a strike with attendant picketing, may seem to indicate the failure of bargaining between the parties. However, these moves may also be critical steps in the sometimes arduous process of reaching a final agreement. As the Supreme Court noted in *NLRB v. Insurance Agents' International Union*,[1] "[t]he presence of economic weapons in reserve, and their actual exercise on occasion by the parties, is part and parcel of the system that the Wagner and Taft-Hartley Acts have recognized."[2]

A. Strikers and Replacement Workers

Strikes are both a critical part of the labor-management relationship and an unfortunate, often self-imposed crisis for both employer and employees. The ability to withdraw the company's labor force *en masse* is a union's principal weapon. The NLRA itself provides specific protection for the strike. In addition to § 7's general protection of employee concerted activity, § 13 provides that: "Nothing in this subchapter, except as specifically provided for herein, shall be construed so as either to interfere with or impede or diminish in any way the right to strike, or to affect the limitations or qualifications on that right."[3]

Under the NLRA, a union is legally entitled to go on strike with relatively little hindrance.[4] Section 8(d) of the Act—part of the Taft-Hartley amendments—does provide a sixty-day written notice requirement if one party wants to change or terminate an existing collective bargaining agreement, including one that is due to expire. A union may not go on strike during that sixty-day period, nor can employers lock out employees during that period; such actions would be considered § 8(a)(5) or 8(b)(3) violations.[5] During this interim

---

1 361 U.S. 477 (1960).

2 Id. at 489.

3 29 U.S.C. § 163.

4 In contrast, under the RLA, the parties may not resort to self-help until after the National Mediation Board makes a proffer of voluntary interest arbitration which, if refused by either party, serves as a declaration of impasse. See 45 U.S.C. §§ 155 First & 156.

5 29 U.S.C. § 158(d)(4).

period, the parties must offer to meet and confer over new terms, and they must notify the Federal Mediation and Conciliation Service (FMCS) and cognate state agencies.

1. Replacement vs. Discharge

Employees cannot be disciplined for participating in a strike, whether or not they are represented, unless they engage in serious misconduct, such as threatened violence or destruction of property.

Although employees cannot be discharged or disciplined for striking, the employer can try to maintain operations by hiring permanent replacements for economic strikers. In *NLRB v. Mackay Radio & Telegraph Co.*,[6] the Court ruled that the employer does not violate the NLRA by hiring permanent replacements for jobs left open as a result of a strike over an economic dispute. "Permanent" means, under this ruling, that the employer has no obligation to bump the replacements in favor of strikers who at the strike's end are ready to return. The replaced strikers, however, retain their employee status under the Act and have a right to be reinstated on a preferential basis once jobs open up.

Mackay Radio's statement about the employer's right to maintain operations during an economic strike by hiring so-called "permanent replacements" was not strictly necessary to the holding because the only issue in the case involved the employer's discriminatory refusal to reinstate active strikers to jobs that had opened up. Even if technically dictum in that case, the employer privilege to refuse to bump permanent replacements in favor of returning economic strikers has been the premise of a dozen Supreme Court cases as well as a series of NLRA amendments now providing in § 9(c)(3)[7] that replaced economic strikers lose any voting rights after being on strike for one year or more.[8]

In some circumstances, where replacement employees continue working or the employer's staffing needs decline at the end of the strike, there may be no practical difference between replacement and discharge of a striker. But there can be important consequences to the distinction. The employer in *NLRB v. Fleetwood Trailer Co.*[9] hired replacements for its striking workers, which was permissible,

---

[6] 304 U.S. 333 (1938).

[7] 29 U.S.C. § 159(c)(3).

[8] See Samuel Estreicher, Collective Bargaining or "Collective Begging"?: Reflections on Antistrikebreaker Legislation, 93 Mich. L. Rev. 577 (1994); Julius G. Getman & Thomas C. Kohler, The Story of *NLRB v. Mackay Radio & Telegraph Co.*: The High Cost of Solidarity, in Labor Law Stories (Laura Cooper & Catherine L. Fisk eds., 2005).

[9] 389 U.S. 375 (1967).

but then hired a new set of employees two months after the end of the strike when it expanded its operations back to pre-strike levels. The employer violated §§ 8(a)(1) and 8(a)(3) by failing to give priority to replaced strikers for the open positions, even if the employer evidenced no overt antiunion animus in making the new hires. In *Laidlaw Corp.*[10] the Board confirmed that replaced strikers remain employees under § 2(3) and must be offered their positions if replacement workers leave or lose their positions or if the employer makes additional hires to the bargaining unit.[11] The employer can refuse to offer reinstatement if the striker has instead found alternative employment or if there are "legitimate and substantial business reasons" for denying reinstatement, such as unprotected conduct during the strike. These rights to continued employment and potential reinstatement are called "*Laidlaw* rights."

A strike can also be a means of protesting the employer's ULPs. The motivation for the strike is important because employees who are striking against ULPs are not subject to the risk of permanent replacement and are treated differently in other respects:

- ULP strikers are entitled to get their jobs back once they make an unconditional offer to return to work, and they receive back pay for the period they remain idle after the unconditional offer.
- ULP strikers can continue to vote in representation elections indefinitely while on strike. Replaced economic strikers, on the other hand, no longer have the right to vote after a year of being on strike.
- The conventional "no-strike" contract clause does not apply to ULP strikes; express language would be required and even then there would be a question of enforceability.[12]
- The union need not follow the sixty-day notification requirement of § 8(d) before going out on a ULP strike because the motivation for the strike is not to terminate or modify the CBA.[13]

---

[10] 171 NLRB 1366 (1968), enforced, 414 F.2d 99 (7th Cir. 1969).

[11] Returning strikers are entitled only to positions that they have previously held or that are substantially equivalent to those positions. Rose Printing Co., 304 NLRB 1076 (1991). The Board's view is that *Laidlaw* reinstatement rights are not time-limited, Brooks Research & Mfg., 202 NLRB 634 (1973), even though replaced economic strikers retain voting rights for only one year under § 9(c)(3). However, the employer can regularly inquire about continuing interest amongst employees to maintain current information.

[12] Mastro Plastics Corp. v. NLRB, 350 U.S. 270, 278 (1956).

[13] Id.

- Under a set of older precedents, the Board may have greater leeway to exercise discretion in reinstating ULP strikers even if they have engaged in some picket-line misconduct.[14] However, since the 1980s the Board has not applied this more lenient standard.[15]

A ULP strike is a work stoppage that is prompted or prolonged in part by the employer's commission of a ULP even when the ULP is not the sole or even primary cause of the strike.[16] In addition, an economic strike can change over to a ULP strike if the employer commits a ULP during the strike and the strike is continued or prolonged in part because of the ULP. In such a case, strikers are not entitled to replace permanent replacements hired before the strike was converted to a ULP strike, but they are entitled to bump employees hired after the conversion. There is no advisory ruling mechanism under the NLRA—no easy assurance that can be given to inform strikers (and to warn employers) that what may have started as an economic strike has been converted into a ULP strike. This issue is decided in after-the-fact NLRB proceedings to determine whether the employer committed ULPs and whether the strike was prolonged by those violations.

2. Role of Duty to Bargain Principles

As suggested by *Insurance Agents,* the duty to bargain in good faith plays only a limited role in regulating weapons of economic conflict. As a general matter, the Board can regulate these weapons only if the employer (or the union) engages in discriminatory conduct violative of §§ 8(a)(3) and 8(b)(1). There are some caveats:

a. The *Katz* doctrine does not require the employer to bargain with replacement workers over the terms of their hiring[17] but does prevent the employer from offering more to hire replacement workers than was offered to the union.[18] At the margin, the value of benefits not given to replacement workers would be factored in.

---

[14] See, e.g., NLRB v. Thayer Co., 213 F.2d 748 (1st Cir. 1954).

[15] See Clear Pine Mouldings, Inc., 268 NLRB 1044 (1984).

[16] Teamsters Local Union No. 515 v. NLRB (Reichold Chemicals, Inc.), 906 F.2d 719, 723 (D.C. Cir. 1990) (*Reichold II*).

[17] Service Electric Co., 281 NLRB 633, 641 (1986).

[18] Burlington Homes, Inc., 246 NLRB 1029 (1979).

b. In *Charles D. Bonanno Linen Service, Inc. v. NLRB*,[19] the Supreme Court constrained the timing and limited the reasons for an employer's withdrawal from a multiemployer bargaining unit. That decision suggests that the Board has some authority to apply good faith bargaining principles to protect the structure of the bargaining relationship.

c. When an employer subcontracts out unit work during a strike, this may be viewed as an attempt to alter terms and conditions of employment. If the subcontract is considered a permanent one, the D.C. Circuit has agreed with the Board there is a duty to bargain over the decision, unless the employer can show business necessity for the subcontracting.[20]

3. Rights of Replacement Workers

What rights do replacement workers have under the NLRA? They are § 2(3) employees within the bargaining unit and have voting rights that are not time-limited as in the case of the economic strikers. Whether or not they keep their jobs at strike's end depends on whether the employer promised them post-strike job security and thereafter resisted any strike settlement agreement that would provide for bumping of replacements with returning strikers. That the replacements were deemed "permanent" replacements does not mean that they can never be fired. The Board has held that permanent replacements can be "at will" employees with no guarantee of future tenure in their position.[21] However, the Board presumes that replacements are temporary unless the employer proves there was a mutual understanding that they were hired to continue on at strike's end.

The employer may negotiate with the union for the reinstatement of economic strikers, even if that requires bumping permanent replacements. In such cases, if the employer has made contractual obligations to the replacements, these workers may bring common-law contract claims against the employer for breach; their suits are not preempted by the NLRA.[22] Replacement workers are

---

[19] 454 U.S. 404 (1982) (holding that impasse, standing alone, was not an unusual circumstance warranting withdrawal of employer from multiemployer bargaining unit).

[20] Land Air Delivery v. NLRB, 862 F.2d 354 (D.C. Cir. 1988); see also Hawaii Meat Co. v. NLRB, 321 F.2d 397 (9th Cir. 1963).

[21] Jones Plastic & Engineering, 351 NLRB 61 (2007), enforced sub nom. United Steel, Paper & Forestry, Rubber, Mfg., Energy, Allied Indus. & Service Workers Int'l Union v. NLRB, 544 F.3d 841 (7th Cir. 2008).

[22] Belknap v. Hale, 463 U.S. 491 (1983).

part of the unit to whom the strikers' union owes a duty of fair representation (DFR). In the abstract, these workers may have a DFR claim against the union for ignoring their interests. In practice, unions will argue that their advocacy for strikers was based on neutral criteria for reinstatement, such as seniority. In addition, the union can, within limits, agree to waive the *Laidlaw* rights of its striking members as part of its negotiations with the employer.[23]

4. Role of Motive vs. Impact Analysis

In general, the employer's motivation to inflict costs of disagreement on the union and the strikers is part and parcel of the model of economic conflict underlying the NLRA and is not evidence of a discriminatory motive under § 8(a)(3). Similarly, the union's motive to inflict economic costs on the employer is not evidence of a discriminatory motive under § 8(b)(2). However, there are some circumstances where the Board, with judicial approval, is willing to infer discriminatory motive from the impact of the bargaining tactic. These employer actions are deemed to be an inherent violation of the Act based on their enduring effects at strike's end.

In *NLRB v. Erie Resistor Corp.*,[24] the employer had given a twenty-year seniority credit to all replacements and strikers who returned to work before the end of the strike. The employer argued that it needed to offer "super-seniority" to attract qualified replacement workers. However, the Board concluded that this provision violated §§ 8(a)(1) and (3) because it discriminated against the striking union workers, regardless of whether the employer needed to provide this credit in order to stay open. Affirming the Board's decision, the Supreme Court agreed that the conduct "*does* speak for itself—it *is* discriminatory and it *does* discourage union membership and whatever the claimed overriding justification may be, it carries with it unavoidable consequences which the employer not only foresaw but which he must have intended."[25]

In its *Erie Resistor* opinion, the Board had differentiated the super-seniority credit from striker replacement under *Mackay Radio* with a detailed assessment of the continuing consequences of super-seniority. The Court agreed. Because the employer was effectively bribing replacements by offering them seniority terms that would have required 20 years of service, such an "extraordinary lure" would defeat almost any strike; moreover, it created "a cleavage in the plant continuing long after the strike ended."[26] As such, reasoning from

---

[23] United Aircraft Corp., 192 NLRB 382, 388 (1971).

[24] 373 U.S. 221 (1963).

[25] Id. at 228 (emphasis in original).

[26] Id. at 231.

effect alone, the Court agreed there was no need to prove independently that the employer acted with a discriminatory purpose.

Erie Resistor makes clear that there are substantive limits to what employers can do to attract replacement workers in order to stay open. The Court framed its analysis in the language of intent and (because of *Insurance Agents*) did not invoke directly "duty to bargain" principles. Arguably, however, the real vice with the super-seniority credit was that the credit represented effectively a bribe.[27] Virtually any strike can be broken by hiring replacement workers at well over the wage (including the value of benefits) offered to the strikers. The fact that the employer can maintain operations by offering such incentives reveals nothing about the reasonableness of the union's demands. Super-seniority credit in fact gave replacement workers and returning strikers a valuable privilege that would have taken 20 years of actual service to earn.

In view of *Erie Resistor* and the *Katz* principle, the employer violates § 8(a)(3) if it offers higher compensation to replacements than it had offered to the union at the bargaining table.[28] Under *Fleetwood* and *Laidlaw,* it cannot hire new workers or recall laid-off replacements[29] after the strike until higher-seniority returning strikers have been offered the open jobs.

Similarly, employers are not required to pay wages or accrue benefits for employees out on strike, but neither can they penalize strikers through discriminatory benefit terms. In *NLRB v. Great Dane Trailers,*[30] the employer refused to pay striking employees their accrued vacation benefits but offered to pay such benefits to replacements, returning strikers, and nonstrikers if they were on the job as of a certain day. The court of appeals denied enforcement of the Board's ULP determination: although the Board had shown discriminatory treatment between strikers and replacements, the court held that the Board had not demonstrated that the employer's intent was to discourage protected activity or interfere with collective bargaining. The Supreme Court ruled that the agency had shown discriminatory treatment, and it was then the employer's burden to

---

27 See Estreicher, supra note 8.

28 Burlington Homes, Inc., 246 NLRB 1029 (1979).

29 Giddings & Lewis, Inc., 255 NLRB 742 (1981), enforcement denied, 675 F.2d 926 (7th Cir. 1982). In Aqua-Chem, Inc., 288 NLRB 1008 (1984), the Board retreated somewhat from *Giddings & Lewis,* holding that employers could extend recall rights to laid-off replacement workers who had "a reasonable expectancy of recall" based on the circumstances of the layoff and what the replacement workers were told.

30 388 U.S. 26 (1967).

identify a legitimate business reason for the treatment, which it had failed to do.

Great Dane articulates a new framework for employer ULPs. The Court distinguished between two categories of employer conduct. The first type has an "inherently destructive" impact on employees' § 7 rights, as in *Erie Resistor*, where the Board can infer unlawful motivation violative of § 8(a)(3) without independent evidence. The second type of conduct has a "comparatively slight" impact, where the Board's General Counsel would have the initial burden of showing discriminatory conduct. In the latter category, if the Board meets its initial burden, the employer must show it was motivated by legitimate business purposes. It is not clear from the *Great Dane* decision whether a burden of persuasion shifts to the employer or is only a burden of production.

The impact of the *Great Dane* framework remains unclear. The Board and the courts have placed very few types of employer decisions or conduct into the "inherently destructive" category. The D.C. Circuit has declined to treat permanent subcontracting of unit work during a strike as "inherently destructive" under *Erie Resistor*.[31] And in *Trans World Airlines, Inc. v. Independent Federation of Flight Attendants*,[32] a case involving the Railway Labor Act (RLA), the Supreme Court further cabined the doctrine. The airline had hired permanent replacement flight attendants during a strike, making clear that the replacement workers and cross-over former strikers would be allowed to keep their particular job assignments and "domiciles" (base of operations) even after the strike, and that even very senior strikers would need to bid on available vacancies in order to be reemployed. The replaced flight attendants would keep their seniority and could bid on future assignments once reemployed on the basis of their seniority.

The Supreme Court held that the employer did not violate the RLA in allowing the cross-over former strikers to retain their job assignments at strike's end. Important to the decision was the fact that the seniority provisions were set to remain in place and would operate to the benefit of returning strikers as to future vacancies once they were reemployed. Because there was no "prospect of a continuing diminution of seniority upon reinstatement at the end of the strike," the employer's measures were distinguishable from *Erie Resistor*'s super-seniority.

The bottom line in these cases may be summarized as this: at strike's end, as in *Mackay Radio*, the employer is not required to

---

31 International Paper Co. v. NLRB, 115 F.3d 1045 (D.C. Cir. 1997).

32 489 U.S. 426 (1989).

bump permanent replacement workers, but once the returning strikers are reemployed, the employer cannot discriminate in favor of those who were hired as replacements. If seniority governs job assignments, say as a matter of contract, reinstated strikers cannot be treated as new employees but can bid for those assignments on the basis of their relative seniority.

5. Representational Issues

Replaced economic strikers retain their voting rights for one year from the commencement of the economic striker.[33] A difficult question is how to resolve representational issues in a unit comprised of former strikers and replacement workers.[34] In considering the preferences of replacements whether or not to be represented by the formerly striking union, the Board has adopted a no-presumption policy. The employer cannot presume that replacement workers are opposed to the union but must have affirmative evidence of their preference to demonstrate the reasonable good-faith doubt or reasonable uncertainty as to the union's majority support that is a prerequisite for an employer representation petition under § 9(c)(1)(B). The Supreme Court sustained the Board's no-presumption policy in *NLRB v. Curtin Matheson Scientific, Inc.*[35] Chief Justice Rehnquist concurred in the majority's opinion but did chastise the Board for making it difficult for the employer to poll employees without first proving reasonable good faith doubt.

B. Lockouts

Lockouts are the employer's version of a strike: the employer shuts down operations and closes its doors to workers. The Board and the courts have separated lockouts into two categories: defensive and offensive. Defensive lockouts are employed to prevent potential strikers from exacting additional economic damage through their control over the timing of the strike or through their conduct while still on the premises. One example of a defensive lockout is when the employer closes down in order to prevent spoilage to its wares; waiting for the employees to strike could make the employer vulnerable to serious losses. Another example is the "whipsaw" strike, in which the union calls a strike against one member of a multi-employer bargaining unit in order to pressure the struck employer to sign a favorable "interim" agreement with the union. In

---

33 29 U.S.C. § 159(c)(3).

34 Replacement workers may bring a decertification petition to remove the union, but striking employees can vote, too (at least for a year), and logistical hurdles may delay any vote for some period of time. This can include a blocking charge filed by the union, if there is a basis for the charge, which may suspend any election until after the charge is resolved.

35 494 U.S. 775 (1990).

response to a whipsaw strike, the other members of the multi-employer unit can call a lockout to equalize the disadvantage for all employers in the unit.[36] Employers who lock out their employees in the face of a whipsaw strike are permitted, like the struck employer, to use supervisors and temporary replacements in order to maintain operations. Using the *Great Dane* test, the Supreme Court held that the aim of the employers was to preserve the multi-employer unit, and the tactic only had a "comparatively slight" tendency to discourage union membership.[37]

Offensive lockouts do not have a defensive rationale but are simply used to put pressure on represented employees in the midst of bargaining or other contexts. The Board originally took the position that offensive lockouts were a violation of §§ 8(a)(1) and (3) since they treated union-represented employees adversely due to their union representation and since such lockouts had the requisite discouraging effect on § 7 activity. The Supreme Court disagreed, holding in *American Ship Building Co. v. NLRB*[38] that the employer had a right to visit costs of disagreements on union-represented employees "in support of [its] legitimate bargaining position." The employer cannot discriminate against represented employees, but "the use of a lockout does not carry with it any necessary implication that the employer acted to discourage union membership or otherwise discriminate against union members as such."[39] In essence, the Court requires the Board to show independent evidence of a discouragement/anti-union motive by the employer because the lockout itself is deemed a legitimate bargaining weapon.

The use of temporary replacements is permissible, even in offensive lockouts. There would seem to be an inherent tension between the closing of a facility as an offensive bargaining tactic and the defensive rationale of hiring replacements in order to stay open during a strike. Nevertheless, the courts of appeals have upheld the use of temporary replacements in both contexts, as long as the decision is not motivated by antiunion animus. These courts have noted certain circumstances present in these cases (without holding that they are necessary features): (1) the lockout is temporary, especially when a definite date has been set; (2) employees have an option to accept the employer's terms and return to work; and (3) the union-security clause remains in effect. Hiring permanent replacements in tandem with a bargaining lockout is so close to

---

[36] NLRB v. Truck Drivers Local Union No. 449 (Buffalo Linen), 353 U.S. 87 (1957).

[37] NLRB v. Brown, 380 U.S. 278 (1965).

[38] 380 U.S. 300 (1965).

[39] Id. at 312.

simply firing the employees that it is likely permissible only as a defensive measure in cases of sabotage or violence.[40]

C. Boycotts and Picketing

The NLRA's restrictions on secondary activity by labor organizations are among the most complicated provisions in the statute. The purpose of the Act's limitations on boycotts and picketing is to cabin labor disputes to the primary disputants and thus prevent spillover effects to other businesses not involved in the dispute. At the same time, appeals to suppliers, customers, and the public are important weapons for unions in securing support for their side of the dispute.

1. Labor Picketing

As a general matter, the Supreme Court has interpreted the First Amendment to allow regulation of labor picketing because such picketing involves a combination of expression and regulable conduct.[41] Picketing has a physical aspect: the patrolling of territory by a group of people accompanied by signs and slogans. Although picketers are generally required under egress and trespass regulations not to block access to entrances or exits, the picketing itself—generally in some proximity to those exits or entrances—can create an intimidating presence beyond the mere words of the picketers. Early cases such as *Vegelahn v. Guntner*[42] held that picket lines were inherently coercive. The judicial view has shifted since then, but there is still a sense that individuals are reluctant to cross a picket line "because of that aspect of the union's efforts to communicate its views that calls for an automatic response to a signal, rather than a reasoned response to an idea."[43] This reasoning is best understood in a period of substantial unionization when background understandings between labor groups (and their supporters) assured a fairly reflexive response to a union picket line.

It may be questioned whether in today's environment a labor picket line still calls for "an automatic response to a signal."[44] The

---

[40] Johns-Mansville Prods. Corp. v. NLRB, 557 F.2d 1126 (5th Cir. 1977).

[41] Teamsters, Local 695 v. Vogt, 354 U.S. 284 (1957).

[42] 167 Mass. 92, 44 N.E. 1077 (1896).

[43] NLRB v. Retail Store Employees Union Local 1001, 447 U.S. 607, 619 (1980) (Stevens, J., concurring in part and concurring in the result).

[44] There are grounds to question whether picketing by nonlabor groups is entitled to more preferential treatment from a First Amendment standpoint. See NAACP v. Clairborne Hardware Co., 458 U.S. 886 (1982). See generally Michael C. Harper, The Consumer's Emerging Right to Boycott, *NAACP v. Clairborne* and Its Implications for American Labor Law, 93 Yale L.J. 409 (1984); Cynthia Estlund, Are Unions a Constitutional Anomaly?, 114 Mich. L. Rev. 169 (2015). Union boycotts

Supreme Court has made clear that handbilling by unions does not generally operate as a "signal" to other labor organizations and should be treated as constitutionally protected expression.[45]

2. Secondary Pressures

As a result of Taft-Hartley, the NLRA prohibits union efforts to exert secondary pressure on third-party neutrals as a means of achieving the union's goals in a dispute with the employer.

The NLRA's statutory prohibitions against secondary activity are laid out in a maze of statutory language that is difficult to navigate. Under § 8(b)(4), a union ULP requires both that the union's conduct involved a prohibited means/conduct and that it furthered a prohibited objective/purpose. Prohibited conduct is set out under prongs (i) and (ii) of the statutory section, and the prohibited purposes are set out in subsections (A)–(D). In order to find a violation under § 8(b)(4), the Board must prove that the union engaged in one of the two types of prohibited conduct and acted for one of the four types of prohibited purposes.

The conduct requirements apply to certain types of picketing, boycotts, or other efforts to discourage engagement with particular businesses. Section 8(b)(4)(i) applies to appeals to workers such as a strike, a refusal to work, or a refusal to use or handle goods, as well as inducing or encouraging other employees to engage in these activities. Section 8(b)(4)(ii) looks more broadly to appeals to management, employees, customers, employer suppliers or competitors, or any other "person engaged in commerce" but requires coercion or restraint—not just appeals. Thus, prong (i) applies only to work stoppages by the employees themselves or efforts to persuade other employees to stop work, while the conduct in prong (ii) applies to coercive activities against economic actors in general.

One of the two conduct requirements must then be paired with one of the four purpose requirements to find a violation. The four purpose requirements are: (A) forcing or requiring an employer to join a labor or employer organization or enter into a "hot cargo" agreement; (B) forcing or requiring a third party to stop handling products or otherwise stop doing business with another firm or forcing or requiring another employer to recognize or bargain with a noncertified union; (C) forcing or requiring employer recognition of

---

directed at workers in other unions are distinguishable from consumer boycotts because of an underlying agreement among unions to honor each other's picket lines. Once this background agreement dissipates, say, with declining union density across broad swaths of the economy, the union boycott increasingly resembles the consumer boycott.

[45] Edward J. DeBartolo Corp. v. Florida East Coast Bldg. & Constr. Trades Council, 485 U.S. 568 (1988) (reading NLRA § 8(b)(4) to avoid constitutional doubts).

one union when another union is already certified; and (D) forcing or requiring the employer to assign work to a particular set of employees in a particular union or trade/craft/class.

Section 8(b)(4)(B), the "secondary boycott" provision, is by far the most commonly-invoked ULP within § 8(b)(4).[46] Under § 8(b)(4)(B), labor organizations are not permitted to mount a picket encouraging other workers not to cross the line in front of a "neutral" secondary employer, even if that employer buys from, sells to, or otherwise interacts with the primary employer. Congress in the Taft-Hartley amendments sought to curb secondary picketing and boycotts as a means of furthering "industrial peace," presumably limiting the spillover effects of a primary labor dispute. The exceptions to this bar include labor appeals directed at secondary companies performing struck work or companies that are part of the same corporate entity as the struck employer. Section 8(b)(4)(B) also specifically exempts primary strikes or primary picketing from its prohibitions, which serves to confirm that the prohibition is not intended to limit the primary strike. "Primary situs" picketing refers to labor appeals at the site of the primary dispute, while "secondary situs" picketing applies to labor appeals at other locations where the products of the primary employer are being processed, used, or sold by others. As a general matter, primary-situs picketing is lawful even if it causes disruption not only to the primary employer but also to businesses seeking to enter the premises of that employer, whereas labor appeals at locations where the primary employer's employees are not present are unlawful.[47] Appeals to other employees and consumers to honor a picket line at the primary site are also exempted. Even if such "primary" picketing thereby has secondary effects, such as missed deliveries from suppliers or missed shipments to customers, it is still considered primary and not prohibited by the Act.

Section 8(b)(4)(B) applies only to pressures directed at "any other person." It does not reach boycotts at other locations or subdivisions of the primary employer.[48] Nor does it reach "allies" of

---

[46] Section 8(b)(4)(B) was § 8(b)(4)(A) prior to the 1959 Landrum-Griffin Act.

[47] See generally Howard Lesnick, The Gravamen of the Secondary Boycott, 62 Colum. L. Rev. 1361, 1414 (1962); Paul C. Weiler, Governing the Workplace: The Future of Labor and Employment Law 267, 271–72 (1990).

[48] Some decisions hold that unincorporated divisions of the same corporate entity may be viewed as separate from the corporate parent for secondary-boycott purposes. In AFTRA v. NLRB, 462 F.2d 887 (D.C. Cir. 1972), the union picketed at a television station with whom it had a primary dispute as well as at a newspaper owned by the same corporate parent. However, the station and the newspaper had different management and different workforces, and the two managements had independent control over their respective day-to-day operations. Agreeing that the picketing of the newspaper violated § 8(b)(4)(B), the court relied on NLRB decisions holding that potential ultimate control by the parent is not sufficient: "There must be in addition

the primary employer, including independent businesses performing "struck work" either by prior agreement or practice, in situations where the primary employer will be paying for such work

When does a secondary employer cross the line to be considered an "ally"? In *NLRB v. Business Machine, Local 459 (Royal Typewriter Co.),*[49] the struck employer Royal told its customers with whom it had a repair contract that they could use any other company during the strike and send the bills for reimbursement to Royal. The union picketed both the customers and the independent repair companies. Although the picketing against the business's customers was held to be unlawful secondary activity, the picketing of the independent businesses was permissible under the ally doctrine. The ally doctrine clearly applies in situations where the primary employer directly transfers or subcontracts out bargaining-unit work to another company.[50] The *Royal* court held that the doctrine also applied where the independent companies had no direct relationship with the primary but were nevertheless performing struck work. The court did hold open the possibility that the potential allies could escape that doctrine if they were unable to determine which work was farmed out from the primary and which was not. The court held that the independent repair companies, however, had made no effort to identify and turn away Royal work, and thus had knowingly enmeshed themselves in the controversy.

A union generally does not violate the Act in picketing wherever the primary employer's employees are working. In some cases, the picketing employer is at a "common situs" where a number of businesses share a particular location. Consider *Sailors' Union of the Pacific and Moore Dry Dock,*[51] a case in which a cargo ship (or, at least, the company that owned the ship) was the primary employer. A union sought to organize the ship company's employees but was denied recognition or access to the ship. It then set up a picket line against the ship company outside the entrance to an independent dry dock where the ship was being serviced. (The union had sought to picket in front of the ship itself, but the dry dock denied them access.) The Board ruled that the picketing of a secondary's premises would be considered primary if:

---

such actual or active common control . . . as to denote an appreciable integration of operations and management policies." Id. at 892, quoting Drivers, Chauffeurs and Helpers Local No. 639 (Poole's Warehousing, Inc.), 158 NLRB 1281, 1286 (1966).

[49] 228 F.2d 553 (2d Cir. 1955).

[50] See, e.g., Douds v. Metropolitan Federation of Architects, Engineers, Chemists & Technicians, Local 231 (Ebasco Services, Inc.), 75 F. Supp. 672, 676 (S.D.N.Y. 1948).

[51] 92 NLRB 547 (1950).

> (a) The picketing is strictly limited to times when the *situs* of dispute is located on the secondary employer's premises; (b) at the time of the picketing the primary employer is engaged in its normal business at the *situs*; (c) the picketing is limited to places reasonably close to the location of the *situs;* and (d) the picketing discloses clearly that the dispute is with the primary employer.[52]

Because the union's picketing met these requirements, it was lawful.

Employers have responded to *Moore Dry Dock* by trying to cordon off labor appeals to employees working for the primary employer from appeals directed the workers employed by secondary employers at the site owned by the primary employer. The Supreme Court recognized the possibility of creating a "reserve gate" within a struck employer's premises for employees of secondary employers in *Local 761, International Union of Electrical, Radio & Machine Workers v. NLRB (General Electric).*[53] At one of its plants in Louisville, Kentucky, General Electric (GE) set up a separate entrance for employees of various independent contractors who worked at the plant. The union representing GE employees picketed at all of the GE gates, including the separate gate for contractor employees. The Court recognized the principle that, even on the premises of the primary employer, unions had to respect separate gates for independent contractors and refrain from picketing. The union would be free to picket the reserve gate, however, if it was regularly used by primary employees, especially during the strike; it would also cease to be considered secondary if employees using the gate performed tasks connected to the normal operations of the struck employer or tasks made possible by the strike. On remand, the Board held that the gates were primary since some aspects of the contractors' work were connected with the company's normal operations.[54]

Construction sites are treated somewhat differently. In *NLRB v. Denver Building & Construction Trades Council*,[55] a union picketed a construction site where a unionized general contractor and a number of union and nonunion subcontractors were working. The union claimed it had a primary dispute with the general contractor, since the general had selected a nonunion subcontractor. Although the union argued that the picketing would have been primary if the general contractor had been using its own nonunion employees for the work, rather than the subcontractor's, the Court held that the

---

52 Id. at 549.

53 366 U.S. 667 (1961).

54 Id. at 680.

55 341 U.S. 675 (1951).

general and the subcontractor were independent entities in a "doing business" relationship for § 8(b)(4) purposes, and the union's purpose in picketing the construction site was to force the general to stop doing business with the subcontractor. Despite the fact the construction site was a common situs, the *Moore Dry Dock* factors did not apply. In sum, the general contractor and subcontractors were viewed as separate entities, even though the general contractor controlled the decision to contract with the subcontractor and these companies were engaged in interdependent tasks at the same site.

The other provisions of § 8(b)(4) outside of § 8(b)(4)(B) are narrower in scope. Section 8(b)(4)(A) is connected to § 8(e) of the Act, the so-called "hot cargo" provision. A product of the 1959 Landrum-Griffin amendments, § 8(e) prohibits unions and employers from entering into agreements that boycott other secondary employers, generally because the other employer's employees are not represented by a union or because they are working on goods produced by the struck employer.[56] Section 8(e) provides exceptions for such agreements in the construction and garment industries. Section 8(b)(4)(C) concerns conflicts between unions over representation, and Section 8(b)(4)(D) applies to work assignment disputes between craft or trade unions.

3. Consumer Appeals

Customer-oriented picketing and boycotts are treated differently under the Act than labor picketing aimed at persuading employees to stop working. In the 1959 Landrum-Griffin Act, Congress added § 8(b)(4)(ii) to the Act so as to prohibit certain kinds of coercion and threats directed at employers through means other than the traditional labor pressures. As the publicity proviso to § 8(b)(4) indicates, unions are permitted to "truthfully advis[e]" the public that a "product" is "being produced by an employer" with whom the union has a primary dispute. In *NLRB v. Servette, Inc.*,[57] the primary employer was a wholesale distributor of specialty products to retail supermarkets. The union appealed to managers at those supermarkets not to stock the primary's wares and threatened to handbill the markets if the goods were stocked. The Court held that the appeal to managers was an effort to induce a certain managerial choice, rather than an effort to have the managers refuse to do their work, and therefore did not involve prohibited means under § 8(b)(4)(i). Neither was § 8(b)(4)(ii) violated, as the threat to handbill was a threat to do an act that was lawful under the publicity proviso. The primary employer had argued that it did not "produce" the goods,

---

[56] 29 U.S.C. § 158(e).

[57] 377 U.S. 46 (1964).

which was seemingly required by the text of the proviso.[58] However, the Court interpreted the proviso to apply to any goods that the primary produces or supplies, or to services which are essential to the goods' production and distribution.[59]

To what extent may a union urge a consumer boycott at the premises of a secondary employer through picketing? In *NLRB v. Fruit & Vegetable Packers, Local 760 (Tree Fruits)*,[60] the Court ruled that unions may engage in consumer-product picketing. The most important condition is that the union must target only the products or services of the primary employer without a "signal" to employees or other labor organizations to withhold their labor. The union picketed and handbilled forty-six Safeway supermarkets that sold apples produced by the primary employer. The pickets appeared only at consumer entrances, and leaflets made clear that the union was not asking Safeway employees (or other employees making deliveries to the stores) to refrain from doing work.

The Court cut back on the potential reach of the *Tree Fruits* doctrine in *NLRB v. Retail Store Employees Union, Local 1001 (Safeco Title Insurance Co.)*.[61] The union picketed secondary employers (local title companies) to advocate for a consumer boycott of the primary employer's wares (title insurance policies). However, unlike the supermarket in *Tree Fruits*, where the apples were only one item among many, in *Safeco* the primary's insurance policies made up over 90% of the business of the secondary title companies. Customers could not honor the picket line without boycotting the title company's entire business. To determine whether the holding of *Tree Fruits* or *Safeco* should apply in a particular case, the Court stated that the Board should determine whether the picketing was "threatening the neutral party with ruin or substantial loss."[62] If so, efforts to encourage a consumer boycott were so harmful to the secondary that they would violate § 8(b)(4). But if such loss is a

---

[58] 29 U.S.C. § 158(b)(4) (allowing unions to "truthfully advis[e] the public . . . that a product or products are *produced by* an employer with whom the labor organization has a primary dispute" (emphasis added)).

[59] The relationship between the product and the distribution of the product can be too attenuated to come within the publicity proviso. In Edward J. DeBartolo Corp. v. NLRB, 463 U.S. 147 (1983) (*DeBartolo I*), the Court held that the union's boycott against all the tenants in a mall was not protected by the publicity proviso when the dispute was with a general contractor doing construction work for the mall owner. The relationship between the contractor and the owner did not extend the publicity proviso to all of the tenants within the mall itself. (However, note that the handbilling in question was ultimately held to not be a ULP in Edward J. DeBartolo Corp. v. Florida Gulf Coast Building & Construction Trades Council, 485 U.S. 568 (1988) (*DeBartolo II*), discussed infra).

[60] 377 U.S. 58 (1964).

[61] 447 U.S. 607 (1980).

[62] Id. at 615 n.11.

product of the extent of the company's dependence on the products or services of the struck employer, in what sense should it be considered a neutral employer for purposes of consumer picketing?

What if a union engages in handbilling, leafleting, or other non-picketing activity to advocate for a consumer boycott of secondary businesses? In *Edward J. DeBartolo Corp. v. Florida Gulf Coast Building & Construction Trades Council (DeBartolo II)*,[63] the union engaged in a leafleting campaign to encourage a consumer boycott of all the stores at a mall, even though its primary dispute was with a general contractor who was building a new store for the mall owner. Such activity was clearly secondary. However, the Supreme Court held that leafleting did not have the "mixture of conduct and communication" that picketing entailed; rather, leafleting was akin to pure speech.[64] Because of that distinction, any prohibition on leafleting would pose serious constitutional questions under the First Amendment. The Court therefore interpreted the statute not to ban consumer appeals via handbills even if those appeals called for a secondary boycott. The secondary boycott in and of itself was not illegal, and the union was therefore entitled to publicize its dispute and its calls for a legal boycott in support of the dispute. In order to fall under the "threaten, coerce, or restrain" language of § 8(b)(4)(ii), the union's activity would need to extend beyond mere calls for a consumer boycott into coercive activity such as labor picketing. If, however, that handbilling or other activity was aimed at work stoppages by secondary employees, rather than being limited to consumer boycotts, it would be prohibited by § 8(b)(4)(i)(B).[65]

The line between picketing, on the one hand, and purer speech activities such as leafleting or demonstrating is an important one, as indicated by the difference in results between *Safeco* (picketing in support of secondary consumer boycott is prohibited) and *DeBartolo II* (leafleting with the same ends is not). This distinction has led to creative approaches whereby the union creates a physical presence urging a boycott but without picketing. For example, unions have used large banners in conjunction with leafleting to promote consumer boycotts; the banners were stationary, held to the side, did not interfere with ingress or egress, and were not accompanied by moving pickets. The Board has held such bannering not to violate the "coercion" requirement in § 8(b)(4)(ii).[66] Along the same lines, the Board has held that a mock "funeral" for workers' rights, along with a large inflatable rat and a display poster, similarly did not constitute

---

[63] 485 U.S. 568 (1988).

[64] Id. at 580.

[65] See Warshawsky & Co. v. NLRB, 182 F.3d 948 (D.C. Cir. 1999).

[66] Carpenters Local 1506 (Eliason & Knuth of Arizona), 355 NLRB 797 (2010).

coercion under the Act.[67] The Board held that the union's conduct was more fairly characterized as persuasion, rather than intimidation, as the union members were stationary, stayed over a hundred feet from the hospital's entrances, did not accost people entering the hospital, and did not carry themselves in a way that could be perceived as labor picket urging other workers to refuse to perform work.[68] Perhaps the most notable presence at these types of demonstrations is a large inflatable rat—sometimes going by the nickname "Scabby"—that has become a regular presence at construction sites.[69] Although the Trump Administration's NLRB general counsel had issued an advice memo arguing that Scabby should be considered coercive and tantamount to picketing (as opposed to an informational demonstration),[70] the Biden Administration Board upheld the use of the balloon rat and his ilk as a permissive form of speech.[71] Should not the question here be whether the demonstration signaled to workers for other companies that they were expected to refuse to deliver services at the struck employer's premises?

4. "Hot Cargo" Clauses

The "hot cargo" prohibition of § 8(e) of the Act was also part of the 1959 Landrum-Griffin amendments designed to target a particular type of secondary activity. The activity in question was the execution of an agreement between a union and an employer whereby the employer agreed not to handle, use, sell, or otherwise deal with the goods of another employer. These clauses were designed to allow unions to circumvent the secondary boycott prohibitions by building them into collective bargaining agreements, thus arguably turning the dispute into a primary one. In *Local 1976, United Brotherhood of Carpenters v. NLRB (Sand Door & Plywood Co.)*,[72] the Supreme Court held that such clauses were not themselves prohibited under the 1947 Act. Section 8(e) closed this gap by making the "hot cargo"

---

[67] Sheet Metal Workers International Association, Local 15 (Brandon Regional Medical Center), 356 NLRB 1290 (2011). The opinion was prompted by a remand from the D.C. Circuit holding that the mock funeral was protected speech and was not coercive. See Sheet Metal Workers' Local 15 v. NLRB, 491 F.3d 429 (D.C. Cir. 2007).

[68] *Brandon Regional*, 356 NLRB at 1292.

[69] Sarah Jones, Leave Scabby the Rat Alone, N.Y. Mag., July 29, 2019.

[70] Jayme L. Sophir, NLRB, Advice Memo, International Brotherhood of Electrical Workers, Local 134 (Summit Design + Build), Case 13–CC–225655, Dec. 20, 2018.

[71] International Union of Operating Engineers, Local Union No. 150 a/w International Union of Operating Engineers, AFL-CIO (Lippert Components, Inc.), 371 NLRB No. 8 (July 21, 2021).

[72] 357 U.S. 93 (1958).

agreements themselves unfair labor practices.[73] In addition, § 8(b)(4)(A) expressly prohibits unions from requiring them or forcing employers to adopt them. Enforcement of such clauses could violate § 8(b)(4)(B).

To what extent, however, is a union entitled to bargain for restrictions on employer practices that have reduced the bargaining unit's work? As an example, consider a work-preservation clause that prohibits the purchase of materials on which certain prior work has been done—work that previously would have been done by members of the bargaining unit. Such a clause is in technical violation of § 8(e), as it requires the employer not to deal with sellers of pre-fabricated materials. However, in *National Woodwork Manufacturers Association v. NLRB,*[74] the Supreme Court interpreted § 8(e) so as to permit clauses designed for the purpose of preserving unit work as opposed to achieving union objectives elsewhere. "The touchstone is whether the agreement or its maintenance is addressed to the labor relations of the contracting employer vis-à-vis his own employees."[75] The Board has held that work-preservation clauses are permissible even when the clauses seek to recapture work that was previously lost[76] or penalize the use of new technology that indirectly cuts into the bargaining unit's traditional work.[77] Work-acquisition clauses, on the other hand, are generally held to be in violation of the hot-cargo prohibition.

While the work-preservation clause may be lawful, its enforcement may impose labor pressures on secondary employers that would violate § 8(b)(4). In *NLRB v. Enterprise Ass'n of Steam Pipefitters,*[78] a subcontractor had a work-preservation agreement with its union which required that pipe threading and cutting be done on the job site. However, the subcontractor executed an agreement with a general contractor for a particular job, and the general required the subcontractor to use pre-threaded and pre-cut pipes from a particular manufacturer. When the pre-threaded pipes arrived at the worksite, the union steamfitters refused to install them. The clause itself was held not to violate § 8(e). However, because the subcontractor did not have the "right to control" the

---

[73] An example of such a clause is: "No employee shall work on any job on which cabinet work, fixtures, millwork, sash, doors, trim, or other detailed millwork is used unless the same is Union-made and bears the Union Label of the United Brotherhood of Carpenters and Joiners of America." See National Woodwork Manufacturers Association v. NLRB, 386 U.S. 612, 615 n.2 (1967).

[74] 386 U.S. 612 (1967).

[75] Id. at 645.

[76] See American Boiler Mfrs. Ass'n v. NLRB, 404 F.2d 547 (8th Cir. 1968).

[77] NLRB v. Int'l Longshoremen's Ass'n, 447 U.S. 490 (1980).

[78] 429 U.S. 507 (1977).

decision over which pipe to use, the union's enforcement of the provision by refusing to install the pre-cut pipe was secondary pressure in violation of § 8(b)(4)(B). Because the general controlled the decision as to pipes, the union's refusal to work had the object of forcing the subcontractor to cease doing business with the general.

In *Heartland Industrial Partners, LLC*,[79] the Board approved an innovative agreement between the Steelworkers union and Heartland, an investment firm, even though it skirted close to the § 8(e) line. The agreement was essentially a card-check and neutrality agreement, with a twist: the investment company was obliged to use its voting power, in companies where it held at least a 50% voting interest, to induce that company to execute a card-check and neutrality agreement with the union. If the company ultimately refused to negotiate such an agreement, an arbitrator was to be called in. The Board held, however, that the arbitrator was not bound to require Heartland to stop doing business with that company. As a result, the provision did not violate § 8(e).

There are two provisos which provide § 8(e) exceptions within certain industries. The garment-industry proviso is fairly broad, allowing garment-industry unions to negotiate hot-cargo clauses as applied to the "integrated process of production in the apparel and clothing industry," and permitting unions to strike and picket to enforce such clauses. The purpose of the exception is to allow unions to attempt to curb practices whereby employers under union contracts farm out work to independent contractors. The construction-industry proviso is significantly narrower, as it applies only to agreements that concern a particular geographical job site. Unions are permitted to execute agreements with owners or contractors allowing only union contractors on a particular site. However, any effort to restrict off-site work over which the signatory employer had no right of control (as in *Enterprise Association of Steam Pipefitters*) would be unlawful. In addition, unions may not enforce job-site clauses through work stoppages, nor may a union negotiate for a union-only job site if it has no represented employee at the site beforehand.[80] However, such union-only provisions, negotiated in the context of a collective bargaining relationship, need not be limited to job sites where union and nonunion workers would have to work alongside each other, even if reducing such frictions was a principal purpose of the exception.[81]

---

79 348 NLRB 1081 (2006).

80 Connell Construction Co. v. Plumbers, Local 100, 421 U.S. 616 (1975).

81 Woelke & Romero Framing, Inc. v. NLRB, 456 U.S. 645 (1982).

5. Work-Assignment Disputes

Employers can be particularly frustrated by inter-union disputes in which each side seeks to enlist the employer as a supporter in the struggle. The employer may, or may not, have a preference as to which union represents its employees, but ultimately it does not have any control over the resolution of the dispute. Under § 8(b)(4)(D), unions are prohibited from picketing, striking, or other coercive behavior with the purpose of forcing the employer to assign work to one labor organization over another. However, the Board has also put into place a system for resolving such disputes. The filing of a § 8(b)(4)(D) charge triggers a Board hearing under § 10(k) to determine who should be assigned the disputed work. The Supreme Court has interpreted § 10(k) to require the Board to make an affirmative award of the work to one of the unions in the dispute.[82] The Board has developed a test for determining work assignments that relies on a variety of factors, including: the skills and work involved; prior certifications by the Board; company and industry practice; agreements between unions and between employers and unions; awards of arbitrators, joint boards, and the AFL-CIO in the same or related cases; the nature of the assignment made by the employer; and the efficient operation of the employer's business.[83]

A union's disagreement with an employer's work assignment may lead to picketing or other conduct to block the assignment. When the employer files a § 8(b)(4)(D) charge, the Board must then begin a § 10(k) hearing unless the parties otherwise agree to resolve the matter on their own. The § 8(b)(4)(D) proceeding is held in abeyance until the work assignment is resolved. If the picketing union loses its work-assignment claim (either through the § 10(k) hearing or through private resolution), then it loses the § 8(b)(4)(D) claim. However, if the union wins its assignment claim, the employer loses its § 8(b)(4)(D) claim, and the union can continue to picket until the work is properly assigned.

As interpreted, the § 10(k) hearing is only used to resolve § 8(b)(4)(D) claims. The Supreme Court has held that employers are entitled to participate in the resolution of union jurisdictional disputes since their workplaces are affected by the resolution. In *NLRB v. Plasterers' Local Union No. 79*,[84] the two unions involved in the jurisdictional dispute agreed to a private method of resolving the dispute. The employer objected to the procedure, however, and the

---

[82] NLRB v. Radio and Television Broadcast Engineers Union, Local 1212, 364 U.S. 573 (1961).

[83] Machinists, Lodge 1743 (J.A. Jones Constr.), 135 NLRB 1402, 1410–11 (1962).

[84] 404 U.S. 116 (1971).

Board continued with the § 10(k) hearing and awarded the work to one of the unions. The court of appeals ruled that the Board could not continue with its hearing once the two unions agreed to arbitration to resolve the matter. The Supreme Court disagreed. It held that the employer could be considered a "party" to the § 10(k) hearing, and that the Board's decision to continue with the hearing was a proper way to resolve the matter, particularly considering the employer's interest.

6. Representational or Organizational Picketing

Picketing for organizational and representational purposes received special treatment as a result of the Landrum-Griffin amendments to the NLRA. The underlying concern is that unions should not be able to use labor picketing to coerce an employer into recognizing a union.

Under § 8(b)(7), a union commits a ULP when it engages in picketing for an organizational or recognitional purpose and comes within one of the subsections of the provision. The conduct in question must be picketing or threats to picket. One of the objects of the picketing must be to compel employer recognition or to compel employees to select the union as their bargaining agent. Section 8(b)(7) does not apply to certified exclusive representatives. In addition, if the purpose of the picketing is to protest the employer's ULPs or to protest the employer's failure to pay "area standards," the picketing is not a violation absent independent evidence of an organizational or representational objective.

Once the prior conditions are satisfied (picketing; seeking to force or require recognition; by a union not currently certified), § 8(b)(7) prohibits representational picketing in each of the three following circumstances:

- where the employer has lawfully recognized another union and the picketing union has no right to raise a question concerning representation (§ 8(b)(7)(A));
- where a valid representation election was held within the past year (§ 8(b)(7)(B));
- where the union has not filed a representation petition within a reasonable period of time from the start of the picketing, not to exceed thirty days (§ 8(b)(7)(C)).

Sections 8(b)(7)(A) and 8(b)(7)(B) are fairly straightforward: the union is not permitted to conduct representational picketing where it cannot lawfully raise a representational claim. So when the employer has already properly recognized another union, or when a valid representation election was held in the last year (raising the election bar for the year), the union is not in a position to be lawfully recognized under the Act as the employees' representative. If the union is protesting the validity of the election, even extended picketing is not within the § 8(b)(7)(B) prohibition.

Representational picketing is allowed under § 8(b)(7)(C) if the picketing union has the opportunity to become the exclusive representative of the employer's employees. However, the union is required to act on its interest within a reasonable period of time, not to exceed thirty days, from the start of the picketing. This two-part requirement provides the union with a chance to begin its picketing, but it must "put up or shut up" within thirty days. By the end of the reasonable-time period, the union must file a representation petition with the Board seeking to represent the employees in question. If it does not, it is vulnerable to a § 8(b)(7)(C) charge for any continued picketing.

If the union does file a representation petition, it is entitled to continue picketing for organizational or recognitional purposes. However, if the employer has filed an § 8(b)(7)(C) charge, the Board treats this petition in an expedited fashion. Section 8(b)(7)(C) states that when a representation petition has been filed in the face of an § 8(b)(7)(C) charge, the Board "shall forthwith . . . direct an election in such unit."[85] The proviso eliminates many of the standard procedures associated with a Board-regulated election, such as the 30% showing of interest by the union and the parties' rights to pre-election hearings to determine the appropriateness of the bargaining unit.[86] The purpose of the expedited election is to resolve the representational quickly and through Board processes. Once the election has been held, the union either becomes the employees' representative, and the picketing is no longer prohibited by § 8(b)(7), or the union is not the employees' representative, and the union is barred from picketing for at least a year under § 8(b)(7)(B). If no § 8(b)(7)(C) charge is filed, the Board will follow its standard procedures as to the representation petition, even if the union is picketing. Thus, if the employer would rather have picketing than an expedited election, it would choose not to file a charge.

There is one other exception within § 8(b)(7)(C), and that applies to "picketing or other publicity for the purpose of truthfully advising the public (including consumers) that an employer does not employ members of, or have a contract with, a labor organization."[87] Thus, rather than being organizational in tenor, the picketing is designed

---

[85] 29 U.S.C. § 158(b)(7)(C).

[86] The Regional Director may conduct a hearing if she thinks it is necessary to resolve substantial issues prior to the election. See 29 C.F.R. § 101.23.

[87] 29 U.S.C. § 158(b)(7)(C).

to advise the public as to the representational status of employees. This proviso may or may not be required under the First Amendment, but it serves a similar purpose to the "publicity proviso" of § 8(b)(4). However, the § 8(b)(7)(C) publicity proviso does not apply if the picketing has a labor signal effect, if "an effect of such picketing is to induce any individual employed by any other person in the course of his employment, not to pick up, deliver or transport any goods or not to perform any services."[88] Also, this proviso does not apply to §§ 8(b)(7)(A) or (B).

Does § 8(b)(7)(C) prohibit picketing when the union has the support of a clear majority of the employees for whom it is picketing to represent? In *International Hod Carriers, Local 840 (Blinne Construction)*,[89] the union had authorization cards from all three employees in the unit when it demanded recognition by the employer. The employer refused to recognize the union and transferred one of the employees to a different unit in retaliation. The union began picketing with three objectives: (1) recognition, (2) payment of area-standard wages, and (3) protesting alleged unfair labor practices by the employer. The union also filed unfair labor practice charges against the employer, including for failure to recognize the union, but did not file a representation petition within thirty days.

The Board held that the union violated § 8(b)(7)(C) with its picketing, even though the union had a clear majority based on authorization cards and had filed ULP charges against the employer. The Board held that the union's majority support did not absolve the union of the responsibility to file a representation petition and seek an election to obtain Board certification. As the Supreme Court indicated in *Linden Lumber*,[90] the employer has the right to insist upon an election, even in the face of majority support for the union. As to the ULP charges, the Board held that the blocking-charge policy applied: an election would not be held until the ULPs were resolved but that did not excuse the union's failure to file a representation charge within the reasonable time period.

As noted above, picketing will be deemed to have a representational object even if it is only one of several objects of the picketing. The question as to the object(s) of the picketing is a question of fact to be resolved by the Board. However, if unions remove any evidence of a representational object from their picketing, the Board will generally view the picketing as nonrepresentational, even if the union might otherwise be interested

---

88 Id.

89 135 NLRB 1153 (1962), supplementing 130 NLRB 387 (1961).

90 Linden Lumber Division, Summer & Co. v. NLRB, 419 U.S. 301 (1974).

in representing the employer's employees. Picketing to protest employer ULPs committed during a representation campaign is deemed not to fall within § 8(b)(7), even though the union's underlying objective is recognitional. Area-standards picking does not violate the provision,[91] but some investigation into the union's conduct and the employer's compensation practices may be required to show that the union is in fact addressing its picketing to those practices.[92]

7. Remedies for Unlawful Picketing and Boycotts

Sections 8(b)(4), 8(e), and 8(b)(7) create union unfair labor practices which can be enforced through traditional Board procedures. Aggrieved employers or other persons in commerce can file charges, and the Board will investigate and prosecute such charges on behalf of the charging party. However, there are two additional aspects to the remedial process for such activities that warrant special mention. First, section 10(*l*) of the Act compels the Board to follow special procedures for violations of §§ 8(b)(4)(A)–(C), 8(e), and 8(b)(7).[93] When such violations are charged, the charges are known as "priority cases," and the Regional Director must give priority to their investigation over all of the other charges before it. If the Board's investigation shows that reasonable cause exists to find a violation, the Regional Director (without the need for Board authorization) must immediately petition a federal district court for an injunction against the behavior. The district court is empowered to provide injunctive relief or even a temporary restraining order if necessary to prevent substantial and irreparable injury. The injunctive relief will generally stay in place pending final Board adjudication of the matter. Section 10(*l*) essentially creates a separate track for these kinds of union violations—a track that surpasses even those charges that are awarded § 10(j) injunctive relief. The justification for this priority treatment is the damage to commerce that can come, quickly, from union secondary boycotts, hot cargo clauses, and extended recognitional picketing.

Second, employers or other victims of union activities under § 8(b)(4) may bring an independent action under § 303 of the Labor Management Relations Act.[94] The action provides damages for any person injured by the unlawful union activity, including the neutral employer, the primary employer, or third parties who have suffered

---

[91] Houston Bldg. & Constr. Trades Council, 136 NLRB 321 (1962); New Otani Hotel & Garden, 331 NLRB 1078, 1079 (2000).

[92] See, e.g., Better Home Deliveries, 274 NLRB 164 (1985).

[93] 29 U.S.C. § 160(*l*).

[94] 29 U.S.C. § 187.

direct and foreseeable economic injury themselves.[95] However, the actions are limited to compensatory damages and do not include punitive damages, unless authorized under state law by a specific (non-preempted) state tort, such as battery or conversion. Section 303 actions are independent of Board charges under § 8(b)(4) and can be brought simultaneously. Although the § 303 claim need not be held off pending Board resolution, courts will generally defer to the Board's findings if the § 8(b)(4) claim is resolved first.[96]

---

[95] See, e.g., W.J. Milner & Co. v. IBEW Local 349, 476 F.2d 8 (5th Cir. 1973) (sales agent of primary employer has a claim for foreseeable lost wages and commissions).

[96] See, e.g., Paramount Transp. System v. Teamsters, Local 150, 436 F.2d 1064 (9th Cir. 1971).

Chapter 9

ENFORCING THE COLLECTIVE BARGAINING AGREEMENT

Up to this point we have described the development of a bargaining relationship between the employer and its employees' collective bargaining representative. In this Chapter, we discuss a mature stage of that relationship, in which the employees have chosen a union, the union has negotiated with the employer, and the two sides have agreed upon a collective bargaining agreement (CBA or agreement) to govern their relationship. Like any contract, the CBA cannot enforce itself; it must be interpreted by the parties, and they may at times disagree over its meaning and potentially breach its requirements. Under traditional common law of contract, these private disputes would be brought to state court to be resolved through the judicial process. But unions and management were relatively early adopters of a private system of dispute resolution: a multi-step grievance procedure culminating in a final, binding arbitration.[1]

A. Overview of the Grievance-Arbitration Process

Arbitration refers to a dispute-resolution system in which a neutral selected by both parties serves to resolve the dispute with a final, binding decision. It differs from mediation in that a mediator seeks to bring the parties to a mutually-agreeable settlement but has no power to impose a resolution. Arbitrators act as judges: they hear evidence, manage the hearing, make credibility assessments, and render a binding decision. It is in many ways a private judicial system.

In the United States, employers and labor unions included arbitration clauses in their agreements even before the enactment of the NLRA. The 1925 Federal Arbitration Act[2] requires federal courts (and, under later interpretations, state courts) to enforce agreements to arbitrate as they would any other contract. With the rise of unions

[1] This Chapter does not discuss arbitration between employers and individual employees outside of the union context. In Gilmer v. Interstate/Johnson Lane Corp., 500 U.S. 20 (1991), the Supreme Court upheld a contract requiring non-union employees to arbitrate statutory discrimination claims. In 14 Penn Plaza LLC v. Pyett, 556 U.S. 247 (2009), the Court extended *Gilmer* to collective bargaining agreements requiring arbitration of individual employee's statutory employment claims. See Section D below.

[2] United States Arbitration Act (now Federal Arbitration Act) of 1925, Pub. L. 68–401, 43 Stat. 883, (February 12, 1925), codified at 9 U.S.C. § 1 et seq.

and collective bargaining first during and after World War I and then during the New Deal, negotiated grievance procedures culminating in final, binding arbitration became increasingly commonplace. Today, almost all CBAs include some form of grievance-arbitration process as the method of dispute resolution.

The grievance-arbitration process is so named because of the "grievance" that must be filed to begin the dispute resolution process.[3] The grievance is similar to a complaint in litigation or a charge filed at the NLRB, although often less formal. The grievance indicates that the grievant believes the CBA has been violated by the actions of the other party. Generally, only unions or employers can file a grievance. Unions often file grievances on behalf of represented employees who have been subject to workplace discipline or termination allegedly in violation of the contract. Other grievances include contract claims, as for example, where an employer has assigned work claimed by the bargaining unit to other workers or third parties. The union is the party to the CBA and decides whether to file a grievance and pursue it to arbitration. If the union chooses not to file a grievance on behalf of the employee, the employee may have a claim against the union for violating its duty of fair representation to the employee, as well as a possible contract action against the employer. This duty of fair representation is discussed further in Chapter 12.

Unions historically have favored arbitration because of the costs of bringing a contract action in the courts as well as concern over the bias of judges. Because arbitrators are jointly selected by the union and the employer, arbitrators will not be chosen unless they are acceptable to both parties. Arbitration also provides the parties with an opportunity to continue the bargaining process and fill gaps left open by the CBA in a private and mutual process. Employers generally agree to arbitration of disputes arising under the CBA as an alternative to other forms of conflict, such as a strike over such disputes in the middle of the contract term.

Arbitrators are also thought to have special expertise concerning what the Supreme Court has called "the common law of the shop."[4] The reference here is to the implied assumptions of the parties in their CBA and the customary norms of labor and management

---

[3] This Chapter addresses "rights arbitration," the arbitration of disputes arising under CBAs. This is to be distinguished from "interest arbitration," where arbitrators resolve bargaining disputes over the content of initial or renewal collective agreements. In the U.S. private sector, interest arbitration is rare. In the public sector it is more common because strikes are generally unlawful and interest arbitration provides a neutral mechanism for resolving bargaining deadlocks.

[4] United Steelworkers of America v. Warrior & Gulf Navigation Co., 363 U.S. 574, 579 (1960).

relations. In some cases, arbitrators sit as umpires for the parties for an extended period of time and come to know the parties and their bargaining and grievance history quite well. In most cases, arbitrators sit on an ad hoc basis but are likely aware of the pattern of arbitral outcomes and the principles arbitrators use in other cases. And because unions often give up the right to strike in exchange for a grievance-arbitration regime, the process allows the parties to work out specific CBA disagreements without the mutual pain of a work stoppage.

Arbitration is private dispute resolution, and in most contexts arbitral decisions remain private. In the labor field, however, there is a history of publication of arbitration awards, although both parties must consent to publication and the practice is by no means universal. Awards have no formal precedential effect, except perhaps if they involve the same CBA. Nevertheless, they provide a source of jurisprudence that helps inform how arbitrators will decide cases.

A number of topics recur in the decisions. Given the frequency of employee grievances over discipline, numerous arbitrators have wrestled with the meaning of "just cause" and subsidiary issues. Employees may have engaged in some misconduct, but the question will often be whether the employer has consistently applied its rules, whether the employee was given sufficient notice, and whether a discharge rather than lesser discipline is appropriate. In one prominent case, the arbitrator determined that an employee could be fired immediately for "proven dishonesty" even when the conduct (a guilty plea to a burglary charge) happened off the job.[5] Arbitrators have had to resolve issues regarding the implementation of seniority provisions in the context of promotions or layoffs, especially when the seniority clause is mitigated by "relative ability" language. Subcontracting is another contentious issue that raises a number of potential questions: Is the subcontracting a breach of the CBA? Does contractual silence as to subcontracting implicitly prohibit such contracting, or does it allow management discretion? In one influential decision, the arbitrator ruled that CBA silence meant that only bad-faith subcontracting (i.e., to avoid the CBA's wage costs) was prohibited.[6]

Another source of controversy concerns the use of past practices in interpreting a CBA's requirements. The well-respected labor law professor and arbitrator Benjamin Aaron argued that the collective history of the parties will sometimes trump the clear language of the

---

5 Safeway Stores, Inc., 74 Lab. Arb. Rep. (BNA) 1293 (1980).

6 Allis-Chalmers Manufacturing Co., 39 Lab. Arb. Rep. (BNA) 1213 (1962).

agreement.[7] Other arbitrators take a more text-bound approach and hew closely to the CBA's written language.

B. Arbitration and the Courts

1. The *Steelworkers* Trilogy

Although common law courts were hostile to arbitration, whether in labor disputes or other contexts, federal judges since the enactment of the NLRA have been quite supportive of the process. An understanding of the jurisprudence surrounding labor arbitration must begin with § 301 of the Labor Management Relations Act (LMRA or Taft-Hartley). Section 301 provides federal courts with jurisdiction to hear disputes involving claimed violations of CBAs. In *Textile Workers Union v. Lincoln Mills of Alabama*,[8] the Supreme Court held that § 301 also empowered the courts to apply a newly-minted federal common law to be "fashion[ed] from the policy of our national labor laws."[9] In that case, the union had filed suit to compel the employer to arbitrate a set of grievances involving workloads and work assignments. The CBA included a no-strike provision, and the Court stated that "the agreement to arbitrate disputes is the *quid pro quo* for an agreement not to strike."[10] The Court held that an injunction was proper notwithstanding the text of the Norris-LaGuardia Act. The Court reasoned that the "congressional policy in favor of the enforcement of agreements to arbitrate grievance disputes" essentially trumped the "literal reading" of the statute.[11]

Lincoln Mills was the beginning of the Supreme Court's foray into the enforcement of collective bargaining agreements. Because arbitration is so central to CBA enforcement, however, much of the Court's jurisprudence in the area is devoted to the allocation of power between arbitrators and courts. In a set of cases all decided on the same day known as the *Steelworkers* Trilogy, the Court established the primacy of arbitration as the method by which disputes under CBAs were to be resolved. Authored by Justice Douglas, who also wrote the *Lincoln Mills* decision, the *Steelworkers* Trilogy is a paean to the role of arbitration within industrial relations. In each of the

---

7 Benjamin Aaron, The Uses of the Past in Arbitration, in Arbitration Today: Proc. 8th Ann. Mtg., Natl. Acad. of Arbitrators 1, 3–7 (J. McKelvey ed. 1955).

8 353 U.S. 448 (1957).

9 Id. at 456. State courts retain jurisdiction over actions brought under § 301, but they are required to apply federal law. Local 174, Teamsters v. Lucas Flour Co., 369 U.S. 95 (1962). One reason the Court recognized a federal substantive law under § 301 may have to been to bypass the common law rule that executory agreements to arbitrate were not enforceable. See Red Cross Line v. Atlantic Fruit Co., 264 U.S. 109 (1924).

10 *Lincoln Mills*, 353 U.S. at 455.

11 Id. at 458–59.

cases, lower courts had taken issues away from arbitrators and resolved the disputes independently. In each one, the Court returned the power to the arbitrators.

In *United Steelworkers of America v. American Manufacturing Co. (Steelworkers I)*,[12] a worker who had been injured on the job sought to return to work under the CBA. The employer, however, refused to accept him back for employment because he had settled a workers' compensation claim on the basis that he was permanently partially disabled. His disability, argued the employer, rendered him unfit to perform the job. The union filed a grievance on the worker's behalf and then sought to compel arbitration. When the employer refused, the union brought suit under § 301. The court of appeals affirmed the district court's dismissal of the case on the ground that the grievance was frivolous, invoking a state-law doctrine that equity would not compel the doing of a frivolous act.[13] The Supreme Court reversed. It was not the role of courts, reasoned the Court, to determine the substantive merits of the claim: "The agreement is to submit all grievances to arbitration, not merely those which the court deem meritorious."[14] The Court placed particular weight on several provisions in the CBA: (a) the arbitration clause, which referred to arbitration of "[a]ny disputes, misunderstandings, differences or grievances . . . as to the meaning, interpretation and application of the provisions of this agreement," (b) the termination and discipline provision, which allowed management to take action against employees "for cause," and (c) the no-strike clause. As the Court noted, "[t]here is no exception in the 'no strike' clause and none therefore should be read into the grievance clause, since one is quid pro quo for the other."[15] Moreover, "[t]he processing of even frivolous claims may have therapeutic values of which those who are not part of the plant environment may be quite unaware."[16]

The Court elaborated on its presumption of arbitrability in *United Steelworkers of America v. Warrior & Gulf Navigation Co. (Steelworkers II)*.[17] In that case, the grievance challenged the company's subcontracting of unit work. Invoking language in the CBA that stated "matters which are strictly a function of

---

12 363 U.S. 564 (1960).

13 United Steelworkers of Am. v. American Mfg. Co., 264 F.2d 624, 628 (6th Cir. 1959), rev'd, 363 U.S. 564 (1960).

14 *Steelworkers I*, 363 U.S. at 568. The Court's opinion singled out a New York state appellate decision for the contrary view. See International Assn. of Machinists v. Cutler-Hammer, Inc., 271 App.Div. 917, 67 N.Y.S.2d 317, affirmed, 297 N.Y. 519, 74 N.E.2d 464 (1947).

15 *Steelworkers I*, 363 U.S. at 567.

16 Id. at 568.

17 363 U.S. 574 (1960).

management shall not be subject to arbitration,"[18] the employer refused to submit the dispute to arbitration. The Supreme Court held that the grievance was arbitrable because it came within the parties' otherwise broad arbitration clause, and the exclusion for "matters which are strictly a function of management" was not self-defining and had to be strictly construed as referring "only to that over which the contract gives management complete control and unfettered discretion."[19] The Court explained: "In the absence of any express provision excluding a particular grievance from arbitration, we think only the most forceful evidence of a purpose to exclude the claim from arbitration can prevail."[20]

Courts, of course, must decide whether the parties agreed to arbitrate the particular dispute.[21] But under the *Trilogy*, they must approach the question with a strong presumption of arbitrability. If the CBA has not yet been ratified or has expired, its arbitration provisions are not binding during such hiatus. Courts generally determine the date on which the contract was formed or renewed in order to determine when the arbitration clause becomes binding.[22] Although the arbitration clause does not survive the expiration date of the contract absent evidence of a status-quo agreement, the parties' agreement to arbitrate still covers disputes that arose under the CBA prior to expiration.[23] According to the Court, "[a] post expiration grievance can be said to arise under the contract only where it involves facts and occurrences that arose before expiration, where an action taken after expiration infringes a right that accrued or vested under the agreement, or where, under normal principles of contract interpretation, the disputed contractual right survives expiration of the remainder of the agreement."[24]

The final leg of the *Steelworkers Trilogy* involved the scope of judicial review of an arbitration award. In *United Steelworkers of*

---

18 Id. at 575.

19 Id. at 584.

20 Id. at 584–85.

21 Whether the parties reached an agreement to arbitrate the particular dispute is a question of "substantive arbitrability" for the courts. By contrast, the determination whether the procedural prerequisites to arbitration have been met, such as compliance with filing periods, waiver, laches, and limitations periods, are issues of "procedural arbitrability" for the arbitrator. These procedural matters are often tied up with the merits and assume there is underlying agreement to arbitrate. See Operating Engineers Local 150 v. Flair Builders, 406 U.S. 487 (1972).

22 Granite Rock Co. v. Teamsters, 561 U.S. 287 (2010).

23 Litton Fin. Printing Div., a Div. of Litton Bus. Sys., Inc. v. NLRB, 501 U.S. 190, 203–04 (1991) (discussing and citing Nolde Bros., Inc. v. Bakery Workers, 430 U.S. 243 (1977)). In *Nolde Brothers*, the Court held that grievances about severance pay should proceed to arbitration even after the expiration of the CBA because the rights to severance arose under the CBA. Id. at 248–49.

24 *Litton*, 501 U.S. at 205–06.

America v. Enterprise Wheel & Car Corp.,[25] the court of appeals refused to enforce an award because it provided back pay for a period after the expiration of the CBA. The Supreme Court reversed: "The refusal of courts to review the merits of an arbitration award is the proper approach to arbitration under collective bargaining agreements."[26] An award is to be enforced by the courts so long as it "draws its essence from the collective bargaining agreement."[27] After *Enterprise Wheel*, it is difficult to challenge a labor arbitration award except in rare circumstances where the arbitrator is relying on a source external to the collective agreement and the parties' related course of dealing under that agreement.

2. "Public Policy" Exception

One recurring issue concerns the extent to which arbitral awards must conform to external legal requirements. Under *Enterprise Wheel*, the arbitrator may not base his or her decision on sources external to the CBA, yet awards that violate external law are not enforceable. In *W.R. Grace & Co. v. Rubber Workers*,[28] the Court held that an arbitrator's award should be enforced unless it violated a "well-defined and dominant" public policy that was "ascertained by reference to . . . laws and legal precedents and not from general considerations of supposed public interests."[29] The Court elaborated on this standard in *United Paperworkers International Union v. Misco*,[30] in which the arbitrator required the employer to reinstate an employee who had been found in a car in the company parking lot with a lit marijuana cigarette. After the court of appeals refused to enforce the award on grounds of public policy, the Supreme Court reversed. It held that the lower court had failed to show that the award conflicted with "a well-defined and dominant [public] policy."[31] The Court left open whether the only ground for refusing to enforce an award on public-policy grounds was that the award itself violates a statute, regulation, or other manifestation of positive law, or compels conduct by the employer that would violate such a law.

The public-policy exception was again at issue in *Eastern Associated Coal Corp. v. United Mine Workers, District 17*.[32] The employer had terminated a worker after two positive drug tests within a sixteen-month period, but the arbitrator had ordered

---

[25] 363 U.S. 593 (1960).

[26] Id. at 596.

[27] Id. at 597.

[28] 461 U.S. 757 (1983).

[29] Id. at 766.

[30] 484 U.S. 29 (1987).

[31] Id. at 44.

[32] 531 U.S. 57 (2000).

reinstatement if certain conditions were met.[33] The lower courts, perhaps learning the lesson of *Misco*, enforced the arbitral award, and the Supreme Court affirmed. The Court specified that "courts' authority to invoke the public policy exception is not limited solely to instances where the arbitration award itself violates positive law."[34] However, the Court confirmed that the public-policy exception was "narrow" and urged "particular caution" in its application.[35] The employer had identified specific areas of public policy as embodied in federal transportation regulations, which were particularly apt since they regulated the employer's business.[36] But the federal regulatory scheme did not require the employee's dismissal, and the arbitrator's award was consistent with aspects of the federal rule that addressed counseling and continued testing.

3. No-Strike Clauses

Courts have generally viewed arbitration clauses as a tradeoff accepted by employers in exchange for a "no strike" clause from the union. To what extent are no-strike clauses enforceable in federal courts under the Norris-LaGuardia Act's prohibition against injunctions in labor disputes? In *Sinclair Refining Co. v. Atkinson*,[37] the Supreme Court initially ruled that federal courts could not enjoin a peaceful strike even if in violation of a no-strike agreement. Eight years later, the Court reversed course in *Boys Markets, Inc. v. Retail Clerks Union, Local 770*[38] and held that an injunction to halt a strike was impliedly permitted by Norris-LaGuardia. Because the no-strike clause was the *quid pro quo* for the arbitration agreement, the Court explained, "[a]ny incentive for employers to enter into such an arrangement is necessarily dissipated if the principal and most expeditious method by which the no-strike obligation can be enforced is eliminated."[39] Damages would often be insufficient on their own to properly enforce a no-strike clause. The Court emphasized that this exception to Norris-LaGuardia was a narrow one, that the traditional requirements for equitable relief (probable success on the merits, inadequacy of the legal remedy, and irreparable injury) still applied,

---

[33] The arbitrator's conditional reinstatement award required the employee to accept a three-month suspension, reimburse the employer and the union for the costs of arbitration, and continue to participate in substance abuse counseling and random drug testing. Id. at 60.

[34] Id. at 63.

[35] Id.

[36] See id. at 63–64 (discussing the Omnibus Transportation Employee Testing Act of 1991 and the U.S. Department of Transportation's implementing regulations).

[37] 370 U.S. 195 (1962).

[38] 398 U.S. 235 (1970).

[39] Id. at 248.

and that the employer could be ordered to arbitrate as a condition of obtaining an injunction against the strike.[40]

The underlying dispute in *Boys Markets* over which the union was threatening to strike was arbitrable; in essence, the union was striking to compel a result outside of the arbitration process. The Court made clear, however, in *Buffalo Forge Co. v. United Steelworkers of America*[41] that the arbitrability of the dispute was a condition of obtaining a *Boys Markets* injunction. In that case, the union arguably violated the contract's no-strike clause in observing another union's picket line. But because the union's strike was in support of a sister union's picket line, it was not striking over an arbitrable dispute, even if the strike was in breach of the CBA.

In *Jacksonville Bulk Terminals, Inc. v. International Longshoreman's Association*,[42] the Supreme Court held that Norris-LaGuardia barred an injunction to compel the union to end its refusal to handle any cargo going to or from the Soviet Union in protest of the Soviet invasion of Afghanistan. Since the underlying dispute was not arbitrable under the CBA, the *Boys Market* exception did not apply.[43]

Unions may pursue "reverse" *Boys Markets* injunctions to preserve the status quo pending arbitration. Although the Supreme Court has not squarely ruled on the issue, the consensus among courts of appeals is that injunctions against employer conduct are appropriate when "necessary to prevent conduct by the party enjoined from rendering the arbitral process a hollow formality."[44] Such circumstances may include such dramatic changes as a plant closing in violation of a successorship clause, but they do not generally include injunctions against employee discharges where an arbitral order of reinstatement with back pay is considered sufficient.[45]

---

[40] See id. at 253.

[41] 428 U.S. 397 (1976).

[42] 457 U.S. 702 (1982).

[43] Id. at 703. Strikes in bargaining conflicts, including strikes not called or condoned by the union, are also generally not strikes over arbitrable disputes. Hence, they would not be enjoinable under *Buffalo Forge*. See Complete Auto Transit, Inc. v. Reis, 614 F.2d 1110, 1114 (6th Cir. 1980), affirmed on other grounds, 451 U.S. 401 (1981).

[44] Lever Bros. Co. v. Chemical Workers Local 217, 554 F.2d 115, 123 (4th Cir. 1976) (plant relocation).

[45] See, e.g., Aluminum Workers, Local Union No. 215 v. Consolidated Aluminum Corp., 696 F.2d 437 (6th Cir. 1982) (vacating injunction against discharges when the district court "fail[ed] to explain why loss of job opportunities and wages constitute irreparable harm").

Although injunctions are available against unions only under limited circumstances, unions are liable for damages under § 301 of the LMRA when they violate the CBA. This liability has two important provisos. First, individual employees are not liable for damages arising from their union's breach of a no-strike clause.[46] Second, unions are only liable if the action can be attributed to the organization by the union's conduct or ratification. In *Carbon Fuel Co. v. United Mine Workers*,[47] the Supreme Court held that the international union was not liable for "wildcat" strikes unauthorized by the union if it had not "instigated, supported, ratified, or encouraged any of the work stoppages."[48]

C. Arbitration and the NLRB

The NLRB does not have authority over CBA violations as such, but there are occasions in which a potential CBA violation will overlap with an alleged unfair labor practice. Two common instances of such overlap include: (1) a dispute over the meaning of or change to the CBA that may raise contractual as well as § 8(a)(5) unfair bargaining claims, and (2) employee discipline or termination for allegedly discriminatory reasons that may violate the CBA as well as §§ 8(a)(1) and/or (3). But overlap may arise in other cases as well.

In *NLRB v. C&C Plywood*,[49] the Supreme Court held that the Board had authority to interpret the CBA in order to determine whether the employer had made a unilateral change violating § 8(d) and thus had committed a § 8(a)(5) ULP. The Board need not wait for an arbitrator's decision about the meaning of a CBA provision in making its own determination of whether a ULP has occurred.[50] Instead, the Board could proceed on its own.

But should it? Whether the Board would wait for an arbitrator to decide and then defer to that decision had been the subject of considerable debate. The Board has largely resolved these issues with twin policies that favor deference to arbitration. The policy of postponing Board action in the midst of a pending arbitration is referred to as *Collyer* deferral, based on the Board's decision in *Collyer Insulated Wire*.[51] And the policy of deferring to an arbitration award once it has issued is known as *Spielberg* deference, based on *Spielberg Manufacturing Co.*[52] In effect, the Board generally will hold

---

[46] 29 U.S.C. § 185(b).

[47] 444 U.S. 212 (1979).

[48] Id. at 218.

[49] 385 U.S. 421 (1967).

[50] NLRB v. Acme Industrial Co., 385 U.S. 432 (1967).

[51] 192 NLRB 837 (1971).

[52] 112 NLRB 1080 (1955).

off resolving cases that are subject to a pending arbitration, and then will defer to the arbitrator's resolution in most circumstances.

In *United Technologies Corp.*,[53] the Board settled on the *Collyer* policy of pre-arbitral deferral for all claims that could be considered by an arbitrator. Prior to *United Technologies*, the Board had oscillated between a policy of deferral only for bargaining disputes that alleged a § 8(a)(5) claim, and a broader policy of deferral for all arbitrable claims. The Board finally settled on the latter approach, concluding that the benefits of arbitration extended broadly.

In *Collyer* deferral cases, the Board orders the charging party to bring the claim to the grievance-arbitration process and retains jurisdiction over the ULP charge. The Board will rescind the deferral if either the dispute is not resolved "with reasonable promptness" after the issuance of the Board's deferral order or if the arbitration process has resulted in an outcome that is "repugnant to the Act."[54] If the process has already been initiated, the Board will hold the charges in abeyance under the policy set forth in *Dubo Manufacturing*.[55]

After the arbitrator has issued an award, the Board under *Spielberg* generally will defer to an arbitration result when the proceedings appear to have been fair and regular, all parties had agreed to be bound to the arbitral award, and the decision of the arbitrator is not clearly repugnant to the purposes and policies of the Act.[56] In its 1984 decision in *Olin Corp.*,[57] the Board confirmed that *Spielberg* deference is appropriate only where "an arbitrator has adequately considered the unfair labor practice if (1) the contractual issue is factually parallel to the unfair labor practice issue, and (2) the arbitrator was presented generally with the facts relevant to resolving the unfair labor practice."[58] Moreover, the arbitrator's award need not be "totally consistent" with Board precedent. "Unless the award is 'palpably wrong,' i.e., unless the arbitrator's decision is not susceptible to an interpretation consistent with the Act, we will defer."[59]

In 2014, the Obama Administration Board in *Babcock & Wilcox Construction Co., Inc.*,[60] ruled that the proponent of deferral would

---

53 268 NLRB 557 (1984).

54 Id. at 561.

55 142 NLRB 431 (1963).

56 *Spielberg*, 112 NLRB at 1082.

57 268 NLRB 573 (1984).

58 Id. at 574.

59 Id.

60 361 NLRB 1127 (2014).

have to "demonstrate that the parties presented the statutory issue to the arbitrator, the arbitrator considered the statutory issue or was prevented from doing so by the party opposing deferral, and Board law reasonably permits the award."[61] This, too, has been a subject of oscillation with each change in administration.[62]

D. Arbitration of Individual Statutory Employment Claims Under Union Auspices

One additional piece of the labor arbitration puzzle involves the arbitrability of individual statutory employment claims that do not arise under the NLRA. Such claims often derive from the antidiscrimination statutes that protect employees against discharge or discipline based on race, ethnicity, sex, age, or disability. In *Gilmer v. Interstate/Johnson Lane Corp.*,[63] the employee alleged that his termination resulted from age discrimination in violation of the Age Discrimination in Employment Act (ADEA).[64] The Court enforced an arbitration agreement between an employer and individual employees directing that any claims related to employment were to be resolved through arbitration.[65] Although the Court retained its settled precedent that employees cannot waive their statutory rights through a contract with the employer,[66] the *Gilmer* Court concluded that arbitration was not a waiver of the employee's claims, but rather a choice by the parties to resolve their disputes in a different forum.[67] In employment, as in a variety of other contexts, arbitration was seen as an appropriate way for the parties to handle their contractual disputes.

Given that employees are free to arbitrate their statutory claims individually, it may seem natural for them to arbitrate such claims with the assistance of union representation. But in the earlier case of *Alexander v. Gardner-Denver Co.*,[68] the Court had held that a union and employer through their CBA could not force arbitration of an

---

61 Id. at 1128.

62 See United Parcel Service, Inc., 369 NLRB No. 1 (Dec. 23, 2019) (returning to the *Olin* test), aff'd in part and vacated and remanded in part, Atkinson v. NLRB, No. 20–1680, 2021 WL 5204015 (3d Cir. Nov. 9, 2021) (unpublished); United Parcel Service, Inc., 372 NLRB No. 158 (Nov. 21, 2023) (returning to *Babcock & Wilcox*).

63 500 U.S. 20 (1991).

64 29 U.S.C. § 621 et seq.

65 The New York Stock Exchange required the employer to adopt the arbitration system as a condition of being licensed as a registered representative under the stock exchange's rules. *Gilmer*, 500 U.S. at 23. See generally Samuel Estreicher, The Story of *Gilmer v. Interstate/Johnson Lane Corp.*: The Emergence of Employment Arbitration, in Employment Law Stories, ch. 8 (Samuel Estreicher & Gillian Lester eds. 2007).

66 See Alexander v. Gardner-Denver Co., 415 U.S. 36 (1974).

67 *Gilmer*, 500 U.S. at 35.

68 415 U.S. 36 (1974).

individual's statutory claim under Title VII of the 1964 Civil Rights Act.[69] The Court's opinion in *Gilmer* had distinguished *Gardner-Denver* on the grounds that the union was the party to the arbitration agreement, rather than the individual employee.[70] Subsequently, however, the Court modified its course from *Gardner-Denver* in *14 Penn Plaza LLC v. Pyett*.[71] The CBA in *14 Penn Plaza* was negotiated between Local 32BJ of the SEIU and NYC's Realty Advisory Board (RAB). One of the CBA's provisions, entitled "NO DISCRIMINATION," prohibited discrimination and required that "[a]ll such claims shall be subject to the [contract's] grievance and arbitration procedures . . . as the sole and exclusive remedy for violations."[72] A group of workers brought grievances alleging violations of the CBA, including age discrimination. The union later withdrew these claims from the arbitration process, and the employees filed age discrimination charges, under the federal Age Discrimination in Employment (ADEA) law, with the relevant federal administrative agency. The employer then filed suit in federal district court seeking to compel arbitration of the ADEA claims. The court of appeals, citing *Gardner-Denver*, ruled that a CBA could not waive the workers' rights to a judicial forum for statutory causes of action. The Supreme Court reversed, holding that "a collective-bargaining agreement that clearly and unmistakably requires union members to arbitrate [statutory age discrimination] claims is enforceable as a matter of law."[73] In *Gardner-Denver*, it was not clear whether the arbitrator had the authority to hear the statutory discrimination claim, whereas this authority was present in the *14 Penn Plaza* collective agreement.

The Court did not resolve what happens if the union chooses not to take a statutory discrimination claim to arbitration. Can the individual employee be barred from a court remedy in such circumstances? The *14 Penn Plaza Court* stated that "although a substantive waiver of federally protected civil rights will not be upheld, we are not positioned to resolve in the first instance whether the CBA allows the Union to prevent respondents from 'effectively vindicating' their 'federal statutory rights in an arbitral forum.' "[74] It would seem doubtful that the union could bar resort to a statutory remedy without allowing the case to go to arbitration. The majority did acknowledge that union intransigence or discrimination against individual employee claims could potentially violate the union's duty

---

69 42 U.S.C. § 2000e et seq.

70 *Gilmer*, 500 U.S. at 34–35.

71 556 U.S. 247 (2009).

72 Id. at 252 (quoting the CBA).

73 Id. at 274.

74 Id. at 273 (quotations and citation omitted).

of fair representation or the antidiscrimination statutes themselves.[75]

[75] Id. at 271–72. See generally Terry McGinniss & Paul Salvatore, The *Pyett* Protocol: Collectively-Bargained Grievance Arbitration as a Forum for Individual Statutory Employment Claims, in Beyond Elite Law: Access to Civil Justice in America, ch. 42 (Samuel Estreicher & Joy Radice eds. 2016).

Chapter 10

LABOR LAW AND BUSINESS CHANGE

A. Labor Law Obligations

Labor law is about the relationships between various legally-defined entities: an employer, a union, and a bargaining unit of employees. In this Chapter, we consider how a change in the employer's ownership or other legal status affects a preexisting collective-bargaining relationship.

In almost all cases, the "employer" will be a legal entity—often a corporation, either publicly or privately held, or perhaps an LLC or partnership. These organizations are generally created through state law provisions that require only the basics to get started. As such, it can be relatively easy for the underlying legal entity to change without any real change in the ongoing business. Imagine that the shareholders of ABC Corporation, a privately held company, create a new corporation, XYZ Inc., and transfer all of ABC's business and assets to XYZ. Nothing may have happened other than the creation of a small stack of paperwork, but the employees now work for a new entity. Can that entity claim that it no longer has any bargaining obligation to the employees' exclusive representative? The answer should clearly be no. The Board has held that bargaining obligations transfer to all "alter egos" of the original entity.[1] Alter-ego entities are those that are "substantially identical" to the original entities, and the Board looks at the two entities' management, business purpose, operating equipment, customers, and supervision as well as common ownership.[2] The purpose behind the creation of the new entity is also relevant to the Board—for example, if the new entity was formed merely to avoid collective bargaining obligations. But the Board treats the employer's purpose as only one factor among many.[3]

---

[1] See Southport Petroleum Corp. v. NLRB, 315 U.S. 100, 106 (1942) (noting that a new company should not be able to evade its labor law obligations if it is "merely a disguised continuance of the old employer").

[2] These are known as the "*Crawford Door*" factors. Crawford Door Sales Co., 226 NLRB 1144 (1976); see also Advance Electric, 268 NLRB 1001, 1002 (1984); Newark Elec. Corp., Newark Elec. 2.0, Inc., & Colacino Indus., Inc., 362 NLRB 345 (2015), vacated by Newark Elec. Corp. v. NLRB, No. 15–1111, 2017 WL 5662145 (D.C. Cir. July 14, 2017). This is also similar to the "single employer" doctrine encountered in connection with union secondary boycotts in Chapter 8.

[3] The courts are split over whether the alter-ego doctrine requires finding an intent on the employer's part to avoid the requirements of the preexisting CBA or the NLRA. See, e.g., Penntech Papers, Inc. v. NLRB, 706 F.2d 18, 24 (1st Cir. 1983). Some courts look to see if there is a reasonably foreseeable legal benefit to the business change, Alkire v. NLRB, 716 F.2d 1014 (4th Cir. 1983), or simply use the Board's test

Under the NLRA, alter egos are treated as the equivalent of the original employer entity and have all of the rights and responsibilities that the original entity had.[4]

When an employer with an existing collective bargaining relationship merges with another company, the new merged entity likely assumes the obligations of the CBA. In *John Wiley & Sons, Inc. v. Livingston*,[5] the Supreme Court held that a merger does not automatically terminate all rights of the employees covered by a preexisting collective agreement, even if that employer no longer exists as an entity. Instead, in appropriate circumstances, the contract continues to exist and the successor employer must arbitrate with the union under the agreement. The circumstances in *Wiley* demonstrated a continuity of the employees' interests: the new company retained all of the merged company's employees and operated the enterprise in a substantially identical manner. The union was therefore able to enforce the agreement through a § 301 action and compel arbitration. Although a company's successor labor obligations are a question of federal law, the *Wiley* Court's treatment of merged companies follows the rules of traditional state corporate law, which generally provides that all premerger assets and liabilities of the original company (including ongoing contractual relationships) become assets and liabilities of the surviving company after the merger.[6]

The Board and the courts draw a distinction between a sale of a company's stock and a sale of a company's assets. Sales of a company through stock purchases, such as through a tender offer, are treated similarly to mergers: there is a strong presumption that the purchaser of the company assumes the CBA and any bargaining obligations with the union. This presumption can be overcome where the purchaser's operations are substantially different than the seller's and the seller's workforce is merged with a much larger workforce not represented by the seller's union or represented by a different union. Assets sales are treated differently both under state law and the NLRA. In *Howard Johnson Co. v. Hotel & Restaurant Employees*,[7] the Supreme Court made clear that the mere purchase

---

as one factor in the mix, Stardyne, Inc. v. NLRB, 41 F.3d 141 (3d Cir. 1994). See generally Drew Willis & Richard A. Bales, Narrowing Successorship: The Alter Ego Doctrine and the Role of Intent, 8 DePaul Bus. & Com. L.J. 151, 153 (2010).

[4] *Newark Elec. Corp.*, 362 NLRB at 354 ("The Board and the courts have applied the alter ego doctrine in those situations where one employer entity will be regarded as a continuation of a predecessor, and the two will be treated interchangeably for purposes of applying labor laws.").

[5] 376 U.S. 543, 548 (1964).

[6] See, e.g., Revised Model Bus. Corp. Act § 11.07(a)(3)–(4); Del. Code Ann. tit. 8, § 259(a).

[7] 417 U.S. 249 (1974).

of all of the predecessor's assets will not create continuing bargaining obligations.[8] In that case, the purchaser hired 45 employees in total, only nine of whom were employees of the predecessor. None of the seller's supervisors were brought over. Under these circumstances, the buyer had no obligation with the union and was not bound by the seller's unexpired CBA. The union may have had a contract claim against the seller under the CBA's successorship clause, but it had no claim against the purchaser.[9]

In cases where the new employer has not taken over the seller's business operations but has hired a majority of its employees from the ranks of the seller's employees, the purchaser will have a bargaining obligation with the seller's union but no duty to maintain the seller's unexpired CBA. In *NLRB v. Burns International Security Services, Inc.*,[10] the Wackenhut Corporation had provided security services for a Lockheed plant for five years. A few months before Wackenhut's contract with Lockheed was to expire, its employees selected union representation, and the company and union negotiated a collective bargaining agreement. Soon thereafter, Lockheed selected Burns International Security Services over Wackenhut for the plant security contract. Burns kept 27 of the guards who had been with Wackenhut and added another 15 to the unit. It then required the Lockheed employees to join a different union, one which already had a relationship with Burns, and refused to negotiate with the prior union. The Board ruled that Burns had violated § 8(a)(2) by giving assistance to the union with which it had a prior relationship, a charge to which Burns eventually acceded. The Board also determined that Burns had violated § 8(a)(5) by failing to negotiate with the prior union and failing to adhere to the Wackenhut CBA.

The Supreme Court held that Burns did in fact have an obligation to bargain with Wackenhut's prior union because it hired a so-called "successor majority"—a majority of its employees from the Wackenhut workforce—and there was no reason to believe that the bargaining unit had changed. The Court explained that "where the bargaining unit remains unchanged and a majority of the employees hired by the new employer are represented by a recently certified

---

8 An assets purchaser may, however, end up assuming a seller's unremedied ULPs. In Golden State Bottling Co. v. NLRB, 414 U.S. 168 (1973), the assets purchaser continued the business without substantial change and was aware of the pending Board proceeding at the time of purchase.

9 The Court distinguished *Wiley* on the grounds that in *Wiley*, the surviving corporation had kept the same business going with all of the predecessor's employees, while in *Howard Johnson*, only twenty percent of the employees came from the prior employer. *Howard Johnson*, 417 U.S. at 256–60.

10 406 U.S. 272 (1972).

bargaining agent, there is little basis for faulting the Board's implementation of the express mandates of § 8(a)(5) and § 9(a) by ordering the employer to bargain with the incumbent union."[11] On the other hand, the Court disagreed with the Board when it came to the ongoing vitality of the Wackenhut-negotiated CBA. According to the Court, Burns had no obligation to follow that CBA, nor did Burns have to use the terms and conditions in the CBA to define the status quo for purposes of bargaining with the union. The Court distinguished its earlier holding in *Wiley* in part by noting that Burns did not merge with Wackenhut, but they were rather "competitors for the same work" that had no organizational or contractual affiliation.[12]

In *Fall River Dyeing & Finishing Corp. v. NLRB*,[13] the prior employer (Sterlingware) had gone out of business, and Fall River Dyeing & Finishing bought key Sterlingware assets and built up its production capabilities over time. In September 1982, it hired its initial employees; by January 1983, it attained its initial goal of one shift and began production. At this point, a majority of Fall River's employees were former Sterlingware employees. When Fall River further expanded to two shifts by mid-April, however, former Sterlingware employees dropped to just below a majority (52 or 53 out of 107). The Sterlingware employees had been represented by a union, which petitioned for recognition in October 1982, but Fall River refused the request.

In *Fall River*, the Supreme Court held that the obligation to recognize and bargain with the union carries over when a majority of the new employer's workforce is comprised of the old employer's employees doing the same work. Fall River had an obligation to bargain with the union even if it was not bound to the prior CBA. The Court also clarified some issues stemming from *Burns*. First, the Court made clear that "a successor's obligation to bargain is not limited to a situation where the union in question has been recently certified."[14] Second, the Court approved of the Board's method of choosing the relevant moment when to judge majority status. Fall River had started with almost all Sterlingware employees until, over time, it ended up with less than half of them. The Board had used a "substantial and representative complement" test to determine when the employee census should be taken. The Court described the test as the point in time "when all [the employer's] job classifications have been filled or substantially filled, when it has hired a majority of the

---

[11] Id. at 281.

[12] *Burns*, 406 U.S. at 286.

[13] 482 U.S. 27 (1987).

[14] Id. at 41.

employees it intends to hire, and when it has begun normal production."[15] The Court rejected the employer's "full complement" test that majority status could only be determined after the complete workforce had been hired. Such an approach, in the Court's view, would delay the representation relationship and could demoralize carryover employees. Applying the Board's approach, the Court agreed that a "substantial and representative complement" had been hired as of January 1983, when a majority of Fall River's employees had been with Sterlingware and presumably continued to support the union.[16] Finally, the Court approved of the Board's "continuing demand" presumption, which provides that "when a union has made a premature demand that has been rejected by the employer, this demand remains in force until the moment when the employer attains the substantial and representative complement."[17] The Court believed that the rule put a "minimal burden" on the successor employer and made sense in light of the employer's better information about when it had begun normal production.

The upshot of these successor decisions is to place a great deal of weight on whether a majority of the new employer's workforce is drawn from the unionized predecessor's workforce. Under *Burns*, the new employer has a right to hire its own workforce, but any discriminatory hiring on the basis of union status would violate § 8(a)(3). The predecessor's workforce represents an experienced group of people doing much the same work as the new employer contemplates; a refusal to hire these workers may be an indication of discrimination. Nor can an employer avoid a successorship determination by assigning the predecessor's employees a temporary or probationary status in the successor's work force.[18] Even if the employer retains the predecessor's employees for a period of time only because a provision of the contract of sale or a non-preempted state or local statute requires it to do so, the Board still looks primarily at the ratio of predecessor employees within the successor's workforce.[19]

To establish a violation of § 8(a)(3) in the successorship context, the General Counsel has the burden to prove that the employer failed to hire employees of its predecessor because they were represented

---

15 Id. at 50.

16 Note that the critical inquiry is "whether a majority of the successor's employees were those of the predecessor," not "whether the successor had hired a majority of the predecessor's employees." Id. at 46 n.12.

17 Id. at 52.

18 GVS Properties, LLC, 362 NLRB 1771, 1774 (2015), vacated 2017 WL 1462124, N.L.R.B., Apr. 20, 2017.

19 Id. at 1776 (holding that successorship obligations may arise before the expiration of the statutory mandatory retention period).

by a union while working for the predecessor.[20] Under a version of *Wright Line*, if the General Counsel establishes this showing, the employer can then attempt to prove its affirmative defense—here, that it would not have hired the predecessor's employees even in the absence of its unlawful motive.

In situations where the successor has violated § 8(a)(3) by strategically failing to hire a majority of its predecessor's employees, the employer is also in violation of § 8(a)(5) for failing to recognize and bargain with the predecessor's union.[21] In contrast, such a discriminating successor does not violate § 8(a)(5) in setting initial terms and conditions of employment unless its hiring discrimination created such uncertainty as to make it impossible to determine whether the employer would have hired all or substantially all of the predecessor employees absent that discrimination.[22]

What if the employer hires a majority of workers from the prior unit, but a majority of workers in the new unit genuinely do not wish to have union representation? How long must the bargaining relationship continue? The Board's current rule imposes a "successorship bar" on challenges to the continuing relationship. As outlined in *UGL-UNICCO Service Co.*,[23] the successorship bar requires that "when a successor employer acts in accordance with its legal obligation to recognize an incumbent representative of its employees, the previously chosen representative is entitled to represent the employees in collective bargaining with their new employer for a reasonable period of time, without challenge to its representative status."[24] The effect of the bar is to create a nearly conclusive presumption of majority status for a reasonable period of time, one that prohibits any challenge to majority status through a decertification petition, poll, or withdrawal of recognition.

The definition of a "reasonable period of time" under the successorship-bar doctrine depends on the context. When the new employer has expressly adopted existing terms and conditions of employment as the starting point for bargaining, without making

---

20 See Planned Building Services, Inc., 347 NLRB 670, 673 (2006) (Board looks to "substantial evidence of union animus; lack of a convincing rationale for refusal to hire the predecessor's employees; inconsistent hiring practices or overt acts or conduct evidencing a discriminatory motive; and evidence supporting a reasonable inference that the new owner conducted its staffing in a manner precluding the predecessor's employees from being hired as a majority of the new owner's overall work force to avoid the Board's successorship doctrine.").

21 See Love's Barbeque Rest. No. 62, 245 NLRB 78 (1979), enforced in relevant part sub nom. Kallman v. NLRB, 640 F.2d 1094 (9th Cir. 1981).

22 See Galloway School Lines, Inc., 321 NLRB 1422 (1996).

23 357 NLRB 801 (2011).

24 Id. at 801.

unilateral changes, the bar will last for six months from the start of bargaining.[25] When, however, the new employer recognizes the union but at the same time unilaterally announces initial terms and conditions of employment before proceeding to bargain, the reasonable period of bargaining will be a minimum of six months and a maximum of one year. The Board also shortened the contract-bar doctrine to two years should the successor enter into a CBA with the union.[26] The reason for the shorter period is to "mitigate the possibility that consecutive application of the successor bar and contract bar doctrines will unduly burden employee free choice by leading to prolonged insulated periods."[27]

In late 2024 the Supreme Court vacated and remanded a D.C. Circuit opinion upholding the *UGL-UNICCO* approach for reconsideration in light of its intervening *Loper Bright* decision, where the Court held that courts decide the meaning of statutes without according any strong measure of deference to the agency's views.[28] This could signal a return to the approach prior to *UGL-UNICCO*, in which the Board found only a rebuttable presumption that the union continued to enjoy support.[29]

B. Bankruptcy

The federal bankruptcy system provides for the restructuring of existing obligations when the debtor is no longer able to meet those obligations. Chapter 11 of the Bankruptcy Code (Code) allows the corporation to avoid liquidation and carry on as a continuing business. In the process of reorganizing, the bankrupt firm may propose the modification or termination of ongoing contracts. In 1984, the Supreme Court in *NLRB v. Bildisco and Bildisco* interpreted the Code to permit a rejection of the CBA if the debtor showed that the CBA burdened the estate and, "after careful scrutiny, the equities balance in favor of rejecting the labor contract."[30] However, Congress shortly thereafter added § 1113 to the Code, requiring a court to find instead that "the balance of the

---

25 Id. at 809.

26 Id. at 810 ("We hold that where (1) a first contract is reached by the successor employer and the incumbent union within the reasonable period of bargaining during which the successor bar applied, and (2) there was no open period permitting the filing of a petition during the final year of the predecessor employer's bargaining relationship with the union, the contract-bar period applicable to election petitions filed by employees or by rival unions will be a maximum of 2 years, instead of 3.").

27 Id. (quotations omitted).

28 Hospital Menonita Guayama, Inc. v. NLRB, No. 24–138, 2024 WL 5112286, at *1 (U.S. Dec. 16, 2024) (remanding for further consider in light of Loper Bright Enterprises v. Raimondo, 603 U.S. 369 (2024)).

29 MV Transp., 337 NLRB 770 (2002)).

30 465 U.S. 513, 526 (1984).

equities clearly favors rejection of such agreement."[31] In addition, the debtor-employer's proposal to the union must "provide[ ] for those necessary modifications in the employees benefits and protections that are necessary to permit the reorganization of the debtor and assures that all creditors, the debtor and all of the affected parties are treated fairly and equitably."[32] The debtor-employer must provide the union with "such relevant information as is necessary to evaluate the proposal."[33] And if the parties confer in good faith but fail to reach an agreement on the employer's proposal, the court must find that the union "refused to accept such proposal without good cause."[34] Courts have ruled that a union does not have "good cause" to refuse a "necessary" and "fair" proposal unless it can come up with a reasonable alternative.[35]

The *Bildisco* Court had also permitted the debtor-employer to unilaterally reject or modify a CBA upon filing the bankruptcy petition under Chapter 11, and before formal acceptance of the petition by the bankruptcy court.[36] Section 1113 does permit, however, the Board to find that a unilateral change prior to the bankruptcy court's order rejecting a CBA is a violation of § 8(a)(5). In order to balance out this restriction on the debtor-employer's freedom of action, particularly in possibly dire financial circumstances, § 1113 places strict time limits on the bankruptcy court's hearing and ruling on an application to reject the CBA. If the court fails to meet the time requirements, the debtor-employer or its trustee may alter or terminate the CBA pending the ruling.[37]

If the bankruptcy court approves the rejection of the CBA, the employer is still under a statutory duty to bargain in good faith with the union concerning terms and conditions of employment. Unions retain bargaining authority during the reorganization process and can go on strike against the debtor if unable to reach an agreement.[38] If the bankruptcy court has approved interim changes pending its

---

31 11 U.S.C. § 1113(c)(3).

32 Id. § 1113(b)(1)(A). Courts have interpreted "necessary" to mean something more than the absolute minimum to permit a reorganization. See Truck Drivers Local 807 v. Carey Transp. Inc., 816 F.2d 82, 89–90 (2d Cir. 1987) (noting that the company's long-term viability must be considered).

33 11 U.S.C. § 1113(b)(1)(B).

34 Id. § 1113(c)(2).

35 See In re Maxwell Newspapers, Inc., 981 F.2d 85 (2d Cir. 1992); In re Allied Delivery Sys. Co., 49 B.R. 700, 704 (Bankr. N.D. Ohio 1985).

36 *Bildisco*, 465 U.S. at 532.

37 11 U.S.C. § 1113(d).

38 But see In re Nw. Airlines Corp., 349 B.R. 338, 361 (S.D.N.Y. 2006) aff'd, 483 F.3d 160 (2d Cir. 2007) (under the RLA, a union cannot strike until all of the RLA bargaining procedures are exhausted or management undeniably acts in bad faith, capriciously, or in violation of the law).

ruling on rejection, these interim changes presumably constitute a new status quo that the employer must maintain until a new contact is negotiated or further changes are made after impasse.[39] The Board's position is that once a CBA has been rejected, the employer may unilaterally implement changes but only with respect to those provisions contained in the debtor's final § 1113 proposal.[40] More often, however, the union wields its influence in the creditor committees. Even though union committee members may have conflicts of interest with other creditors, courts have appointed them to represent the interests of the bargaining-unit employees. Any potential conflicts are thought mitigated by the fact that a majority of the committee represents the other creditors.[41]

---

[39] See In re D.O. & W. Coal Co., 93 B.R. 454 (Bankr. W.D. Va. 1988) (interim order continues in effect after expiration of CBA and becomes part of the status quo the employer must observe); see generally Donald B. Smith & Richard A. Bales, Reconciling Labor and Bankruptcy Law: The Application of 11 U.S.C. § 1113, 2001 L. Rev. Mich. St. U. Det. C.L. 1145, 1146 (2001).

[40] See Advice Memo, In re Apple Tree Markets, Inc., 1993 WL 726774, at *2 (NLRB G.C., Feb. 26, 1993); Advice Memo, In re Amherst Sparkle Market, 1988 WL 489921, at *4 (NLRB G.C., Feb. 25, 1988).

[41] See In re Altair Airlines, Inc., 727 F.2d 88, 90 (3d Cir. 1984) ("There is no reason why the voice of the collective bargaining representative should be the one claimant voice excluded from the performance of that statutory role."); Matter of Schatz Fed. Bearings Co., Inc., 5 B.R. 543 (Bankr. S.D.N.Y. 1980). See generally Michael E. Abrams & Babette Ceccotti, Protecting Union Interests in Employer Bankruptcy, in Labor Law and Business Change: Theoretical and Transactional Perspectives Ch. 17 (Samuel Estreicher & Daniel G. Collins eds. 1988).

For a discussion on union representation of creditor interests within the context of the public sector, see Alvin Velazquez, Lucha Si, Entrega No: How an "Awkward Power Sharing Arrangement" Enabled Retirees to Upend a Plan of Adjustment, 97 Am. Bankr. L.J. 836, 836 (2023).

Chapter 11

LABOR AND THE ANTITRUST LAWS

Reflecting federal policy in favor of union organization and collective bargaining, the courts have recognized two areas of exemption from the federal antitrust laws: a statutory labor exemption and a "non-statutory" exemption. The statutory exemption, based on the Clayton Act of 1914 and the Norris-LaGuardia Act of 1932, shields unions and their members from antitrust liability if they act alone and not in combination with business groups. The non-statutory exemption is based on the pro-collective bargaining policies of the NLRA and RLA, and it protects unions and employers from antitrust liability in negotiating and entering into contracts that do not involve price-fixing or other direct restraints on product-market competition.

There are several reasons why Congress decided labor needs exemption from the antitrust laws. One is historical. Whether and to what extent the antitrust laws apply to union organizations, strikes, and boycotts has been, as Chapter 2 illustrates, an area of much-contested terrain resulting in several legislative attempts to develop rules of accommodation. Second, at a general level, union objectives are anticompetitive. A union seeks either to control the supply of labor or to organize all product market competitors who will agree to union standards. Society may benefit from the realization of these objectives—that, too, is contested—but consumer welfare narrowly viewed is not maximized by "taking wages out of competition." A third reason is that the antitrust laws can be used as a bludgeon as they carry treble damages and criminal penalties. At least since the 1947 Taft-Hartley amendments, which added union ULPs dealing with the most contentious union weapons—the secondary boycott and unlimited recognitional picketing—the argument could be made that the more focused labor law prohibitions coupled with administrative enforcement do a better job of curbing the harms of certain union practices at less cost of inhibiting legitimate union activities.

A. Statutory Labor Exemption

The first labor exemption—the "statutory" exemption—is drawn from Sections 6 and 20 of the Clayton Act with an assist from the Norris-La Guardia Act. As the Supreme Court held in its 1941 ruling in *United States v. Hutcheson,*[1] a labor union's picketing of an

---

[1] 312 U.S. 219 (1941).

employer to compel it to assign particular work to that union rather than another was not criminal activity under the Sherman Act.[2] Because the union was acting alone and not in concert with business groups, it could not be enjoined by a federal court under the Clayton and Norris-LaGuardia Acts. Therefore, the Court insisted, it could not be the subject of an antitrust criminal indictment. This exemption from the antitrust laws is an exemption for labor organizations "acting alone" and not in combination with "nonlabor groups." Thus, in *Hunt v. Crumboch*,[3] a union's arson of a plant violated state criminal and tort law but did not violate the antitrust laws. Similarly, in *Apex Hosiery v. Leader*,[4] the union's shutting down production in a hosiery plant was not unlawful under the antitrust laws.

The statutory exemption extends to certain combinations of unions and "labor groups." The Supreme Court has recognized two kinds of labor groups who come within the statutory exemption. One category involves independent contractors, such as owner-operators of trucks, that are in direct job or wage competition with labor unions.[5] The explanation for the exemption is that the union acting alone does not contravene the antitrust laws when it seeks to impose the same labor standards as govern its members on contractors functioning as direct competitors of its members.[6]

The second category of labor groups covers businesses, like theatrical and sports agents, who function as intermediaries in the labor market.[7] These businesses do not compete with represented employees but do compete with labor unions concerning their bargaining and contract-administration functions. If the union has representational authority for the bargaining unit, it could in theory centralize all contractual relations with the employer, as we saw in connection with *J.I. Case Co. v. NLRB*.[8] In certain settings where there are significant skill and wage differences among represented employees, the union may negotiate minimum "scale" but allow above-scale negotiations between individual talent and the employer through the use of agents. The entertainment and sports industry unions issue licenses to agents and require represented employees in

---

2 That activity could be a ULP under § 8(b)(4)(D) of the NLRA after the 1947 Taft-Hartley amendments. 29 U.S.C. § 158(b)(4)(D).

3 325 U.S. 821 (1945).

4 310 U.S. 469 (1940).

5 American Fed'n of Musicians of U.S. & Canada v. Carroll, 391 U.S. 99 (1968).

6 Id. at 106.

7 H.A. Artists & Associates v. Actors' Equity Assn., 451 U.S. 704 (1981).

8 321 U.S. 332 (1944).

the bargaining unit to deal with employers only through licensed agencies.[9]

Open questions regarding the statutory exemption include how far unions can go in setting the prices charged by independent businesses in direct job or wage competition with represented employees,[10] and how far they can go in regulating the business of theatrical and sports agencies.[11] In addition, there is the question whether individuals excluded from coverage under the NLRA and the RLA can organize as a group to improve their compensation and work standards and avoid antitrust scrutiny. The application of antitrust laws to platform-economy workers such as Uber and Lyft drivers has become a hot topic. Are they merely sellers of labor falling squarely within Section 6 of the Clayton Act? Does the fact that they may own the car they drive turn them into independent businesspersons who may not combine free of antitrust scrutiny? Should a car that can be used both for personal and business purposes be treated as an indicator of entrepreneurial status, or is that no different from the general-purpose work tools that workers have historically brought with them to work? Can all professional service providers, like doctors and lawyers, combine to carve markets or fix prices, or are they entrepreneurs because they provide their services through a business in which they have made significant capital investments?

An employer's classification of workers as independent contractors does not necessarily foreclose their being laborers within the statutory labor exemptions if they are merely providing labor services without significant capital investment,[12] In January 2025, the Federal Trade Commission (FTC) issued a policy statement affirming that the statutory exemption applied to gig workers and that the agency would not seek antitrust enforcement against them.[13]

B. The "Non-Statutory" Exemption

The so-called "non-statutory" exemption from the antitrust laws covers certain labor-management agreements. It is "non-statutory"

---

[9] See Collins v. National Basketball Players Assn., 850 F. Supp. 1468 (D. Colo. 1991).

[10] See Am. Fed'n of Musicians of U. S. & Canada v. Carroll, 391 U.S. 99, 116–17 (1968) (White, J., dissenting); cf. Metropolitan Life Insurance Co. v. Massachusetts, 471 U.S. 724, 752 (1985) (referring to *Oliver I*).

[11] See *H.A. Artists*, 451 U.S. at 722 (questioning "union extraction of franchise fees from agents").

[12] See Samuel Estreicher & Jack Samuel, Labor's Antitrust Exemption for Independent-Contractor Workers, 59 Wake Forest L. Rev. 1020 (2024).

[13] FTC, Enforcement Policy Statement on Exemption of Protected Labor Activity by Workers from Antitrust Liability, Jan. 14, 2025, at: https://www.ftc.gov/legal-library/browse/enforcement-policy-statement-exemption-protected-labor-activity-workers-antitrust-liability.

because is based on the policies of the NLRA and RLA which contemplate collective bargaining agreements as the ultimate objective for labor organization. Union agreements with a single employer generally do not raise antitrust concerns. The need for the exemption arises most particularly in connection with multi-employer agreements where unions strive, with varying degrees of success, to bring all of the competitors in the same product market to the bargaining table. Absent the non-statutory exemption, the meetings and agreements of the multiemployer association as well as "me too" agreements with other companies could be subject to possible antitrust liability as unlawful combinations.

Just because the union is negotiating with employers in a multi-employer unit and the subjects of the agreements reached ostensibly concern wage, hours, and working conditions does not mean that the actions of the parties are free of all antitrust scrutiny. To the extent the agreement deals with prices[14] or allocates territories or business opportunities among employers[15] or seeks to drive competitors out of business,[16] the union and the employers will be subject to the antitrust laws. Some subjects like hours of operation may be shown in a given case, however, to be a legitimate means of dealing with labor conditions such as working hours.[17]

One area of continuing controversy concerns the extent to which employers, whether part of or outside of formal multiemployer bargaining, can attempt to mitigate the effect of whipsaw strikes by forming a mutual aid pact whereby they agree to share revenues during any strike. The state of California charged a group of grocery stores with antitrust violations for entering into such an agreement. The Ninth Circuit, sitting *en banc*, held that the agreement was not a *per se* illegal conspiracy in restraint of trade under "quick-look"

---

14 See Local Union No. 189, Amalgamated Meat Cutters v. Jewel Tea Co., Inc., 381 U.S. 676 (1965).

15 Cf. Allen Bradley Co. v. Local 3, IBEW, 325 U.S. 797 (1945).

16 United Mine Workers of America v. Pennington, 381 U.S. 657 (1965). The Court draws a distinction within "me too" agreements, which provide that if the union negotiates more favorable terms with other companies those terms will be made applicable to the contracting employers, and would generally not create antitrust issues, and "they too" agreements, which provide that the terms of the CBA will be made applicable to other employers outside the contracting parties. This would seem a formal point since unions are expected by all contracting employers to impose the terms that have been agreed to with one union on their competitors.

17 *Jewel Tea*, 381 U.S. at 696–97 (marketing-hour restriction found necessary to prevent non-butchers from performing bargaining unit work or to require night employment of butchers).

antitrust review, but nor did it escape judicial examination because of the labor exemption.[18]

In professional sports leagues, players' associations have used the antitrust laws to pry open owners' rules that made it difficult for players to leave teams in search of better compensation and other terms.[19] The leagues have used collective bargaining to provide for salary caps for individual teams. Until the Supreme Court's decision in *Brown v. Pro Football, Inc.*,[20] the courts of appeals generally required that any league restraint on players' mobility and compensation required the consent of the players in order to be antitrust-exempt. In *Brown*, the National Football League (NFL) unilaterally implemented its proposed salary cap after bargaining to impasse with the players' association. The Court held that implementation of the salary cap was part and parcel of the multiemployer collective bargaining process and was antitrust-immune under the non-statutory exemption. The Court, per Justice Breyer, cautioned that not "every imposition of terms by employers" would be free of antitrust scrutiny "for an agreement among employers could be sufficiently distant in time and in circumstances" that such scrutiny "would not significantly interfere with that process."[21]

The NFL players' association picked up on the suggestion in *Brown* and decertified themselves in 2011. The players attempted to use the antitrust laws to enjoin an NFL lockout during collective bargaining, but the Eighth Circuit held that the injunction was prohibited by the Norris-LaGuardia Act.[22]

---

[18] See State of California v. Safeway, Inc., 651 F.3d 1118 (9th Cir. 2011) (en banc).

[19] Major League Baseball does not need the labor exemption, as baseball is statutorily exempt from federal antitrust laws. See, e.g., Flood v. Kuhn, 407 U.S. 258 (1972).

[20] 518 U.S. 231 (1996).

[21] Id. at 250.

[22] Brady v. National Football League, 644 F.3d 661 (8th Cir. 2011).

Chapter 12

REGULATION OF THE EMPLOYEE-BARGAINING AGENT RELATIONSHIP

The NLRA and the RLA empower the recognized or certified majority labor organization to represent the interests of all the employees in the bargaining unit, whether they are members of the union or not. At one level these laws give labor unions economic power that resembles a state's ability to bind all members of the polity, including those opposed to the law in question. Exclusive representation provides special powers to unions when they are chosen to act as the collective bargaining representative for a specific bargaining unit of employees. The employer must bargain in good faith with the union over the terms and conditions of employment for those employees. The union represents all members of the bargaining unit, and the terms that the union and employer negotiate apply to everyone in the unit. When unions are exclusive bargaining agents, they have a duty under the NLRA and RLA fairly to represent all workers in the bargaining unit, even if they are not union members or are dissidents disliked by the union leadership.

At the same time, unions are private organizations that are run by their members. Employees represented by a union are often members of the union, but they need not be. Thus, a labor union has a dual role, a dual capacity: it can be both the statutorily-endowed exclusive bargaining agency for all unit employees as well as a private membership organization attentive to the interests of its members. Although they have political interests as organizations, unions are also not normally political agents for represented workers. Workers generally select unions to represent them on economic issues; they are not authorizing as their agents on general political matters unrelated to their wages, hours and working conditions.[1]

In this Chapter, we shift our attention from the relationship between employers and employees (and their collective representatives) to the relationship between the labor union and represented employees.

---

[1] For a different view, see Benjamin I. Sachs, The Unbundled Union: Politics Without Collective Bargaining, 123 Yale L.J. 148 (2013).

A. The Relationship Between Union Representation and Union Membership

1. Union-Security Arrangements

In the early days of the NLRA, unions would negotiate, or impose through their bargaining strength, a "closed shop"—namely, the requirement that all employees were union members for both initial and continued employment. The 1947 Taft-Hartley amendments to the NLRA outlawed this practice, as it was seen to be giving unions too much power over employees. (A similar prohibition obtained under the RLA.) In its wake, other union-security practices have developed:

- The "union shop," in which employers hire whomever they want but employees must join the union, in the "financial core" sense of paying unions dues or their financial equivalent, and maintain their membership as a condition of continued employment (discussed further below);
- The "agency shop" or "agency fee," under which employees need not join the union but must pay agency fees in order to maintain employment; and
- "Maintenance of membership," under which employees are not required to join the union, but if they do, they must remain members for the duration of the agreement.

When the union seeks to require membership or fees as part of the employment relationship, it will generally seek a "dues checkoff" clause from the employer; this clause provides that union dues or fees will be taken by the employer from the employees' paycheck and paid directly to the union.[2]

There are three important limitations on union-security arrangements. First, the NLRA permits individual states to ban union-shop and agency-fee agreements between unions and employers. A significant number of states have passed these so-called "right-to-work" laws which prohibit union shops or union-security clauses. In these states, unions must individually negotiate with their members to pay the costs of union representation.[3]

---

[2] The employer can deduct dues automatically from the employee's paycheck under LMRA § 302(c)(4), 29 U.S.C. § 186 (c)(4), as long as the employer receives from the employee written permission that is not irrevocable for more than one year.

[3] Most supporters of unionism also support the enforceability of union security arrangements to avoid "free riding" by employees who benefit from union

Second, even in states that allow union-shop clauses, such clauses can only require that all represented employees be union "members" in the sense of "financial core" membership. In *NLRB v. General Motors Corp.*,[4] interpreting the proviso to § 8(a)(3) that allows such clauses, the Supreme Court held that the union may require employees to pay for their representation but may not require them to actually join the union. Employees who elect this status are non-members of the union; they do not have the rights of members to vote in internal union elections or contract ratification, but they are not subject to union discipline.[5] The Court has also ruled that the employees' right to refrain from concerted activities under § 7 gives them a right to withdraw from union membership at any time, even in the midst of a strike.[6]

Third, in order to avoid constitutional doubts under the First Amendment, both the NLRA and RLA have been interpreted to require unions, at the request of non-members, to refund any portion of their compelled dues or fees spent on political or other matters not "germane" to the unions' collective-bargaining and grievance-adjustment functions; and to establish a procedure for challenging the allocation of the fees between chargeable and nonchargeable expenditures.[7] These rights are referred to "*Beck* rights" in the NLRA context because they were formally introduced in the Supreme Court's decision in *Communications Workers of America v. Beck*.[8]

Recognition of the individual right of represented employees to abstain from paying for a union's political activities has led to the development of procedures to help enforce that right. In *Ellis v.*

---

representation but will not pay their share of its costs. Some union supporters have argued that a right-to-work regime requires unions to do a better job in keeping their represented employees happy with their services. See, e.g., George W. Brooks, The Strengths and Weaknesses of Compulsory Unionism, 11 N.Y.U. Rev. L. & Soc. Change 29, 35 (1982) ("Compulsory unionism begins as a device for protecting the union and its members against an anti-union employer. It ends as a device by which the employer protects the union against reluctant or critical members. The erosion of vitality of the union at the workplace is an inevitable consequence. . . .").

For an argument that the "individual freedom" arguments in favor of right-to-work are "misleading and unhelpful," see Mancur Olson, The Logic of Collective Action: Public Goods and the Theory of Groups 88–97 (1971 ed.).

4 373 U.S. 734 (1963).

5 In Marquez v. Screen Actors Guild, Inc., 525 U.S. 33 (1998), the Supreme Court held that the union did not act in bad faith by negotiating union security clause that tracked the language in § 8(a)(3) requiring union "membership."

6 Pattern Makers' League of North Am. v. NLRB, 473 U.S. 95 (1985).

7 See International Assn. of Machinists v. Street, 367 U.S. 740 (1961) (RLA); Communications Workers of America v. Beck, 487 U.S. 735 (1988) (NLRB). Congress added § 19 of the NLRA during the 1974 amendments to give religious objectors the option to pay an amount equivalent to union dues to a list of charities listed in the CBA or chosen by the employee. See 29 U.S.C. § 169.

8 487 U.S. 735 (1988).

Brotherhood of Railway, Airline & S.S. Clerks,[9] the Court held that the union was required under the RLA to provide a pre-expenditure objection procedure to prevent even interim use of an objecting employee's dues for political purposes. The NLRB has similarly developed a set of procedures requiring notice to employees of the union's expenditures, the right to object to expenditures not germane to core union collective-bargaining and grievance-adjustment functions, and the right to challenge the union's calculation of chargeable expenses.[10] The specifics have been refined over time. A union violates the NLRA if it fails to act promptly in response to a request to exercise *Beck* rights.[11] *Beck* objectors are also entitled to ask the union to provide independent verification of the information provided by an auditor.[12]

As to the line between chargeable and nonchargeable expenses, the Supreme Court determined in *Ellis* that expenses for national conventions, social activities, and nonpolitical union publications were related to collective bargaining, while costs for organizing employees outside of the bargaining unit and litigation unrelated to representational issues were not.[13] The Board has found that litigation expenses can count as related to collective representation if they "may ultimately inure to the benefit" of the unit employees.[14] In addition, organizing expenses are related to the union's bargaining function "at least with respect to organizing activity within the same competitive market as the bargaining unit employer."[15] The Board also requires evidence that "there is a direct, positive relationship between the wage levels of union-represented employees and the level of organization of employees of employers in the same

---

[9] Ellis v. Brotherhood of Railway, Airline & S.S. Clerks, 466 U.S. 435 (1984).

[10] California Saw & Knife Works, 320 NLRB 224 (1995), enf. sub nom. Machinists v. NLRB, 133 F.3d 1012 (7th Cir. 1998), cert. denied mem. sub nom. Strang v. NLRB, 525 U.S. 813 (1998). In United Nurses and Allied Professionals (Kent Hospital), 367 NLRB No. 94, at 5 (Mar. 1, 2019), the Board held unions "must provide audit verification to adequately ensure the reliability of the financial information provided to objectors." In that case, the union was held to have violated § 8(b)(1)(A) by using general operating funds for lobbying activity in support of legislative bills that did not relate closely enough to the union's bargaining obligations.

[11] Int'l Bhd. of Teamsters Loc. 385 (Walt Disney Parks & Resorts U.S., Inc. d/b/a Walt Disney World Co.; United Parcel Serv., Inc.), 366 NLRB No. 96 (June 20, 2018) (finding a ULP when the union "repeatedly and deliberately" failed to respond to requests made by letters, telephone calls, and in-person inquiries regarding revocation of their dues checkoff authorizations).

[12] United Nurses and Allied Professionals (Kent Hospital), 367 NLRB No. 94 (Mar. 1, 2019).

[13] *Ellis*, 466 U.S. at 448–54.

[14] Id. at 238.

[15] United Food & Commercial Workers Locals 951, 7 & 1036 (Meijer, Inc.), 329 NLRB 730, 733–34 (1999), enforced in relevant part, 307 F.3d 760 (9th Cir. 2002) (en banc).

competitive market."[16] As to political lobbying expenses, the Board held in *United Nurses and Allied Professionals (Kent Hospital)* that these are not chargeable expenses, even if they may ultimately relate to what could be a subject of bargaining.[17]

The limits on the use of dues for political purposes are part of a larger system of regulation of union political activity.[18] Labor unions are restricted in their ability to participate in the political process. The 1947 Labor Management Relations Act prohibited unions from contributing to federal election campaigns.[19] The provision was construed narrowly by the Supreme Court, allowing unions to donate to campaigns as long as the monies were paid out of voluntary, separately-administered political funds.[20] The prohibition has been fleshed out in subsequent legislation.[21] More recently, the McCain-Feingold Act extended the restrictions on political advocacy to include all "electioneering communications."[22] In *Citizens United v. FEC*,[23] however, the Court struck down on First Amendment grounds legislative restriction on independent expenditures by unions and corporations in support of or against particular political candidates.[24]

In *Janus v. AFSCME*,[25] the Supreme Court overruled longstanding precedent and held that states cannot require public-sector employees to contribute any dues to the union. Prior to *Janus*, public-sector collective bargaining agreements could require payment of the nonpolitical portion of dues to the union, even in the case of non-members.[26] The division between bargaining-related

---

16 Teamsters Local 75, Affiliated with Int'l Bhd. of Teamsters, Chauffeurs, Warehousemen & Helpers of Am. (Schreiber Foods), 349 NLRB 77, 82 (2007).

17 *United Nurses*, 367 NLRB No. 94, at *7.

18 For criticism of the existing jurisprudence, see Matthew T. Bodie, Mother Jones Meets Gordon Gekko: The Complicated Relationship between Labor and Private Equity, 79 U. Colo. L. Rev. 1317, 1353 (2008); Alan Hyde, Economic Labor Law v. Political Labor Relations: Dilemmas for Liberal Legalism, 60 Tex. L. Rev. 1, 33 (1981).

19 Labor Management Relations Act, Ch. 120, § 304, 61 Stat. 136, 159–60 (1947).

20 See United States v. CIO, 335 U.S. 106 (1948); Pipefitters Local 562 v. United States, 407 U.S. 385 (1972).

21 Section 304 was repealed by § 201(a) of the Federal Election Campaign Act Amendments, Pub. L. No. 94–283, 90 Stat. 475, 496 (1976), and replaced by § 112(2) of the Federal Election Campaign Act Amendments, Pub. L. No. 94–283, 90 Stat. 475, 486–490 (1976) (codified as amended at 2 U.S.C. § 441b). Section 441b prohibits the use of dues or agency fees by unions in connection with federal elections. See 2 U.S.C. § 441b (1982), transferred to 52 U.S.C. § 30118(b)(3)(A). This provision was further modified by the McCain-Feingold Act. See Bipartisan Campaign Reform Act of 2002, Pub. L. No. 107–155, Title II, §§ 203, 204, 214(d), 116 Stat. 91, 92, 95.

22 2 U.S.C. § 441b (b)(2), transferred to 52 U.S.C. § 30118(b)(2), (c).

23 558 U.S. 310 (2010).

24 Id. at 886.

25 585 U.S. 878 (2018).

26 See Abood v. Detroit Bd. of Ed., 431 U.S. 209 (1977), overruled by Janus v. Am. Fed'n of State, Cty., & Mun. Employees, Council 31, 585 U.S. 878 (2018).

expenses and political expenses largely mirrored the lines drawn in the private-sector context. The *Janus* Court nevertheless held that the First Amendment prohibits states from requiring employees to pay for speech with which they did not agree, including union negotiations over terms and conditions, due to the implications for matters of public interest.

B. Internal Union Discipline

Union members are subject to internal union discipline for violating union rules and policies, including fines, suspension, and expulsion from membership. As a general matter, union discipline violates §§ 8(b)(1)(A) and 8(b)(2) of the NLRA if it adversely affects the employment rights of represented employees. Union fines and other non-employment discipline are permitted. In *NLRB v. Allis-Chalmers Manufacturing Co.*,[27] the union fined members who had returned to work in the midst of a strike. The employer filed a charge with the Board claiming that the union had restrained or coerced the strikebreaking employees in the exercise of their § 7 rights.[28] The Board found no violation under § 8(b)(1)(A), and the Supreme Court agreed. Noting that the strike had been approved by two-thirds of the membership and that the union imposed the fines after following its internal processes,[29] the Court concluded that the NLRA did not prohibit union fines as a mode of discipline for returning to work during a strike. The Court relied in part on the proviso in § 8(b)(1)(A), which states that: "this paragraph shall not impair the right of a labor organization to prescribe its own rules with respect to the acquisition or retention of membership therein."[30] If a union had the power to expel a member, reasoned the Court, it also had the power to impose a reasonable fine.

The union's power to impose fines extends only to its members. Non-members in the bargaining unit are not subject to fines. Nor are members who have resigned from the union—even in the midst of a strike. In *Pattern Makers' League of North America v. NLRB*,[31] the union constitution prohibited members from resigning during a strike or when a strike was imminent. When ten members resigned during a strike and returned to work, the union charged them with violations and ultimately fined them the amount of money they had

---

27 388 U.S. 175 (1967).

28 See NLRA § 8(b)(1)(A), 29 U.S.C. § 158(b)(1)(A).

29 The union convened local trial committees to adjudicate the charges, and the charged members were represented by counsel. *Allis-Chalmers*, 388 U.S. at 177.

30 29 U.S.C. § 158(b)(1)(A).

31 473 U.S. 95 (1985).

made from their employment when the strike was ongoing.[32] The Board determined that the union's sanctions violated § 8(b)(1)(A), and the Supreme Court upheld the Board's order. Mid-strike resignations may, however, affect internal union governance rights. The Board found no violation when a union suspended the voting rights and eligibility for office of members who resigned during a strike but rejoined afterwards.[33]

Unions also are given some leeway in imposing discipline that affects an employer's operations, provided the discipline does not affect the employment status of the employee-union member. In *Scofield v. NLRB*,[34] the employer maintained an incentive policy for its production goals: it provided bonus pay or allowed employees to bank the excess production for future use. A union rule prohibited members from accepting any incentive pay for production above a certain union-imposed ceiling. If employees accepted such pay, the union would impose a fine; non-payment of fines could lead to eventual expulsion from the union and a court action to enforce the fines. The Board ruled that the union's attempt to collect these fines by court action did not violate the NLRA. The Supreme Court, per Justice White, agreed. The Court noted that the parties had bargained extensively over the union's production ceiling, but that the CBA did not bar the union-imposed ceiling. The Court stated that it found "no basis in the statutory policy encouraging collective bargaining for giving the employer a better bargain than he has been able to strike at the bargaining table."[35] Moreover, the union was not restraining or coercing employees (in violation of § 8(b)(1)(A)) or causing the employer to discriminate against employees (in violation of § 8(b)(2)) because the employees had the choice whether to be a union member without losing their jobs.

In contrast, in the 1978 case *American Broadcasting Company v. Writers Guild of America*,[36] the Supreme Court held that the union had committed a ULP by fining its supervisor-members for working during a strike. Employers were permitted to count on the continued performance of their supervisory employees during a strike, and it was improper interference for the union to fine them for doing their supervisory duties. The Court made clear that situation might have been different had the supervisors been doing the work of the striking rank-and-file employees.[37] Because they simply continued to perform

[32] Id. at 96–97.

[33] Machinists Lodge 1233 (General Dynamics Corp.), 284 NLRB 1101 (1987).

[34] 394 U.S. 423 (1969).

[35] Id. at 433.

[36] 437 U.S. 411 (1978).

[37] Id. at 430.

their own supervisory roles, however, the union discipline interfered with the employer's control over its own representatives in violation of § 8(b)(1)(B).

Although the Board has the power to police union discipline under § 8(b)(1)(A), the reasonableness of union fines has been left to state law. In *NLRB v. Boeing Co.*,[38] employees who had worked during a strike charged the union with a § 8(b)(1)(A) violation for imposing a fine of $450, which was the equivalent of three to six weeks of base pay. The Supreme Court agreed with the Board that the NLRA did not provide authority for regulating the reasonableness of the size of the fine; rather, reasonableness was a matter governed by state law regarding contracts, voluntary associations, or other equitable principles.[39]

C. The Union's Duty of Fair Representation

Unions owe an implied duty of fair representation (DFR) to fairly represent all employees in the bargaining unit, whether they are full-fledged union members or not.

In *Steele v. Louisville & Nashville Railroad*,[40] the union, which had a whites-only membership policy but also purported to be the exclusive representative for a bargaining unit that included African-Americans, negotiated with the employer a 50% cap on African-American employees in certain positions and a limit on their promotions. Although the Railway Labor Act did not expressly impose a statutory duty of fair representation on unions, the Supreme Court held that such a duty was implied from the RLA's grant of exclusive representation. The duty required the union to "exercise fairly the power conferred upon it in behalf of all those for whom it acts, without hostile discrimination against them."[41] The Court recognized that the union must be free to make certain distinctions among its members based upon seniority, type of work performed, and skill. However, the union was not free to determine job opportunities on the basis of characteristics such as race, which was "obviously irrelevant and insidious."[42] Union members could bring a court action under the RLA for injunctive relief and other customary remedies against the union.

---

38 412 U.S. 67 (1973).

39 Id. at 74.

40 323 U.S. 192 (1944).

41 Id. at 202–03.

42 Id. at 203. Compare Ford Motor Co. v. Huffman, 345 U.S. 330, 331 (1964) (sustaining the validity of collective-bargaining agreements in which employees receive credit for pre-employment military service).

The Taft-Hartley Act added a set of union unfair labor practices in § 8(b) of the Act. Section 8(b)(1)(A) makes it a ULP for the union to "restrain or coerce employees in the exercise of [their § 7] rights."[43] Section 8(b)(2) prohibits the union from causing the employer to discriminate against an employee because of the employee's union activity.[44] Although neither of these provisions specifically refers to a duty of fair representation, the Board has held that a union violates §§ 8(b)(1)(A) and 8(b)(2) by failing to represent its bargaining-unit employees fairly. The Board's *Miranda Fuel* doctrine allows individual employees to bring claims to the Board for breach of the union's DFR.[45] But does the Board's exercise of jurisdiction over these claims mean that the Board has exclusive jurisdiction? Are employees required to file DFR claims only with the NLRB, as they are for other § 8 violations?

In *Vaca v. Sipes*,[46] the Supreme Court said no. The Court held that the *Miranda Fuel* doctrine did not foreclose the individual employee from pursuing a DFR claim in the courts. If employees were limited to the Board, "the individual employee injured by arbitrary or discriminatory union conduct could no longer be assured of impartial review of his complaint since the Board's General Counsel has unreviewable discretion to refuse to institute an unfair labor practice complaint."[47] In addition, the Court cited to a more practical concern in the adjudication of individual employee claims for improper employer discharges. As discussed in Chapter 9, most CBAs provide for an extensive grievance-arbitration process to resolve contractual disputes. The union controls which grievances it is willing to take through the grievance process and ultimately to arbitration. In *Vaca*, the employee had been terminated for poor health after a series of employer efforts to manage his hypertension. The union represented the employee through four steps in the grievance procedure but ultimately decided not to take his case to arbitration. The employee then claimed that not only did the employer improperly fire him in violation of the contract, but also the union improperly failed to represent him by not arbitrating his claim. Because the employee's § 301 claim against the employer was intertwined with his unfair representation claim against the union,

---

43 29 U.S.C. § 158(b)(1)(A).

44 29 U.S.C. § 158(b)(2).

45 Miranda Fuel Co., 140 NLRB 181 (1962).

46 386 U.S. 171 (1967).

47 Id. at 182.

the Court held that as a pragmatic matter, the employee should be permitted to bring both claims to court.[48]

Violations of the union's DFR are limited to those incidents in which "a union's conduct toward a member of the collective bargaining unit is arbitrary, discriminatory, or in bad faith."[49] In *Vaca,* the union had not ignored the employee's grievance or treated it in a "perfunctory manner;" instead, it had taken it to the fourth step.[50] The Court found no breach of the union's duty.

In finding DFR violations, courts and the Board generally look for one of two scenarios: (1) the union has utterly failed to exercise care in performing its representational duties, or (2) the union has discriminated against the employee based on an improper motive. Examples of improper motives would be racial animus, as in *Steele*, or retaliation for an internal political dispute. For example, if a union rank-and-file member ran for union office against the incumbent local president, lost, and thereafter had a grievance against the employer, and then the union intentionally ignored the grievance in retaliation, the union would have violated its DFR. It is not clear whether the DFR includes union liability for negligently processing an employee's grievance.[51] The Supreme Court appears to have rejected liability for negligence, albeit in dicta.[52]

When it comes to resolving DFR claims that are paired with § 301 claims against an employer, the *Vaca* Court instructed that both the union and the employer would bear responsibility for remedying meritorious claims. The Supreme Court's "governing principle" is "to apportion liability between the employer and the union according to the damage caused by the fault of each."[53] The Court further refined this allocation in *Bowen v. United States Postal Service.*, finding the union liable for the period after which it had stopped the grievance-arbitration process.[54]

The union's duty of fair representation also extends to its collective-bargaining function. The Supreme Court applied *Vaca*'s

---

48 Employees must file their hybrid § 301/DFR claims within six months of the alleged violations, which is also the limitations period for ULP charges generally. See Del Costello v. Teamsters, 462 U.S. 151 (1963).

49 386 U.S. at 190.

50 Id. at 194.

51 See, e.g., Ruzicka v. General Motors Co., 523 F.2d 306 (6th Cir. 1975) (union liable for "negligently and perfunctorily handling" of grievance).

52 United Steelworkers v. Rawson, 495 U.S. 362, 372–73 (1990) ("The courts have in general assumed that mere negligence, even in the enforcement of a collective-bargaining agreement, would not state a claim for breach of the duty of fair representation, and we endorse that view today.").

53 *Vaca*, 386 U.S. at 197.

54 459 U.S. 212, 226 (1990).

tripartite test to contract negotiations in *Air Line Pilots Association v. O'Neill*.[55] In *O'Neill*, represented employees alleged that the union had botched negotiations with the employer, resulting in a settlement that was worse than simply ending the strike without an agreement. The union argued that the DFR required only nondiscriminatory treatment. The Court disagreed, holding that the union's duty in contract negotiations also extended to avoiding "arbitrary" conduct. But the Court also made clear that the union had "wide latitude" in its negotiations, violating the duty only if it acted "so far outside a wide range of reasonableness that it was wholly irrational and arbitrary."[56] Given this deferential standard, the union's negotiation decisions in that case were "by no means irrational" and did not violate the union's duty.[57]

There are few reported decisions finding a union to have breached its DFR in contract negotiations. One typical scenario involves a merger of plants in which the union must reconcile the seniority lists in the two plants. If the union seeks "endtailing" of the lists—favoring the employees at one plant over the other—as opposed to "dovetailing," some courts might search for an improper motive, such as political expediency, that harms a certain identifiable group within the unit.[58]

Employees can also sue the union for improper administration of union hiring halls. Hiring halls help manage the labor supply for employers with short-term positions, especially in the construction industry. In *Breininger v. Sheet Metal Workers' Local Union No. 6*,[59] an employee alleged that he had been unfairly passed over by the union even when employers had specifically requested him pursuant to the hiring-hall rules. The Supreme Court declined to rest exclusive jurisdiction with the Board and allowed the employee to bring an independent federal claim under the implied duty of fair representation. The Court reiterated that "[t]he duty of fair representation is not intended to mirror the contours of § 8(b); rather, it arises independently from the grant under § 9(a) of the NLRA of the union's exclusive power to represent all employees in a particular bargaining unit."[60] The union could be held liable for arbitrary, discriminatory, or bad faith conduct but not for errors stemming from

---

[55] 499 U.S. 65 (1991).

[56] Id. at 78.

[57] Id. at 79.

[58] See, e.g., Barton Brands, Ltd. v. NLRB, 529 F.2d 793, 798 (7th Cir. 1976) (finding that the union acted "solely on grounds of political expediency" in agreeing to a reduction in the accumulated seniority of employees at one plant in favor of the more numerous employees at the other plant).

[59] 493 U.S. 67 (1989).

[60] Id. at 69.

mere negligence, even in the context of a union-administered hiring hall.[61]

D. The Regulation of Internal Union Governance

Theoretically, under the NLRA a labor union could take a variety of entity forms: nonprofit corporation, for-profit corporation, partnership, LLC, voluntary association, or even sole proprietorship.[62] Unions representing employees under the NLRA are, however, almost always nonprofit associations for three principal reasons. Historically, unions were reluctant to form corporations for fear of making themselves easily amenable to lawsuits. In addition, the Clayton Act provides antitrust exemption for those labor organizations "instituted for the purposes of mutual help, and not having capital stock or conducted for profit."[63] This exemption does not include for-profit unions. Nonprofit status also affords certain tax benefits.[64]

Perhaps decisive to the choice of entity are the requirements of the Labor-Management Reporting and Disclosure Act (LMRDA or Landrum-Griffin Act), which establish certain requirements for labor organizations.[65] The LMRDA was enacted in 1959 after extensive hearings into internal union corruption.[66] The statute's central premise was that "unions should be democratic and that the law should prescribe minimum standards of democratic process in the conduct of internal union affairs."[67] The act is broken down into six titles. Title I provides for a "bill of rights" for union members.[68] Title

---

[61] Steamfitters Local Union No. 342 (Contra Costa Electric), 336 NLRB 549 (2001).

[62] The Board will not certify a labor organization as an exclusive bargaining representative if it suffers from a conflict of interest. See, e.g., St. John's Hosp. & Health Ctr., 264 NLRB 990, 993 (1982) (disqualifying a union that provided ancillary employment referral services); Sierra Vista Hosp., 241 NLRB 631, 633 (1979) (discussing how the presence of supervisors in policymaking positions creates a conflict of interest and may disqualify a union).

[63] Clayton Act, § 6, 38 Stat. 730 (1914), 15 U.S.C. § 17.

[64] I.R.C. § 501(c)(5) (2000).

[65] The definition of labor organization under the LMRDA is also fairly broad, suggesting that almost all unions representing employees under the NLRA as well as unions representing government employees must meet the LMRDA's requirements. 29 U.S.C. § 402(i), (j).

[66] The hearings were conducted by the United States Senate Select Committee on Improper Activities in Labor and Management, chaired by Senator John McClellan. The chief counsel and investigator for the McClelland Committee was Robert F. Kennedy. See Benjamin Aaron, The Labor-Management Reporting and Disclosure Act of 1959, 73 Harv. L. Rev. 851, 883 (1960) (discussing "the sordid record, gathered by the McClellan Committee, of the misuse of union funds by some officers and employees").

[67] Clyde W. Summers, Democracy in A One-Party State: Perspectives from Landrum-Griffin, 43 Md. L. Rev. 93, 94 (1984).

[68] 29 U.S.C. §§ 411–415.

II provides for extensive disclosure and reporting by labor organizations, officers, and employees.[69] Title III restricts the ability of national and international unions to impose trusteeships on local union chapters.[70] Title IV regulates internal union elections.[71] Title V places fiduciary obligations on union officers and prohibits certain transactions with conflicts of interest.[72] Finally, Title VI contains a series of miscellaneous provisions relating to extortionate picketing, union discipline in retaliation, and the use of force or violence.[73]

The union members' "bill of rights," as enacted in LMRDA Title I, § 101, was meant to "bring to the conduct of union affairs and to union members the reality of some of the freedom from oppression that we enjoy as citizens by virtue of the Constitution of the United States."[74] The statute provides for equal rights for members, freedom of speech and assembly within the union, membership's right to approve dues increases, and the right to certain procedural safeguards in union elections.[75] Also protected are the rights to sue and to petition the union's internal governing bodies, as well as to appear as a witness in a proceeding.[76] These rights are designed to protect the ability of union members to participate in internal union elections as candidates, voters, and advocates. They may be enforced through individual lawsuits.[77] Balanced against these rights, however, are the interests of unions in managing their own internal affairs. As private organizations, unions often desire the same flexibility that other organizations—including corporations—have enjoyed.

The LMRDA's protections for free speech and assembly provide that members have "the right to meet and assemble freely with other members; and to express any views, arguments, or opinions; and to express at meetings of the labor organization his views, upon candidates in an election of the labor organization or upon any business properly before the meeting."[78] The union also has the right to adopt and enforce "reasonable rules" that may limit a member's

---

[69] Id. §§ 431–441.

[70] Id. §§ 461–466.

[71] Id. §§ 481–483.

[72] Id. §§ 501–504.

[73] Id. §§ 521–531.

[74] 105 Cong. Rec. 6472 (1959) (statement of Sen. McClellan).

[75] 29 U.S.C. § 411.

[76] Id.

[77] Id. § 412. The member must exhaust internal union remedies before bringing suit, but such procedures are not to exceed four months. Id. § 411(a)(4). Attorneys' fees are not specifically provided for, but may be awarded under the equitable discretion of the court. Hall v. Cole, 412 U.S. 1 (1973).

[78] 29 U.S.C. § 411(a)(2).

freedoms.[79] On the whole, this has meant that unions may adopt "time, place, and manner" restrictions similar to those permitted under the First Amendment, but they generally may not discipline members for the content of their speech. This protection extends even to speech that may be considered libelous in another context but nevertheless concerns internal union governance matters: the allegedly libeled individual may bring suit, but the union may not discipline the member for such speech.[80]

Union rules barring access of dissident candidates to the union newspaper and website raise LMRDA concerns. But unions have a free hand in setting their internal campaign financing rules. In *United Steelworkers of America v. Sadlowski*,[81] the Court held that a union's prohibition against financial contributions to union candidates from non-members was "rationally related to the union's legitimate interest in reducing outsider interference with union affairs."[82]

Union officials generally may make patronage appointments and dismissals. In *Finnegan v. Leu*,[83] the Court held that it was lawful for the incoming president to replace those business agents that had opposed his candidacy with agents "whose views are compatible with his own."[84] However, the union's authority does not extend to the removal of elected officials. In *Sheet Metal Workers' International Associate v. Lynn*,[85] an elected union official was removed for expressing his opposition to a dues increase; this removal violated the LMRDA. The majority distinguished *Finnegan* on the ground that the official had been elected by the membership, as opposed to appointed by a higher official. Concurring, Justice White suggested that a better distinction would be "whether an officer speaks as a member or as an officer in the discharge of his assigned duties."[86]

With regard to union discipline, the LMRDA's Bill of Rights requires unions to give their members the following procedural protections: the member must be "(A) served with written specific charges; (B) given a reasonable time to prepare his defense; and (C)

---

79 Id.

80 Salzhandler v. Caputo, 316 F.2d 445 (2d Cir. 1963).

81 457 U.S. 102 (1982).

82 Id. at 112.

83 456 U.S. 431 (1982).

84 Id. at 441. Justice Blackmun, concurring, maintained that the majority's holding did not apply to "nonpolicymaking employees, that is, rank-and-file member employees." Id. at 443 (Blackmun, J., concurring).

85 488 U.S. 347 (1989).

86 Id. at 360 (White, J., concurring).

afforded a full and fair hearing."[87] According to the Supreme Court, the provision does not permit courts to scrutinize the substance of the charges brought; instead, the charging party need only provide "some evidence" to support the charges made.[88] In addition, the due-process provision applies only to "punishment authorized by the union as a collective entity to enforce its rules," rather than to any act by a union official.[89]

Under LMRDA Title II, unions and their officers and employees must file extensive reports with the Department of Labor regarding assets, liabilities, salaries, and other proprietary information.[90] Since 1960 the Department of Labor has provided forms through which unions meet the disclosure requirements under Landrum-Griffin. Form LM-1 provides for disclosure of dues, fees, and organizational structure under § 201(a) of the Act.[91] Forms LM-2, LM-3, and LM-4 are the annual reports that cover a union's organizational and financial disclosure under LMRDA § 201(a) and (b).[92] Along with these annual forms are specific forms for certain types of disclosures, such as Form LM-30, which pertains to potential conflicts of interest, and Form LM-10, which requires employers to disclose payments made to unions. Further disclosure is required in several specific areas. Section 201(a) requires a union to provide the Department of Labor with a copy of its constitution and bylaws, as well as the union's initiation fee and the regular dues or payments required to remain a member.[93] LMRDA § 201(b) requires that unions file annual reports, signed by the president and treasurer, disclosing details about the union's financial condition and operations.[94] Section 202 requires union officers and employees to disclose a wide array of potential conflicts of interest.[95] These disclosures include any financial interests held by an employee in a business represented by the union, any transactions between such a business and a union employee, and any payments made by a represented business to the union or its employees.

Employers have their own set of disclosures related to potential conflicts of interest. The LMRDA requires that employers disclose any payments made to union officials or employees—a reciprocal

---

[87] 29 U.S.C. § 411(a)(5).

[88] International Brotherhood of Boilermakers v. Hardeman, 401 U.S. 233 (1971).

[89] Breininger v. Sheet Metal Workers' Local Union No. 6, 493 U.S. 67 (1989).

[90] 29 U.S.C. § 431.

[91] 29 C.F.R. §§ 402.2–402.3.

[92] 29 U.S.C. § 431.

[93] Id. § 431(a)(3)–(4).

[94] Id. § 431(b).

[95] Id. § 432.

obligation to the union's.[96] Employers must also disclose any payments made to employees or to outside labor consultants in an effort to persuade employees to exercise or not to exercise their collective rights.[97] Such payments include those designed to interfere in collective rights or to obtain information on employee or union efforts related to a dispute with the employer.[98]

Title III of the Landrum-Griffin Act concerns the imposition of trusteeships upon local unions or councils by their national or international governing organizations. Unions that place a chapter under trusteeship must file a specific set of reports that include "a detailed statement of the reason or reasons for establishing or continuing the trusteeship."[99] Those reasons are circumscribed under the LMRDA: the trusteeship must be imposed "for the purpose of correcting corruption or financial malpractice, assuring the performance of collective bargaining agreements or other duties of a bargaining representative, restoring democratic procedures, or otherwise carrying out the legitimate objects of such labor organization."[100] In addition, the union's constitution or other governing document must authorize the organization's power to place subordinate units under trusteeship.[101] If the union's constitution fails to provide for such power specifically, it will not be able to impose it under its general grants of authority.[102]

The LMRDA regulates the mechanisms of internal union elections under Title IV. Section 401 of the Act provides a set of requirements for such elections:

- § 401(a): National and international unions must hold elections at least every five years and must either use a secret ballot or hold a convention of delegates elected by secret ballot.
- § 401(b): Local unions must hold their elections at least every three years by secret ballot.
- § 401(c): Unions must comply with all reasonable requests to distribute campaign literature from any candidate, as long as such distribution is at the candidate's expense. Candidates must also be allowed

---

96 Id. § 433(a)(1).

97 Id. § 433(a)(2)–(5).

98 Id. § 433(a)(4).

99 Id. § 461.

100 Id. § 462.

101 Id.

102 United Brotherhood of Carpenters v. Brown, 343 F.2d 872 (10th Cir. 1965).

to inspect membership lists and have an observer at the polls and at the counting of the ballots.

- § 401(e): The nomination process for candidates must offer a "reasonable opportunity" to all members, and all members in good standing shall have the right to vote. Notice of the election must be provided to all members at least fifteen days prior to the election.
- § 401(g): Unions cannot use dues monies to promote candidates.
- § 401(h): If the union does not have a process for handling misconduct by elected officers, the Department of Labor may conduct a secret-ballot election to remove an officer guilty of serious misconduct.[103]

Neither Title IV nor the rest of the LMRDA require elections for decisions to authorize a strike or ratify a CBA. These are governed by the internal union constitution or by-laws. If unions do conduct such elections, however, they must abide by the "bill of rights" set forth in Title I. Any such votes would be open only to union members.[104]

Unlike Title I, which is enforceable through a private right of action, Title IV is enforceable (with one exception) only by the Secretary of Labor.[105] Union members must exhaust their internal union remedies and then file a complaint with the Secretary, who then investigates the charge. If probable cause is found, the Secretary can then pursue injunctive relief against the union to set aside the election, remove officers from office, and/or direct a new election. The Secretary has discretion in deciding to bring a case, but if suit is not brought, the Secretary must provide at least a statement explaining the reasons why and may not refuse to sue for "arbitrary and capricious reasons."[106]

This process is the exclusive remedy for election violations (other than the distribution of literature exception).[107] This restriction under Title IV has led some private litigants to reframe their election

---

[103] 29 U.S.C. § 481.

[104] See, e.g., American Postal Workers Union, Headquarters Local 6885 v. American Postal Workers Union, 665 F.2d 1096 (D.C. Cir. 1981) (requiring that all members have "equal rights" pursuant to LMRDA § 101(a)(1) to vote on ratification decisions).

[105] 29 U.S.C. § 482. The one exception is that individual union candidates may sue to compel union distribution of campaign literature under § 401(c).

[106] Dunlop v. Bachowski, 421 U.S. 560 (1975).

[107] 29 U.S.C. § 483.

challenges as Title I "bill of rights" lawsuits, but the Supreme Court has held that such suits are subject to the exclusive Title IV remedy.[108] Specifically, the Court has required: "[i]f the remedy sought is invalidation of the election with court supervision of a new election, then union members must utilize the remedies provided by Title IV."[109] To the extent such suits deal only with Title I rights and contemplate "less intrusive remedies sought during an election," the district court may proceed notwithstanding Title IV.[110]

Eligibility requirements for union office have been the subject of frequent litigation. A union requirement that all officer candidates must have previously been chosen for some lower office provides a fairly obvious method by which incumbents can curtail opposition forces.[111] Requirements that the candidates attend a certain number of union meetings can be unreasonably onerous. In *Local 3489, United Steelworkers of America v. Usery*,[112] the union required candidates to have attended at least half of the union's meetings in the prior 18 months. As a result, however, 96.5% of the membership was disqualified for office, and of the 23 eligible members, nine were incumbent officers. The Supreme Court agreed with the Secretary that the requirement was not a "reasonable qualification." A requirement that candidates be "literate and otherwise competent" has been stuck down,[113] while courts have split over an election rule that rendered members ineligible if they had applied for a management position within the last two years.[114]

The final two titles of the LMRDA address union corruption. Title V imposes a general fiduciary duty on union officials and requires that officials who handle funds be bonded in case of loss.[115] Unions are also prohibited from making loans in excess of $2,000 to officers and employees, and cannot allow candidates with a record of certain felony convictions to take office.[116] Title VI gives general

---

[108] Calhoon v. Harvey, 379 U.S. 134 (1964) (lawsuit regarding union's eligibility requirements for office).

[109] Local No. 82, Furniture & Piano Moving Drivers v. Crowley, 467 U.S. 526, 550 (1984).

[110] Id.

[111] Wirtz v. Hotel, Motel & Club Employees Union, Local 6, 391 U.S. 492, 494 & n.1 (1968).

[112] 429 U.S. 305 (1977).

[113] Donovan v. Local Union No. 120, Laborers' Int'l Union of N. Am., AFL-CIO, 683 F.2d 1095, 1104 (7th Cir. 1982).

[114] Compare Martin v. Branch 419, National Association of Letter Carriers, 965 F.2d 61 (6th Cir. 1992) (qualification is reasonable), with McLaughlin v. American Postal Workers Union, Miami Area Local, 680 F. Supp. 1519 (S.D. Fla. 1988) (qualification is not reasonable).

[115] 29 U.S.C. §§ 501 & 502.

[116] 29 U.S.C. §§ 503 & 504.

investigatory powers to the Secretary of Labor and contains specific regulations against extortionate picketing, retaliatory discipline, and use of force or violence.[117] The title also makes clear that state and federal laws regulating unions remain in place.[118]

The LMRDA's strict requirements regarding union democracy remain controversial. The Act has been said to do too much, with regard to election rules,[119] and do too little, with regard to contract ratification and strike authorization.[120] At the same time, the Act has also been called a "watershed moment" that "encouraged dissidents, reformers, radicals, and mainstream unionists who resisted repression, stolen elections, or corruption in their unions."[121] In the uniquely American approach of exclusive representation, some system of regulation is necessary to handle the agency-cost problems created by the separation of union leadership from the general membership. And for the foreseeable future, the current approach seems likely to remain unchanged.

---

117 29 U.S.C. §§ 521, 522, 529 & 530.

118 29 U.S.C. § 523; see also 29 U.S.C. § 413.

119 Samuel Estreicher, Deregulating Union Democracy, 2000 Colum. Bus. L. Rev. 501, 503 ("The pursuit of union democracy is also counterproductive because it (i) imposes unnecessary compliance costs on unions; (ii) weakens (or complicates) their ability to wage economic struggle with employers; and (iii) most importantly, unnecessarily requires that bargaining agents assume a certain organizational form in order to obtain and retain bargaining authority.").

120 Id. at 504 (proposing mandatory bargaining-unit votes for contract ratification and strike authorization).

121 Herman Benson, Landrum-Griffin Act at 50: Has It Been Good or Bad for Unions?, New Politics, at 29 (Winter 2011).

Chapter 13

PREEMPTION OF STATE LAW

The U.S. Constitution imposed our system of federalism on the existing sovereign states. One aspect of that system is the notion of federal supremacy: federal law trumps state law when the two conflict. The Supremacy Clause effectuates this concept through its command that the Constitution and laws made pursuant to its powers are "the supreme law of the land."[1] It is important to remember that the Supremacy Clause does not just provide that federal law trumps state laws that are in direct conflict with it. The reach of federal preemption extends further to state laws that fall within the zone of coverage for the federal statutory scheme. If Congress decides to leave an area that is otherwise within the reach of a federal law altogether unregulated, states may not be permitted to fill that void with their own efforts if the federal statute is deemed to occupy the field.

Congress can exercise its preemption powers to a greater or lesser extent as to each piece of legislation it enacts. In the employment arena, the Fair Labor Standards Act expressly reserves to the states the power to enact standards that are more protective of employees than those that it imposes.[2] ERISA, the federal law regulating employee pension and welfare benefit plans, contains a very broad express preemption provision.[3] However, as happens in many federal statutes, Congress did not include any specific preemption provision within the NLRA as to its effect on state law. The Act expressly allows states to prohibit union-security clauses,[4] and it provides that states may regulate labor disputes over which the Board has declined to exercise jurisdiction.[5] Otherwise, the NLRA is silent as to preemption. Despite this silence—or, perhaps, because of it—the Supreme Court has interpreted the NLRA to provide for a fairly robust set of preemption doctrines.

There are three preemption doctrines that may be invoked to block state regulation of labor relations activity. The first—*Garmon*

---

1 U.S. Const. Art. VI.

2 29 U.S.C. § 218(a).

3 Id. § 1144; see also id. § 1132.

4 Id. § 164(b); see Retail Clerks Local 1625 v. Schermerhorn, 375 U.S. 96 (1963) (interpreting 29 U.S.C. § 164(b)).

5 29 U.S.C. § 164(c)(2). The provision was added by the 1959 Landrum-Griffin Act, after a 1957 Supreme Court case held that states were preempted from regulating labor relations even if the Board did not exercise jurisdiction. Guss v. Utah Labor Relations Board, 353 U.S. 1 (1957).

preemption—concerns the core of the activity covered by the Act: states cannot regulate acts that are prohibited or protected by the Act, or arguably prohibited or protected by the Act. The second type is *Machinists* preemption, which deals with areas of labor relations activity that Congress wished to be determined by the free play of economic forces, rather than any regulation. Finally, § 301 preemption requires that federal common law be used to interpret and enforce collective-bargaining agreements (CBAs) that are governed by § 301 of the Taft-Hartley Act, including state common law claims based on or derived from obligations in the CBA.[6]

A. *Garmon* Preemption: Activity Protected, Prohibited, or Arguably Protected or Prohibited by the NLRA

In *San Diego Building Trades Council v. Garmon*,[7] California state courts found that union picketing was a violation of § 8(b)(2) of the NLRA because it sought to pressure the employer to require its employees join the union. The union started picketing after the employer refused to sign a members-only collective agreement. The employer filed a petition for a representation election with the NLRB, but the Board refused to take the case because it found that the employer's business fell outside the Board's jurisdictional limits. The employer then took its case to state court, where the courts enjoined the picketing and imposed damages on the union for the loss of business. The Supreme Court in *Garmon* held that both the injunction and the damages were preempted by the NLRA.

Garmon's facts and result may seem confusing because many states operate "mini-Wagner Acts" which regulate the labor relations of smaller employers. In this case, however, the California courts were not proceeding under such a statute but rather were deciding on their own interpretation of the NLRA that the union committed a violation and should be enjoined. Because the state court averred that it was in part interpreting the NLRA in reaching its decision, the Supreme Court overruled that court and held that the Board had sole jurisdiction over enforcement of the NLRA. The Court stated: "When it is clear or fairly may be assumed that the activities which a State purports to regulate are protected by § 7 of the Act, or constitute an unfair labor practice under § 8, due regard for the federal enactment requires that state jurisdiction must yield."[8] Moreover, it was up to the Board to determine whether a particular activity was regulated by the Act, as this fell with the "exclusive

---

[6] 29 U.S.C. § 185.

[7] 359 U.S. 236 (1959).

[8] Id. at 244.

primary competence" of the Board.[9] And—stretching out the contours of the Board's authority even further—the Court held that states were preempted from acting even when an activity was *arguably* prohibited or protected by the Act.[10] Said the Court: "The governing consideration is that to allow the States to control activities that are potentially subject to federal regulation involves too great a danger of conflict with national labor policy."[11]

The four branches of *Garmon* preemption that should be considered in applying the doctrine are: (1) activity protected by the NLRA, (2) activity prohibited by the Act, (3) activity arguably protected by the Act, and (4) activity arguably prohibited by the Act. The first is the easiest to understand: states cannot regulate and deter those activities that the Act specifically protects. The biggest area of potential conflict concerns strikes, picketing, and other protected concerted activity under § 7. States can deal with traditional areas of local concern like violence and mass picketing, but *Garmon* preemption bars application of state laws that curb protected activity.

The second branch of *Garmon* preemption concerns activity prohibited by the NLRA. This branch concerns the Board's jurisdiction and the particular balance of rights and remedies reflected in the Act. For example, in *Wisconsin Dep't of Industry v. Gould*,[12] the Supreme Court held that the *Garmon* doctrine preempted a Wisconsin statute that barred the state from doing business with companies found to have violated the NLRA. Even though the statute relied on determinations made by the Board and enforcing courts, the *Gould* Court held that the state law added penalties for prohibited conduct exceeding the NLRA remedies Congress had chosen to provide.[13]

The Court has recognized two general exceptions to the *Garmon* rule that apply with special force in the prohibited-activity category: if the activity concerns a "merely peripheral concern" of the Act, or if it concerns "interests so deeply rooted in local feeling and responsibility" that preemption would be inappropriate.[14] The NLRA does not preclude state regulation of mass picketing and threats of violence under traditional criminal, tort, and property law, even

---

9 Id. at 245.

10 Id. at 246.

11 Id.

12 475 U.S. 282 (1986).

13 For a discussion of the states as market actors, as opposed to market regulators, see Chapter 13.B. infra.

14 *Garmon*, 359 U.S. at 243–44.

though such activity may also be impermissible under the NLRA.[15] Such conduct has been traditionally regulated by the states and the NLRA deals with the subject only indirectly. Also, within certain limits, state-law claims for defamation[16] and intentional infliction of emotional distress[17] are not preempted. These are areas of traditional state concern where state law is based on common law antecedents. New regulatory regimes directed at economic conflict between unions and companies do not fall under this exclusion to NLRA preemption. Thus, for example, the Supreme Court has struck down state efforts to regulate strikes at public utilities or transit companies as exceeding the traditional state concern over "emergency conditions of public danger."[18]

The remaining two branches of *Garmon* preemption deal with activity that is arguably protected and activity that is arguably prohibited by the NLRA. The party claiming preemption has the burden of demonstrating arguable NLRA protection or arguable NLRA prohibition.[19] Difficulties with the arguably-protected prong are illustrated by *Sears Roebuck & Co. v. San Diego County District Council of Carpenters* and the absence of a declaratory remedy under the NLRA.[20] In that case, the "area standards" union picketing on the company's property was not easily categorized under *Garmon*: the union contended that the picketing was protected concerted activity under § 7, while the employer argued it was prohibited under § 8(b)(7)(C) as unlawful recognitional picketing or under § 8(b)(4)(D) as an unlawful secondary boycott. The employer had invoked state law by seeking an injunction against the picketing for trespass on its own property.

The California Supreme Court declined to enjoin the union because of the NLRA preemption concern. If that decision were left to stand, the employer would have been left without a remedy unless it committed a ULP prompting Board review. Since the union could have filed a ULP charge against the employer if it had been removed from the property under state law, the U.S. Supreme Court held that

---

15 UAW v. Russell, 356 U.S. 634 (1958); United States Construction Workers v. Laburnum, 347 U.S. 656 (1958).

16 Linn v. Plant Guard Workers, 383 U.S. 53 (1966).

17 Farmer, Special Administrator v. United Brotherhood of Carpenters, 430 U.S. 290 (1977).

18 Div. 1287, Amal. Ass'n of Street, Elec., Ry. & Motor Coach Employees v. Missouri, 374 U.S. 74 (1963); see also Amal. Ass'n of Street, Elec., Ry. & Motor Coach Employees v. Wisconsin Employment Relations Bd., 340 U.S. 383 (1951).

19 See Chamber of Commerce of the United States of Am. v. City of Seattle, 890 F.3d 769, 795 (9th Cir. 2018) (holding that a theory of *Garmon* preemption required a showing that Uber and Lyft drivers covered by a Seattle ordinance were arguably employees subject to the NLRA).

20 436 U.S. 180 (1978).

it was better to allow the employer to pursue its traditional property law remedies in state court rather than effectively requiring the employer to commit a ULP.[21] In effect, the Court narrowed the arguably-protected branch of *Garmon* where the controversy potentially to be presented to the NLRB would not be the same as the controversy before the state court.

In *Glacier Northwest, Inc. v. International Brotherhood of Teamsters Local Union No. 174*,[22] the Court held that state tort claims involving damage to the employer's property were not preempted when the union strikers had not taken reasonable precautions to protect that property from imminent danger. Cement-mixer drivers at a ready-mix concrete contractor had walked off the job in the midst of their work, leaving the trucks vulnerable to damage and rendering the concrete useless. Under the Board's existing interpretation of the right to strike, workers are not protected if they have "failed to take reasonable precautions to avoid foreseeable, aggravated, and imminent harm" to the employer's property.[23] The Court determined that, as alleged in the employer's complaint, the union had failed to take such reasonable precautions and that its activity would not be even arguably protected under *Garmon*.[24]

What happens when one party brings a state law claim against another in retaliation for that party's protected activity under the NLRA? The Board has held that such retaliatory lawsuits can constitute ULPs and can be remedied through injunctions and attorney's fees. To constitute a ULP the lawsuit must be unreasonable as well as motivated by a desire to retaliate against protected concerted activity.[25] However, the Board may not enjoin such a suit until a state tribunal has had an opportunity to determine its merit.[26]

---

[21] Id. at 207. On remand the California Supreme Court held that the employer was not in fact allowed to evict the picketers under state law. Sears Roebuck & Co. v. San Diego County District Council of Carpenters, 599 P.2d 676 (Cal. 1979).

[22] 598 U.S. 771 (2023).

[23] Id. at 783.

[24] Id. at 785 ("Because the Union took affirmative steps to endanger Glacier's property rather than reasonable precautions to mitigate that risk, the NLRA does not arguably protect its conduct."). But see id. at 790 (Jackson, J., dissenting) (pointing to the complaint filed by the NLRB regional office alleging the walk-off to be protected activity as evidence that the activity was at least arguably protected).

[25] BE & K Construction Co., 351 NLRB 451 (2007), on remand from BE & K Construction Co. v. NLRB, 536 U.S. 516 (2002).

[26] See Bill Johnson's Restaurants, Inc. v. NLRB, 461 U.S. 731 (1983).

B. *Machinists* Preemption: Activity That Congress Intended to Leave Unregulated

The *Machinists* preemption doctrine creates a zone free from state law interference even on subjects that NLRA does not directly regulate. The doctrine stems from *Lodge 76, IAM (Machinists) v. Wisconsin Employment Relations Commission*,[27] in which the state labor relations agency held that a union's partial strike—requiring its members not to work any overtime—was in violation of state law. In issuing its decision, the state agency noted that partial strikes were not protected by the NLRA, and thus the state was free to regulate them.[28] The state courts affirmed the agency's decision. The Supreme Court reversed, holding that NLRA preemption extended beyond conduct that was prohibited or protected (or arguably so) under *Garmon*. The Act also precluded state regulation of conduct that Congress intended to "be unregulated because left to be controlled by the free play of economic forces."[29]

Peaceful economic conflict is one such area. Congress allowed each party to keep "permissible economic weapons in reserve" in order to enable each side to bargain in good faith while insisting on their ultimate positions.[30] If states were allowed to jump in and restrict those activities in favor of one side or the other, the balance struck by the Act and the Board would be undone. Thus, for example, courts have struck down under the *Machinists* rationale state laws that prohibit the hiring of replacement workers[31] and laws that require firms to honor the collective bargaining agreements of other firms that they acquire.[32] States are also barred from carving out "labor dispute" exceptions from their general criminal trespass laws.[33]

One area of recent activity is the regulation of so-called "captive audience" meetings, in which employers mandate employee attendance at a session promoting anti-union sentiments. Ten states have passed laws outlawing captive audience meetings with respect to political or religious matters, in which "political" is defined to

---

27 427 U.S. 132 (1976).

28 Id. at 151.

29 Id. at 140.

30 Id. at 141.

31 See Employers Ass'n, Inc. v. United Steelworkers of Am., 32 F.3d 1297 (8th Cir. 1994).

32 Steelworkers v. St. Gabriel's Hospital, 871 F. Supp. 335 (D. Minn. 1994).

33 Rum Creek Coal Sales, Inc. v. Caperton, 926 F.2d 353 (4th Cir. 1991). But see NLRB v. Arizona, 2012 WL 3848400 (U.S. Dist. Ct. D. Ariz. Sept. 5, 2012) (not reported in F. Supp.) (dismissing on prematurity grounds a preemption challenge to a state constitutional provision requiring secret-ballot elections as a condition of collective bargaining representation).

include membership in labor organizations.[34] Prior to the Board's 2024 decision in *Amazon.com Services LLC*, [35] employers argued that the Board intentionally left captive audience meetings unregulated (outside the 24-hour pre-election period), making any state prohibitions preempted by *Machinists*. The Board's *Amazon* decision would seem to move these statutes from *Machinists* preemption into *Garmon* preemption, but that decision is expected to be overturned by the Trump II Board when given a quorum.

As a general matter, collective bargaining occurs against a backdrop of state law, both contract law and statutory "minimum terms" legislation. Such state law regimes are generally not preempted under *Machinists* principles. Neither is the local regulation of independent contractors preempted under an "implied" preemption theory, according to the Ninth Circuit.[36]

In *Metropolitan Life Insurance Co. v. Massachusetts*,[37] the state required all health insurance plans to provide mental health care benefits. Insurers challenged the measure as preempted by ERISA as well as the NLRA. The Court ruled that the state law was not preempted by either federal statute. As to NLRA preemption, the Court determined that "[m]inimum state labor standards affect union and non-union employees equally, and neither encourage nor discourage the collective bargaining processes that are the subject of the NLRA."[38] In *Restaurant Law Center v. City of New York*,[39] the Second Circuit held that a provision requiring just cause termination in the fast food industry was not preempted. The court noted that the regulation made no distinction between unionized and non-unionized fast-food employees and merely formed part of the backdrop of mandatory employment terms.[40]

The rights of replacement workers present another context where the Supreme Court has considered *Machinists* preemption. In *Belknap, Inc. v. Hale*,[41] the employer contended that the NLRA preempted state-law contract claims by replacement workers who

---

[34] See, e.g., Conn. Gen. Stat. Ann. 31–51q, (2022); Minn. Stat. 181.531 (2023); N.Y. S.B. S4982 (2023); Or. Rev. Stat. Ann. 659.785 (2009); Wisconsin Fair Employment Act, Wis. Stat. 11.31 *et seq.* (2010).

[35] 373 NLRB No. 136 (Nov. 13, 2024).

[36] See Chamber of Commerce of the United States of Am. v. City of Seattle, 890 F.3d 769, 791 (9th Cir. 2018).

[37] 471 U.S. 724 (1985).

[38] Id. at 755.

[39] 90 F.4th 101 (2d Cir. 2024).

[40] Id. at 113 ("[T]he NLRA leaves intact states' broad authority under their police powers to regulate substantive labor standards, which serve as the backdrop for the employment negotiations governed by federal law.").

[41] 463 U.S. 491 (1983).

were fired after the employer and union negotiated a strike settlement. The employer argued that allowing state-law suits for breach of contract would discourage resolutions of strikes—an area where the free play of economic forces rather than state regulation should control. The Court disagreed, holding the argument to be "mystifying" and noting that employers had to live by their contractual requirements. Otherwise, the parties would be privileged "to injure innocent third parties without regard to the normal rules of law governing those relationships."[42] A reinstatement remedy might be problematic by interfering with the ongoing relationship between the employer and the union, but a damages remedy would not be. The Court did not deal with whether the NLRA preempted state law tort actions against the union for negotiating the bumping of replacement workers by returning strikers.

State laws of general application that exclude union-represented workers from coverage also come in for *Machinists* scrutiny. These laws' objectives may be benign, but their effect is to exclude workers from protective laws because they have engaged in § 7 protected activity. Thus, a state's effort to deny unemployment benefits to employees who filed an ULP charge has been held preempted,[43] as has a state's refusal to enforce a wage payment law for claims by employees working under a CBA.[44]

One significant exception to the general *Machinists* standard is the "market participant" doctrine. The state is preempted only when it is acting as a regulator, not when it is acting as a market participant. In *Building & Construction Trades Council v. Associated Builders & Contractors (Boston Harbor)*,[45] a Massachusetts state agency was negotiating with private construction companies to clean up the Boston Harbor. The agency chose a general contractor to manage the project, and this contractor requested that the state agree to a recognition and pre-hire agreement with a construction union trades council. The Board held that this agreement would have been lawful for private employers under §§ 8(e) and 8(f),[46] but a group of non-union contractors challenged the agreement as preempted.

---

42 Id. at 500.

43 Nash v. Florida Industrial Comm'n, 389 U.S. 235 (1967).

44 Lividas v. Bradshaw, 512 U.S. 107 (1994). Because of Congressional intent behind unemployment insurance legislation, states have been allowed to adopt different eligibility requirements in deciding whether to extend unemployment compensation to strikers. See New York Telephone Co. v. New York State Department of Labor, 440 U.S. 519 (1979). States have also been allowed to exclude employees working under a CBA from coverage for statutory severance pay in the event of a plant closing. See Fort Halifax Packing Co. v. Coyne, 482 U.S. 1 (1987).

45 507 U.S. 218 (1993).

46 The Court held that the NLRA did not apply to the state's actions in any event. Id. at 231.

The Supreme Court held that the state agency's agreement was permissible, since it was acting as a purchaser within the market and was permitted to make choices about its own labor relations.[47] As the Court stated, "To the extent a private purchaser may choose a contractor based upon that contractor's willingness to enter into a pre-hire agreement, a public entity as purchaser should be permitted to do the same."[48]

The line between market-participant and regulator is not always a clear one. The Court in *Wisconsin Dep't of Industry v. Gould*[49] held that a Wisconsin statute could not bar the state from doing business with companies found to have violated the NLRA three times within five years. Although the state was a market participant, the purpose of the state law was determined to be regulatory—to deter NLRA violations by attaching sanctions to such violations.[50] The Court also struck down a California agency's decision to condition the renewal of a taxicab license on the resolution of a labor dispute by a certain date.[51] Although state and local governments have a fair amount of discretion in the granting of taxicab and other licenses, they are not permitted to use those powers to tilt the bargaining field in one direction or another.

And more recently, the Court ruled that California's restriction of government contractors' use of state funds "to support or oppose unionization" also fell within *Machinists* preemption.[52] Upon first blush, the state may appear to be acting like a proprietor since it is conditioning simply the use of its own funds. However, the state imposed complicated compliance burdens on employers to show that none of the funds they received ended up funding opposition to a union organizing campaign. Given Congress's special concern for employer speech, as indicated in § 8(c),[53] the effect of the restriction was to chill employer speech. Moreover, the California statute exempted any expenses related to union access to the employer's property or carrying out a voluntary recognition agreement, suggesting a regulatory purpose.[54] Under *Machinists*, the Court held

---

[47] The Court noted that the state agency was not acting as an employer in the case. Id. at 227.

[48] Id. at 231.

[49] 475 U.S. 282 (1986).

[50] Id. at 287.

[51] Golden State Transit Corp. v. City of Los Angeles, 475 U.S. 608 (1986).

[52] Chamber of Commerce v. Brown, 554 U.S. 60 (2008).

[53] 29 U.S.C. § 158(c).

[54] *Brown*, 554 U.S. at 63.

that the state provision intruded too deeply, and too one-sidedly, into labor relations matters.[55]

Finally, the Supreme Court has extended the *Machinists* doctrine to the regulation of supervisors who seek to unionize. The NLRA does not prohibit unionization or collective bargaining by supervisors, but it does explicitly exclude them from its protections. The Court has inferred an implied policy in the Act to shield employers from any law mandating or pressuring employers to engage in collective bargaining with their supervisors. Thus, the Court held that states could enjoin picketing by a supervisor's union, even though that picketing was not regulated by the NLRA.[56] Similarly, states cannot punish employers for discharging supervisors based on their union activity, even though such discharges were not regulated by the NLRA.[57] The difference between the two situations was that the state was permitted to protect employers against secondary pressure but was not permitted to punish employers for insisting on supervisory loyalty. In situations where supervisory status is a contested issue, the Board must be given the chance to determine the matter.[58]

C. Section 301 Preemption: Claims "Dependent" on or Requiring Interpretation of a CBA

Section 301 of the Labor Management Relations Act (LMRA) establishes federal court jurisdiction over claims involving violations of agreements between labor unions and employers.[59] Pursuant to this jurisdictional grant, federal courts have generated a federal common law of collective-bargaining-agreements.[60] As discussed in Chapter 9, the Supreme Court's *Steelworkers Trilogy* affirmed the centrality of arbitration in resolving CBA disputes. Section 301 is viewed as a complete preemption doctrine that operates even if there is no federal question on the face of the complaint; defendants can remove a case to federal court based on a § 301 preemption defense.[61]

---

55 For the argument that states should be able shape labor policy through "tripartite labor lawmaking" whereby the state or local government agrees to provide benefits to a certain business if and only if the business agrees to new organizing and bargaining rules for its workers, see Benjamin I. Sachs, Despite Preemption: Making Labor Law in Cities and States, 124 Harv. L. Rev. 1153, 1174 (2011).

56 Hanna Mining Co. v. District 2, Marine Engineers Beneficial Ass'n, 382 U.S. 181 (1965).

57 Beasley v. Food Fair of North Carolina, 416 U.S. 653 (1974).

58 See Marine Engineers Beneficial Ass'n v. Interlake S.S. Co., 370 U.S. 173 (1962).

59 29 U.S.C. § 185.

60 See Textile Workers Union v. Lincoln Mills of Alabama, 353 U.S. 448 (1957).

61 See Avco Corp. v. Machinists, 390 U.S. 557, 558 (1968). Removal is generally not permitted based on *Garmon* or *Machinists* preemption.

The critical inquiry in a § 301 preemption case is whether the claim is based on or derived from rights created under the CBA or § 301 decisional law or, instead, is independent of that agreement or law. An employee seeking punitive damages for a claim of breach of a CBA would be blocked by § 301 preemption because the claim is based on the CBA, even though the particular remedy is not usually authorized by a CBA. Similarly, an employee's claim to disability payments under state tort law was held preempted in *Allis-Chalmers Corp. v. Lueck*.[62] The employee contended that the employer had interfered in bad faith with his disability payments due under the CBA's benefit plan. Although the claim sounded in tort, rather than contract, it derived from rights created by the CBA's plan—specifically, whether the payments were improperly withheld and whether the employer or the union had any obligations under the CBA with respect to the proper handling of disability claims. The Court explained that "[b]ecause the right asserted not only derives from the contract, but is also defined by the contractual obligation of good faith, any attempt to assess liability here inevitably will involve contract interpretation."[63]

In contrast, the Supreme Court in *Lingle v. Norge Div. of Magic Chef, Inc.*[64] allowed an employee to pursue a state wrongful-discharge action after he was allegedly terminated for filing a workers' compensation claim. The employee arguably would have had a contractual CBA claim for being fired without just cause. The wrongful-discharge claim, however, was based on the state workers' compensation law and operated independently of the labor agreement, and "resolution of the state-law claim does not require construing the collective-bargaining agreement."[65] The Court refined this analysis in *Lividas v. Bradshaw*[66] to make clear that a CBA could provide the source for determining damages in a work-related dispute. Mere consultation of a CBA would not trigger preemption because virtually any claim authorizing back wages would require consulting the labor agreement for the wages paid. The question is whether an element of the state-law claim required an interpretation of the CBA, which is the exclusive province of the labor arbitrator chosen by the employer and the union.

Section 301 also preempts suits against unions for duties arising from collective bargaining agreements. The Court has found a claim against a union for failing to provide a safe workplace to be

---

62 471 U.S. 202 (1985).

63 Id. at 218.

64 486 U.S. 399 (1988).

65 Id. at 407.

66 512 U.S. 107 (1994).

preempted, as such a duty would have arisen under a collective agreement,[67] as well as a claim against a union for failing to inspect safety conditions in a mine.[68] These were, at bottom, contractual obligations of the union to be interpreted in the grievance-arbitration process, not by state law.

---

[67] International Bhd. of Electrical Workers v. Hechler, 481 U.S. 851 (1987).

[68] United Steelworkers v. Rawson, 495 U.S. 362 (1990).

TABLE OF CASES

INDEX

References are to Pages